CW01187467

OFFICIAL YEARBOOK 2006-07

Head of Communications: Gary Sherrard

Communications Officer: Marc Heywood

Statistics provided by SFMS Limited

Photography: Tiger Images, Getty Images, Action Images

Contact the Tigers ticket office on 08701 28 34 30 or email: *tickets@tigers.co.uk*

ISBN 0-9554366-0-5
978-0-9554366-0-4

Copyright © 2006 Leicester Football Club

All rights reserved. No part of this publication may be reproduced, stored in a retrieval system, or transmitted, in any form or by any means, without the prior written permission of the publisher, nor be otherwise circulated in any binding or cover other than that in which it is published and without a similar condition being imposed on the subsequent purchaser.

Design and Print: Soar Valley Press Limited

Copyright © Soar Valley Press Limited 2006

BRADSTONE

Inspirational Gardens & Driveways

Bradstone has a superb collection of inspirational ideas and imaginative materials to help you create your ideal garden and driveway

For more information or a FREE COPY of our brochure please contact 01335 372289 quoting ref TIGER06
www.bradstone.com

An AGGREGATE INDUSTRIES business

CONTENTS

- 4 Fixture List
- 5 Contact the Club
- 6 Corporate Partners
- 7 Roll of Honour
- 8 Milestones

Welcome to Welford Road
- 14 Bar Guide
- 16 Community
- 18 Members Evenings
- 20 JTC Application Form
- 21 JTC
- 22 Conference & Events
- 23 Matchday Hospitality
- 24 Matt Hampson Trust

Player Profiles
- 30 Marcos Ayerza
- 31 Luke Abraham
- 32 Scott Bemand
- 33 James Buckland
- 34 Paul Burke
- 35 George Chuter
- 36 Martin Castrogiovanni
- 37 Matt Cornwell
- 38 Martin Corry
- 39 Jordan Crane
- 40 Tom Croft
- 41 Leo Cullen
- 42 Brett Deacon
- 43 Louis Deacon
- 44 Harry Ellis
- 45 Daryl Gibson
- 46 Andy Goode
- 47 James Hamilton
- 48 Gavin Hickie
- 49 Dan Hipkiss
- 50 Michael Holford
- 51 Ian Humphreys
- 52 Shane Jennings
- 53 Ben Kay
- 54 Leon Lloyd
- 55 Lewis Moody
- 56 Alejandro Moreno
- 57 Frank Murphy
- 58 Geordan Murphy
- 59 Johne Murphy
- 60 Ian Nimmo
- 61 Seru Rabeni
- 62 Graham Rowntree
- 63 Matt Smith
- 64 Ollie Smith
- 65 Alesana Tuilagi
- 66 Anitelea Tuilagi
- 67 Henry Tuilagi
- 68 Tom Varndell
- 69 Sam Vesty
- 70 Julian White
- 71 David Young

Coach Profiles
- 74 Pat Howard / Neil Back
- 75 Richard Cockerill / Jo Hollis
- 76 Dr Mukul Agarwal / John Dams
- 77 Jamie Hamilton / Dusty Hare
- 78 Julie Hayton / Andy Key
- 79 Ollie Richardson / Cliff Shephard
- 80 Paul Stanton / Craig White

Season Review 2005-06
- 84 Season Review
- 88 Northampton Saints
- 90 Wasps
- 92 Bath
- 94 Leeds Tykes
- 96 Dragons
- 98 Worcester Warriors
- 100 Newcastle Falcons
- 102 Clermont Auvergne
- 104 Stade Français
- 106 Worcester Warriors
- 108 Gloucester
- 110 Sale Sharks
- 112 London Irish
- 114 Northampton Saints
- 116 Ospreys
- 118 Ospreys
- 120 Bristol
- 122 Saracens
- 124 London Irish
- 126 Stade Français
- 128 Clermont Auvergne
- 130 Sale Sharks
- 132 Gloucester
- 134 Worcester Warriors
- 136 Newcastle Falcons
- 138 Wasps
- 140 Leeds Tykes
- 142 Barbarians
- 144 Bath
- 146 Bath
- 148 Northampton Saints
- 150 Wasps
- 152 Saracens
- 154 Bristol
- 156 London Irish
- 158 Sale Sharks

Development Team
- 162 Guinness A League Review
- 164 Guinness A League Final
- 166 Matt Hampson Challenge
- 168 Academy Structure
- 170 Academy Coaches
- 172 Academy Review
- 174 Academy Profiles

Guinness Premiership Guide
- 182 Club Details
- 184 Bath
- 190 Bristol
- 196 Gloucester
- 202 Harlequins
- 208 Leicester Tigers
- 214 London Irish
- 220 London Wasps
- 226 Newcastle Falcons
- 232 Northampton Saints
- 238 Sale Sharks
- 244 Saracens
- 250 Worcester Warriors

www.leicestertigers.com

FIXTURE LIST 2006/07

2006

Date	Match	KO	Comp
Thu 3 Aug	Castres Olympique	20:15	F
Sat 5 Aug	Stade Francais	18:00	F
Sat 12 Aug	Middlesex 7s	11:00	
Fri 18 Aug	**Toulon**	**19:45**	**F**
Fri 25 Aug	Munster	19:00	F
Sun 3 Sep	**Sale Sharks**	**16:00**	**GP**
Sat 9 Sep	Bath Rugby	14:15	GP
Sat 16 Sep	**Gloucester Rugby**	**15:00**	**GP**
Sat 23 Sep	NEC Harlequins	18:15	GP
Sat 30 Sep	**Newport Gwent Dragons**	**17:30**	**EDF**
Sat 07 Oct	Worcester Warriors	TBC	EDF
Sat 14 Oct	Northampton Saints	15:00	GP
Sun 22 Oct	**Munster**	**15:00**	**HC**
Sun 29 Oct	Cardiff Blues	15:00	HC
Sat 4 Nov	**Worcester Warriors**	**15:00**	**GP**
Sun 12 Nov	Saracens	15:00	GP
Sat 18 Nov	**London Irish**	**14:45**	**GP**
Sun 26 Nov	London Wasps	15:00	GP
Sat 3 Dec	Northampton Saints	TBC	EDF
Fri 8 Dec	Bourgoin	20:30	HC
Sat 16 Dec	**Bourgoin**	**14:45**	**HC**
Fri 22 Dec	**Bristol Rugby**	**19:45**	**GP**
Tue 26 Dec	London Irish	14:15	GP

2007

Date	Match	KO	Comp
Mon 1 Jan	**Saracens**	**14:45**	**GP**
Sun 7 Jan	Newcastle Falcons	15:00	GP
12/13/14 Jan	**Cardiff Blues**	**TBC**	**HC**
19/20/21 Jan	Munster	TBC	HC
Sat 27 Jan	**Newcastle Falcons**	**15:00**	**GP**
Sat 17 Feb	Worcester Warriors	15:00	GP
Sat 24 Feb	**Northampton Saints**	**14:45**	**GP**
Sat 3 Mar	**NEC Harlequins**	**15:00**	**GP**
Sat 10 Mar	Gloucester Rugby	15:00	GP
Sat 17 Mar	**Bath Rugby**	**14:45**	**GP**
24 Mar	Semi-final		EDF
30/31 Mar	Quarter-final		HC
Fri 6 Apr	Sale Sharks	19:45	GP
Sun 15 Apr	Bristol Rugby	15:00	GP
14/15 Apr	Final		EDF
21/22/23 Apr	Semi-final		HC
Sat 28 Apr	**London Wasps**	**15:00**	**GP**
5/6 May	Semi-final		GP
12/13 May	Final - Twickenham		GP
20 May	Final - Twickenham		HC

Key:

Bold – Home Fixtures

GP – Guinness Premiership

HC – Heineken Cup

EDF – EDF Energy Cup

F – Friendly

Please note all fixtures may be subject to change.

www.leicestertigers.com

CLUB CONTACTS

Leicester Tigers
Welford Road Stadium
Aylestone Road
Leicester LE2 7TR

Phone: 08701 28 34 30
Fax: 0116 2854 766
Email: tigers@tigers.co.uk

Chairman Peter Tom C.B.E.

Chief Executive Peter Wheeler

Managing Director David Clayton

Company Secretary Mary Ford

Directors
David Abell, Garry Adey, John Allen, Bob Beason, Roy Jackson, David Jones, David Matthews, Sir Digby Jones

President Roy Jackson

Head Coach Pat Howard

Life Members
John Allen, Jerry Day, Martin Johnson C.B.E., David Matthews

Press & PR
Gary Sherrard
Phone: 0116 2171 284
Fax: 0116 2171 291
Email: gary.sherrard@tigers.co.uk

Charity Requests
Email: charity@tigers.co.uk

Corporate Sales
Phone: 0116 2171 287
Fax: 0116 2171 292
Email: sales@tiges.co.uk

Ticket Office
Laura Horne
Phone: 08701 28 34 30
Fax: 0116 2171 263
Email: tickets@tigers.co.uk

Conference and Banqueting
Phone: 01116 2171 281
Email: cab@tigers.co.uk

Community
Phone: 0116 2171 221
Email: community@tigers.co.uk

Merchandise
Sara Watson
Phone: 0116 2171 267
Email: shop@tigers

Supporter Services
Paul Hayes
Phone: 0116 2171 226
Email: paul.hayes@tigers.co.uk

Stadium Management
Jack Russell
Phone: 0116 2171 255
Email: jack.russell@tigers.co.uk

www.leicestertigers.com

CORPORATE PARTNERS 2006-2007

BRADSTONE
OFFICIAL MAIN SPONSOR

STAND SPONSORS
Alliance Leicester
NEXT

SHIRT SPONSOR
AGGREGATE INDUSTRIES

TECHNOLOGY PARTNER
hp invent

ASSOCIATE SHIRT SPONSORS
FLOGAS – people with energy
BARDON CONTRACTING

OFFICIAL VEHICLE SUPPLIER
VAUXHALL

PLAYER OF THE MONTH SPONSOR
Lumbers

KIT SPONSOR
Cotton Traders

TIGER CUP SPONSORS
Prima Solutions

OFFICIAL SPORTS DRINK SUPPLIER
Lucozade Sport

OFFICIAL ALE SUPPLIER
Everards Established 1849

RISK MANAGEMENT PARTNERS
OVAL

LEGAL PARTNER
Harvey Ingram LLP solicitors

OFFICIAL SPORTS SUPPLEMENTS SUPPLIER
EAS – active lifestyle nutrition

ASSOCIATE SPONSORS
Millington Travel
Reflex Design International Ltd – Signs and Graphics
BAXI
Starflight Aviation
SITE COAT SERVICES
The Nautilus Health & Fitness Group
National Car Rental

BOX HOLDERS
Tony Green Associates
KCT Holdings
HBJ Gateley Wareing LLP
Vantis Numerica
Royal Bank of Scotland
Orange
HSBC Holdings
FreethCartwright
Greatline Developments
PricewaterhouseCoopers
Browne Jacobson
Barclays Bank
W R Refrigeration
Lafarge Aggregates
Mr David Abell
Sowden Group
The Danwood Group
CJC Development
George Wimpey East Midlands
Masterplug UK
Haas Automation
Aggregate Industries
Harvey Ingram Owston
PKF
Mondi Packaging
David Wilson Homes
Bostik Findley UK
NIG
Caterpillar Logistics Services (UK) Ltd
Galliford Try
Artisan Press
Alliance & Leicester

EXECUTIVE CLUB MEMBERS
Flogas
Vauxhall Motors Ltd
Guinness
AMG
Goy Harris Cartwright & Co
GE Sensing
Glaxo Smith Kline
Manor House Securities
Matlock Garden Centre
Town & Country
What Records
Forest Gate Corby
BCG Associates

PREMIER CLUB MEMBERS
Persimmon Homes
JTM Property Developers
Pick Everard
Widdowson Group
Amwell Consultancy & Training
LTS Interiors
Taurus Infomatics
Linde Material Handling
AON Ltd
Scott Wilson Group
Trafalgar Eurotech
Cunnington Clark

To discuss partnership and sponsorship opportunities at Leicester Tigers, please call our sales team on 0116 2171 287

www.leicestertigers.com

ROLL OF HONOUR

Honours

European Champions
2001 - 2002
2000 - 2001

English Champions
2001 - 2002
2000 - 2001
1999 - 2000
1998 - 1999
1994 - 1995
1987 - 1988

English Cup Winners
1996 - 1997
1992 - 1993
1980 - 1981
1979 - 1980
1978 - 1979

Championship Winners
2000 - 2001

Most Points

Name	Career	Games	T	C	PG	DG	GM	Pts
Dusty Hare	1976 - 1989	393+1	87	779	820	47	–	4,507
John Liley	1988 - 1997	226+4	74	417	449	2	–	2,518
Tim Stimpson	1998 - 2003	141+10	29	223	372	2	–	1,713
Andy Goode	1998 - 2006	128+21	22	195	204	27	-	1,193
Jez Harris	1984 - 1996	213+12	23	165	178	70	–	1,171
Harold Day	1919 - 1929	212	108	281	81	4	2	1,151
Bob Barker	1968 - 1979	318+2	158	92	107	2	–	1,117

Most Appearances

Name	Career	Games
David Matthews	1955-1974	502
Sid Penny	1896-1910	491
John Allen	1961-1975	457
Doug Norman	1920-1933	453
Paul Dodge	1975-1993	434+3
Graham Rowntree	1990-present	361+36
Dusty Hare	1976-1989	393+1
Pedlar Wood	1906-1922	388
Garry Adey	1967-1981	381
John Wells	1982-1997	360+7
Steve Kenney	1975-1990	361+4
Les Cusworth	1978-1990	365
George Ward	1910-1926	361
Jacky Braithwaite	1895-1906	359
Billy Foreman	1893-1906	358
Bob Rowell	1962-1978	355

Most Tries

Name	Career	Games	Tries
Percy Lawrie	1907-1924	318	206
Barry Evans	1981-1995	273	170
John Duggan	1970-1980	302	158
Bob Barker	1968-1979	320	158
Harry Wilkinson	1895-1905	233	153
Teddy Haselmere	1918-1923	180	136
Rory Underwood	1983-1997	236	134
David Matthews	1955-1974	502	119
Neil Back	1990-2005	311	118
Ralph Buckingham	1924-1935	325	117
Harold Day	1919-1929	212	108
Dean Richards	1982-1997	314	105
Pedlar Wood	1906-1922	388	102

TIGERS MILESTONES

1880

Aug 3 – Leicester Football Club formed in a meeting at the George Hotel in Leicester from an amalgamation of three clubs: Leicester Societies AFC, Leicester Amateur FC and Leicester Alert.

Oct 23 – First match against Moseley, played at the Belgrave Cricket and Cycle Ground, ends in a nil-all draw. Original club colours were black and Leicester were known as "The Death or Glory Boys".

Jan 8 – First game at Victoria Park, new home venue.

1882

Oct 7 – Return to the Belgrave Cricket and Cycle Ground for one season only.

1885

Feb 21 – The earliest reference to the now famous Tiger nickname appears in the Leicester Daily Post stating "the Tiger stripes were keeping well together."

1888

Sep 29 – Club move back to the Belgrave Cricket & Cycle Ground from Victoria Park.

1889

Apr 4 – Leicester reach their first ever final, but lose to Coventry 0-8 at Rugby in the Midland Counties Cup.

1891

Leicester wear their famous scarlet, green and white colours for the first time although in a vertical stripe formation.

1892

Sep 16 – The current home ground, Welford Road, opens with a game against the Leicestershire Rugby Union, won 17-0.

1895

Sep 25 – Club switch to scarlet, green and white hoops for the first time.

1898

Apr 6 – The Tigers win their first ever trophy by beating Moseley 5-3 in the final of the Midland Counties Cup at Coventry. They go on to win this competition for the next seven seasons until retiring "to give other teams a chance".

1902

Feb 8 – Welford Road's first international match sees England beat Ireland 6-3.

1903

Jack Miles becomes the club's first international player.

1909

Sep 4 – New Clubhouse opened for game vs Stratford-upon-Avon containing, for the first time, dressing rooms at the ground.

29 Dec – First fixture against the Barbarians ends in a 9-all draw.

1912

Mar 9 – Harry Lawrie becomes the first Tiger to be sent off in a game at Harlequins by referee HA Taylor

1918

Dec 26 – New Members' Stand officially opened for the first Tigers game in 3 1/2 years for the game against the 4th Leicestershire Regiment. On the same day Percy Lawrie with his 154th try overtakes Harry Wilkinson as the club's leading try scorer. He eventually finishes with a still unsurpassed 206 tries.

1920

Oct 2 – New stand (later named the Crumbie Stand) opened by President of the Rugby Union, Ernest Prescott.

1922

Dec 30 – Alastair Smallwood sets a club record by scoring seven tries in the same game in the 36-0 hammering of Manchester at Welford Road.

TIGERS MILESTONES

1923

Feb 10 – England beat Ireland 23-5 at Welford Road in the last England home international played away from Twickenham until 1992.

1926

Sep 4 – The Leicester forwards first regularly wear letters as a means of identification against Bath at Welford Road.

1927

Mar 26 – Harold Day becomes the first Tiger to score 1,000 career points at home to Old Merchant Tailors.

1928

Mar 13 – Tom Crumbie, Honorary Secretary from 1895, dies in office.

1930

Nov 29 – The first BBC radio broadcast of a Tigers game sees Leicester beat Waterloo 21-5 at Welford Road.

1931

Sep 5 – Against Bath at Welford Road marks the first occasion that an entire Leicester team is lettered.

1946

Dec 14 – Leicester's first replacement is Haydn Thomas who takes over from JCK Campbell at Blackheath when the former is late in arriving.

1951

Feb 3 – First TV appearance, against London Scottish on the Richmond Athletic Ground, won 14-0.

1956

Nov 18 – Tigers' first game on a Sunday sees them lose to Old Belvedere in Dublin 3-23.

1959

Oct 22 – Clocks unveiled on stands as a tribute to the late Eric Thorneloe who was Honorary Secretary between 1928-57.

1960

Feb 13 – Tigers' first game under lights was at Newport, which they lost 9-19.

1963

Dec 14 – David Matthews misses the visit of Blackheath to Welford Road and thus breaks his run of 109 successive first team appearances stretching back to January 1961.

1964

Oct 8 – Floodlights first used at Welford Road for a game against a Midlands XV, won 31-8.

1971

Nov 21 – Leicester's first 'modern' cup tie sees them lose 3-10 to Nottingham at Beeston on a Sunday in the first round of the RFU Knockout Cup.

1973

Apr 21 – David Matthews breaks Sid Penny's club appearance record with his 492nd First XV game at Broughton Park. He goes on to make 502 appearances.

1977

Sep 6 – New scoreboard unveiled.

1978

Apr 15 – The club reach their first Twickenham final but are beaten 3-6 by Gloucester.

Dec 27 – Clubhouse extension opened.

1979

Apr 21 – Leicester win the John Player Cup for the first time, beating Moseley 15-12 in the final at Twickenham.

TIGERS MILESTONES

1980

Apr 19 – Dusty Hare breaks Harold Day's record Tigers career points aggregate with his 1,152nd point, kicked on the day that Leicester retained the John Player Cup with a 21-9 victory over London Irish at Twickenham.

Aug 6 – To honour the centenary of the club's foundation, Leicester become the first English club side to embark on a tour to the Southern Hemisphere. They play six games in Australia and Fiji, only losing the opening game to Queensland.

1981

May 2 – Tigers win the John Player Cup for a 3rd successive season when they beat Gosforth 22-15 in the final, and are allowed to keep the original trophy which is now on display at the Clubhouse.

1984

Feb 18 – A club record seven players appear in England team against Ireland at Twickenham.

1985

Sep 14 – New changing room, medical and weights rooms opened under the Crumbie Stand.

1986

Sep 17 – Dusty Hare scores a club record 43 points in a game in the 95-6 trouncing of Birmingham at Welford Road.

1988

Apr 4 – Leicester are confirmed as the inaugural Courage League champions with a 39-15 victory over Waterloo at Welford Road.

1989

Jan 28 – Les Cusworth drops a club record 4 goals at Liverpool St Helens in the 3rd round of the cup.

1990

Summer – Tony Russ is appointed the club's first full-time coach.

1991

Oct 13 – New Zealand beat Italy 31-21 in the qualifying stages of the World Cup at Welford Road.

1992

Apr 11 – Tigers achieve their record points total in a game by demolishing Liverpool St Helens 100-0 at Welford Road.

Sep 5 – Welford Road celebrates its centenary with two special matches. The first sees Leicester lose out 11-18 to an England XV and then overcome a Leicestershire XV 40-20 four days later.

1993

May 1 – Leicester win the Pilkington Cup by beating Harlequins 23-16 in the final at Twickenham.

Sep 18 – The new 18-foot electronic scoreboard is unveiled for the match against Orrell.

1995

Apr 29 – Tigers win the Courage League for a second time after beating Bristol 17-3 in front of 13,000 at Welford Road.

Sep 23 – The new 3,000-seat Alliance & Leicester Stand is used for the first time for the visit of Bath, and officially opened with a game against Transvaal on 20 November.

1996

Jan – Peter Wheeler is appointed the club's first Chief Executive.

May 30 – Bob Dwyer is appointed Director of Rugby.

TIGERS MILESTONES

1997

Jan 25 – Tigers reach the final of the Heineken European Cup after English teams enter the competition for the first time. In the final at Cardiff Arms Park they are overwhelmed 28-9 by a superb team performance from French side Brive.

Apr 2 – A record six Leicester players are named in the British Lions squad to tour South Africa, including the captain Martin Johnson. Later the same day, Tigers beat Wasps 18-12 in front of a record English league crowd of 17,000 at Welford Road.

May 10 – Leicester win the Pilkington Cup by beating Sale 9-3 in the final at Twickenham.

Dec 8 – Tigers become a plc after a successful share issue raises vital funds.

1998

Feb 17 – Dean Richards takes over as Director of Rugby.

1999

May 2 – Tigers clinch a third league title when they take the Allied Dunbar Premiership with a 21-12 victory over Newcastle Falcons at Kingston Park.

Oct 10 – Welford Road hosts a Rugby World Cup game for the second time as Tonga shock Italy 28-25.

2000

May 14 – Leicester claim a second successive Premiership crown following a 30-23 win at Bristol's Memorial Stadium.

2001

Mar 17 – Take a third Premiership crown in a row when Bath beat Wasps at the Rec, an hour or so after the Tigers had demolished the Falcons 51-7 at Welford Road.

May 13 – Leicester claim the inaugural Zurich Championship crown when they beat Bath 22-10 in the final at Twickenham.

May 19 – Tigers win the European Heineken Cup for the first time, beating Paris-based Stade Français in the final at Parc des Princes 34-30.

Summer – Martin Johnson becomes the first player ever to captain the British Lions on two separate tours, when he leads them in Australia.

2002

Apr 13 – A fourth consecutive Premiership is wrapped up with a 20-10 victory over Newcastle at Welford Road.

May 25 – Leicester become the first club to retain the European Heineken Cup by beating Irish province Munster 15-9 in the final at Cardiff's Millennium Stadium.

2003

May 31 – Tigers qualify for the 2003/04 European Heineken Cup with a thrilling extra-time victory over Saracens at Franklin's Gardens, Northampton to pick up the Zurich Wildcard.

2004

May 29 – Tigers book their place in the 2004/05 Heineken Cup season with a comprehensive 48-27 victory over Sale Sharks at Twickenham to claim the Zurich Wildcard.

2005

April 30 – Leicester Tigers top the Zurich Premiership after 22 games in the regular season, comfortably beating London Wasps 45-10 in their last league match, before losing to the self-same Wasps in the final two weeks later. Tigers were the only English team to qualify for the Heineken Cup semi-finals, going out to eventual winners, Toulouse, in the first-ever rugby match played at the Walkers Stadium.

WELCOME TO WELFORD ROAD

www.leicestertigers.com

WELCOME TO WELFORD ROAD

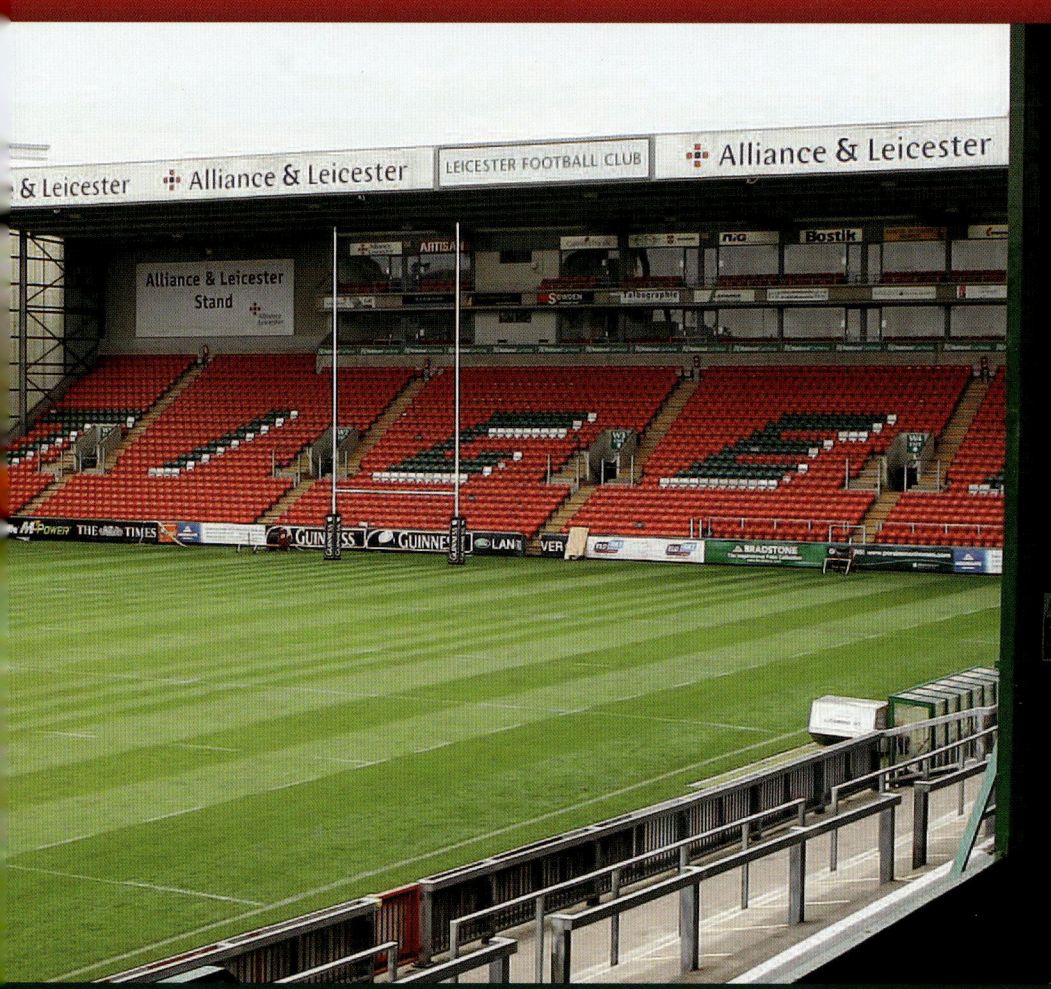

www.leicestertigers.com

TIGERS BAR GUIDE

Bars & Restaurants

1. Barbarians Lounge
2. Tiger Bar
3. European Suite
4. Leicestershire Room
5. Captain's Bar
6. Droglites
7. Dusty's Bar
8. Underwood Suite
9. Lions Bar
10. Members' Bar
11. ABC Bar
12. Crumbie Lounge

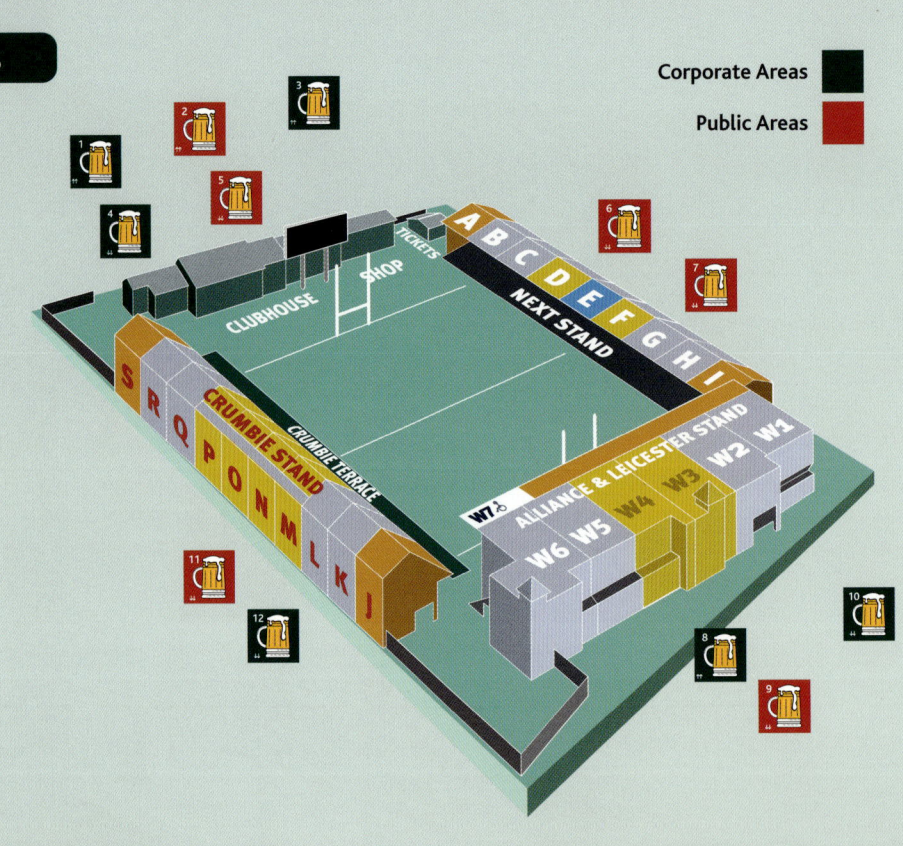

Corporate Areas
Public Areas

14 www.leicestertigers.com

TIGERS BAR GUIDE

Lions Bar

Captain's Bar

Tiger Bar

www.leicestertigers.com   15

COMMUNITY

It's been another great year for the Tigers Community team. We have worked hard to increase participation in rugby and raise awareness of the club within primary and secondary schools, universities, community groups, rugby clubs and Tigers supporters.

TIGERS RUGBY COURSES

Our week-long courses give players aged between 8-16 the chance to experience top-quality coaching in a professional environment. Playing up to 5 hours of rugby each day the children work on their 8 Star Award which tests individual skills. Each day they work on all aspects of rugby, from defence and ball retention to unit skills and conditioned games as well as nutrition advice and video analysis work. The courses have been hugely successful and have meant that this year we have expanded to run 22 courses throughout the region. For more information contact the community team on 0116 2171 283.

ALLIANCE & LEICESTER TAG

The continuation of this great programme has allowed us to go into even more primary schools to coach tag rugby. Using teaching training seminars, tag coaching and tag festivals we aim to enthuse the young people we coach. At the tag festivals children have the chance to practise their newly-learned skills against other local schools. There is also opportunity for them to meet professional Tigers players who come to watch the rugby, show their support and sign autographs. Winners of the local festivals are invited to Welford Road to play in their area finals, where 17,000 Tigers supporters cheer them on before a Tigers match.

VARSITY MATCHES

The men's and women's teams yet again played their annual varsity fixture at Welford Road in front of over 4,000 students.

KICK SMOKING INTO TOUCH

Children from all over Leicestershire and Rutland have been learning about the health problems associated with smoking and designing their own 'Kick Smoking Into touch' posters.

COMMUNITY

TLC

The Tigers Learning Centre aims to provide out-of-hours learning and extra curricular support for selected pupils from Leicester's inner-city schools. This has been another successful year for TLC, accommodating 15 children from four primary and secondary schools each term. The 10-week programme uses rugby themes to educate the children in ICT, literacy and numeracy. The children also get a chance to try some tag rugby in the local park with our own community rugby coaches. The children's hard work is rewarded at their 'graduation' ceremony where a first-team player presents certificates and prizes. After the programme each child receives a free ticket for a Tigers home match where they enjoy a lap of honour around the pitch.

TIGERS LEADERSHIP PROGRAMME

This programme aims to improve children's interpersonal and leadership skills as well as raise self-esteem using tag rugby. The programme builds children's confidence so that in the final week they can coach their peers using a number of simple techniques.

MATCHDAY COACHING CLINICS

Held on matchday mornings, our coaching clinics have been a huge success, providing a unique experience for both players and coaches. Groups meet at our purpose-built training ground, Oval Park, and begin their day with a coaching session from the Tigers coaches and community team. The coaching is followed by a question and answer session with a member of the Tigers first-team squad. For more information contact the community team on 0116 2171 283.

HEALTHY SCHOOLS PROGRAMME

The Tigers Health Education Officer has been visiting inner-city schools all over Leicester, educating children on the virtues of a healthy lifestyle, including a healthy and balanced diet, fluid intake, exercise and dental care.

PRIMA TIGER CUP

Under-10's teams from all over the region took part in this year's Prima Tiger Cup. The tournament began in local festivals with the winners coming to Welford Road and playing before a Tigers home match to decide who are the Prima Tiger Cup champions.

www.leicestertigers.com

MEMBERS EVENINGS

August 9 2006
Season Preview – Pat Howard & Richard Cockerill

September 13 2006
Returning Tourists – Ben Kay, Andy Goode & Tom Varndell

October 11 2006
Heineken Cup Preview – Geordan Murphy, Harry Ellis & James Hamilton

November 15 2006
Meet the New Guys – Jordan Crane, Gavin Hickie, Frank Murphy, Martin Castrogiovanni, Marcus Ayerza & Paul Burke

December 13 2006
Christmas Party
Three-course sit-down meal
Seru Rabeni, Shane Jennings & Leo Cullen

January 24 2007
Captains' Thoughts
Martin Corry & Daryl Gibson

February 21 2007
Quiz Night (Weakest Link meets Who Wants to be a Millionaire)
Danny Hipkiss, Brett Deacon, James Buckland, Leon Lloyd, Luke Abraham, Matt Cornwell, Sam Vesty & Michael Holford

March 21 2007
Secrets of the Front Row
Julian White, George Chuter & Alex Moreno

April 11 2007
Members Player of the Season Awards

Ticket Prices
Season ticket holders/members: £17
Non members: £20

Christmas Party
Season ticket holders/members: £25
Non members: £30

Player Awards
Season ticket holders/members: £22
Non members: £25

All events include a hot fork buffet meal

To book your place contact the Ticket Office on 08701 28 34 30 or email tickets@tigers.co.uk

N.B. We will try to keep to the above programme of events but players & dates may occasionally be changed due to fixtures and training schedules

FANS

www.leicestertigers.com   19

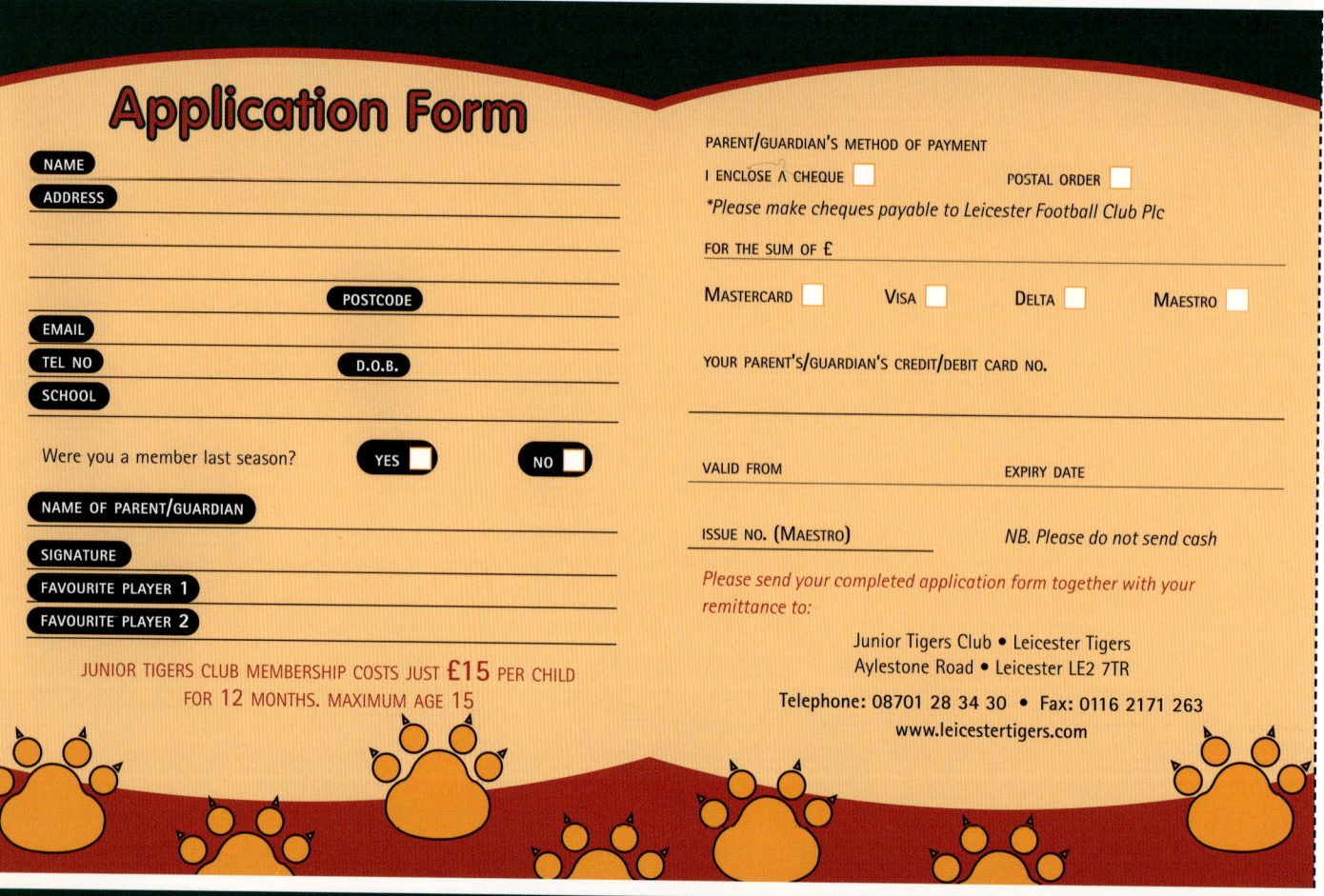

JUNIOR TIGERS CLUB APPLICATION FORM

Application Form

NAME

ADDRESS

POSTCODE

EMAIL

TEL NO

D.O.B.

SCHOOL

Were you a member last season? YES ☐ NO ☐

NAME OF PARENT/GUARDIAN

SIGNATURE

FAVOURITE PLAYER 1

FAVOURITE PLAYER 2

JUNIOR TIGERS CLUB MEMBERSHIP COSTS JUST £15 PER CHILD FOR 12 MONTHS. MAXIMUM AGE 15

PARENT/GUARDIAN'S METHOD OF PAYMENT

I ENCLOSE A CHEQUE ☐   POSTAL ORDER ☐

*Please make cheques payable to Leicester Football Club Plc

FOR THE SUM OF £

MASTERCARD ☐   VISA ☐   DELTA ☐   MAESTRO ☐

YOUR PARENT'S/GUARDIAN'S CREDIT/DEBIT CARD NO.

VALID FROM   EXPIRY DATE

ISSUE NO. (MAESTRO)   NB. Please do not send cash

Please send your completed application form together with your remittance to:

Junior Tigers Club • Leicester Tigers
Aylestone Road • Leicester LE2 7TR

Telephone: 08701 28 34 30 • Fax: 0116 2171 263

www.leicestertigers.com

www.leicestertigers.com

JUNIOR TIGERS CLUB

Hi Kids

I'm Harry Ellis, a Leicester Tigers player, and I'm also very proud to be president of the Junior Tigers Club – JTC

What is the Junior Tigers Club?
A club just for kids who are mad about Tigers - it's the best supported kids rugby club in the whole country.
Junior Tigers have their own clubhouse where they can play games on computers, have their faces painted, enjoy free fruit and have lots of fun before the match. Doesn't that sound great? And, if you become a Junior Tiger, you'll get to see a whole lot more!

Who can be a Junior Tiger?
Anyone, as long as you are a Tigers fan aged between 0-14 years old.

How much does it cost?
It costs only **£15** a year to join the Junior Tigers Club.

Membership Includes:

- The chance to be a mascot at Welford Road - how good is that!
  You'll walk out with the team in front of the whole crowd and be given a FREE team kit to keep
- The chance to ask your favourite player questions for the matchday programme
- £1 off all home games - The Guinness Premiership and Heineken Cup pool games only. When booked in advance
  (Under 14s must be accompanied by an adult)
- A special present for joining
- Your own unique membership card
- A birthday card each year - signed by all the players
  Have fun in the JTC Clubhouse on matchdays with computer games and FREE fruit (open on first team matchdays only)
- An invite to the Junior Tigers Club Christmas Party
- JTC newsletters with stories, competitions and much more...

Plus
- Discounts in the club shop (available on selected items only)

How do I become a Junior Tiger?
It's easy. Just get an adult to fill in this form for you, then send it to us and we'll do the rest.

So, what are you waiting for?
Check out our club, come to watch Tigers, make friends and join in the fun!

Contact Details

For further information contact:

Junior Tigers Club
Leicester Tigers
Aylestone Road
Leicester LE2 7TR

Telephone: 08701 28 34 30
Fax: 0116 2171 263

www.leicestertigers.com

CONFERENCE AND EVENTS

Leicester Tigers provides a wide selection of elegantly-decorated rooms and a variety of menus put together by our Head Chef, from a light working lunch for a business meeting to a wedding breakfast for your special day.

The Conference & Events team look forward to working alongside you to arrange all your specific needs – whatever they may be. Successful events are held throughout the year and range from birthday parties, christenings and weddings to small business meetings, conferences and exhibitions.

We are also taking a few last-minute bookings for Christmas 2006 with traditional dinners and lunches served before you let your hair down to live bands, solo artists and discos. Something for everyone...

As a season ticket holder and member you are also entitled to a 10% discount on all room hire charges when ordering food and on Christmas 2006 bookings.

Call the Conference & Events team today on 0116 2171 278.

www.leicestertigers.com

MATCHDAY HOSPITALITY

Join the rush to be a Tigers VIP

If you want to make your day at Welford Road that extra special surprise for a friend or relative, then why not treat them to a VIP match day hospitality package at one of our home matches during the 2006/2007 season. More and more people are treating their friends and loved ones to an unforgettable day of entertainment that allows them to get up close and personal with some of Leicester Tigers' stars.

The Tigers experience is meticulously planned with reserved car parking allowing you to arrive in style, Whatever the reason for your day with us, all our guests agree that the three-hour complimentary bar is a great way to prepare for the day ahead. A superb four-course lunch is served fresh from the kitchen by our dedicated catering staff allowing you time to browse the complimentary match day programme and enjoy your personalised gift.

A visit from members of our first team squad is the highlight of the day for many of our guests, young and old.

Our Tigers players take part in Q&A sessions and take the time to chat wth our guests, sharing a drink and signing autographs. This also provides some great help with forecasting the score for our match day competitions, with great prizes on offer for the lucky winners.

VIP MATCHDAY HOSPITALITY PACKAGE
This package is for two or more persons.

- Complimentary pre-match bar
- Joined by players for questions/answers
- Four-course pre-match meal with wine
- Souvenir programme for each guest
- Reserved grandstand seating
- Post-match afternoon tea
- Commemorative gift for each guest
- Competitions and prizes
- Reserved car parking

www.leicestertigers.com

MATT HAMPSON TRUST FUND

Matt - the Current Situation

Matt Hampson is a young Tigers prop forward who suffered a serious neck injury whilst at England U-21 training in March 2005. Matt returned home in early August 2006, after spending 17 months recovering from his injuries at Stoke Mandeville Hospital. He is currently paralysed from the neck down and is still unable to breath unaided.

Despite the nature of his injuries, Matt continues to show great courage in the face of adversity. He is constantly looking to raise the profile of other paralysis victims and is determined to become heavily involved in publicising research into spinal injuries.

The Matt Hampson Trust Fund

A large amount of fundraising has taken place both inside and outside the rugby community since Matt's tragic injury - something for which Matt and his family have expressed their heart-felt gratitude and even surprise. However, if Matt is to continue to make progress, he will need our support for many years to come.

How You Can Help

If you would like to raise money for the Matt Hampson Trust, cheques can be made out to the Matt Hampson Trust Fund and posted to Leicester Tigers, Aylestone Road, Leicester LE2 7TR.

If you would like more information, please email mht@tigers.co.uk

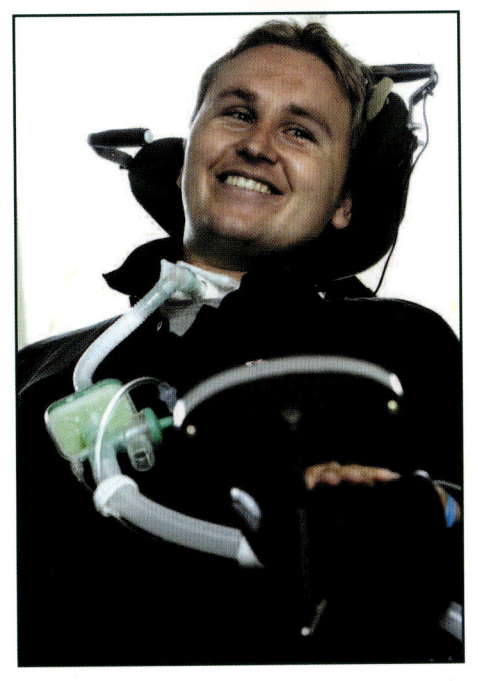

MATT HAMPSON TRUST FUND

Matt Hampson Polo Shirts

Why not make your support of Matt even more visible by proudly wearing a Matt Hampson Trust polo shirt. These stylish black tops are available from www.matthampson.co.uk for only £20. The shirts range in size from small to XXL, giving you the perfect opportunity to show your support for Matt. The more people who know about Matt's situation, the more chance we have of raising funds.

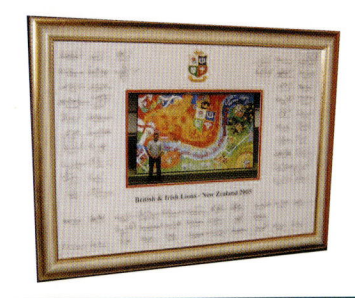

Legends International

Legends International, an internet sporting memorabilia site, has become a central figure in the on-going fund-raising efforts. They have a fantastic range of unique and collectable items, with prices designed to suit all purse strings. The website is a great way to lend your support to Matt, whilst also giving you a chance to get your hands on your very own piece of sporting history.

For a full range of Legends International products, log onto www.matthampson.co.uk and remember...
ALL PROCEEDS GO DIRECTLY TO MATT'S FUND.

Tigers Friendship Bands

In typical fashion, Tigers supporters have lent their support to Matt, with a host of local pubs and rugby clubs raising thousands of pounds. Two Welford Road regulars, Jacqui Haines and Jan Sawbridge, have also done their bit, with the production of Matt Hampson friendship bracelets, which are on sale for £2 at the club shop.

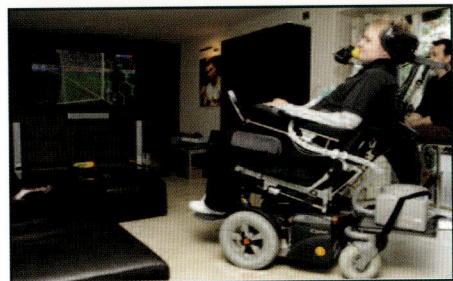

LEICESTER TIGERS SQUAD 2006/07

www.leicestertigers.com

LEICESTER TIGERS SQUAD 2006/07

www.leicestertigers.com

PLAYER PROFILES

www.leicestertigers.com

PLAYER PROFILES

www.leicestertigers.com

PLAYER PROFILES

Marcos Ayerza

Loosehead prop Marcos Ayerza joined Leicester Tigers in the summer of 2006 having previously played his club rugby for Cardinal Newman in Buenos Aires.

After representing Argentina at U21 level, playing for them in both the 2003 and 2004 IRB U21 World Cups, in England and Scotland respectively, he made his debut at senior level in December 2004 against the touring Springboks.

He has since played in both tests against Wales on their tour to Argentina in June, and two 2007 World Cup qualifiers, versus Chile and Uruguay in July. His only test try to date came in his second appearance v Japan in Buenos Aires, April 2005.

MARCOS AYERZA

Position	Prop
Date of birth	12.01.83
Height	6'1"
Weight	16st 9lb
Tigers Debut	
Yet to make Tigers Debut	

Previous Clubs	
	Cardinal Newman (Arg)
Rep Hons	Argentina (8)

PLAYER PROFILES

Luke Abraham

Luke joined the Tigers Academy at the age of 15, only three years after he took up the sport at Bushlow High School and became a member of his local club, Leicester Vipers.

He has played for Tigers' Youth team; was a member of the U21 squad that claimed the 2002/03 League title and appeared regularly in the Tigers Extras team that won the Zurich A League in 2004/05. Luke was selected for the England U18 Schoolboys squad to face New Zealand Schoolboys at Twickenham at the end of January 2001, and then elevated to the U19 team, playing against Ireland and France in their shadow Six Nations. He played in the FIRA U19 Junior World Championship in Italy in March 2002 and more recently has represented England U21A. A back row forward, Abraham also tried out at hooker, a move which led to a brief trip to New Zealand playing for Nelson Bays club, Stoke, during the summer of 2005. He has since returned to the back row position.

LUKE ABRAHAM			
Position	Back Row	**Tigers Record**	7 + 19 apps
Date of birth	26.09.83		1 try
Height	6'2"		5 pts
Weight	16st 5lb	**Previous Clubs**	N/A
Tigers Debut		**Rep Hons**	England U21A
21.01.02 v Worcester Warriors			

www.leicestertigers.com

PLAYER PROFILES

Scott Bemand

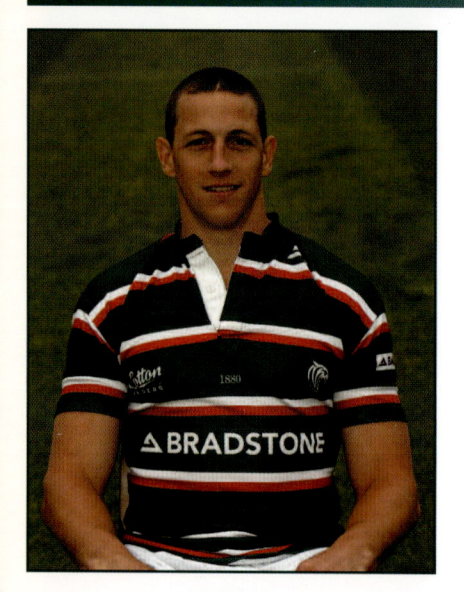

Educated at the Bishop of Hereford's Bluecoat School and Harper Adams University College, Scott played for Luctonians First XV as an 18-year-old, before moving to Moseley Colts in 1997/98, the season they won the National Colts Cup.

He made his debut in the Allied Dunbar Premiership Two for Moseley in 1998, and was selected for England Students whilst with the club; he went on to captain the Students the following season. Scott signed for NEC Harlequins in the summer of 2001, and made 30 Premiership appearances for the club; his last game for Quins was the Parker Pen Cup final in May 2004 when he helped the team to a 27-26 win over French side Montferrand. Since joining Leicester Bemand has captained the Tigers' Extras during their successful Zurich A League campaign in 2004/05. A broken ankle during pre-season training, which required an operation that kept him out of action for four months, delayed his start to the 2005/06 season, but his return to form was such that he competed with Harry Ellis at scrum-half for both club and country; Scott was selected for the England touring party to Australia in the summer although he did not take part in either Test. An all-round sportsman, Scott played junior County Cricket from Under 13 to Under 16 level.

SCOTT BEMAND

Position	Scrum-Half
Date of birth	21.09.78
Height	5'11"
Weight	13st 8lb
Tigers Debut	
11.09.04 v Leeds Tykes	

Tigers Record	18 + 14 apps
	2 tries
	10 pts
Previous Clubs	Luctonians, Moseley, NEC Harlequins
Rep Hons	England Students

32 www.leicestertigers.com

PLAYER PROFILES

James **Buckland**

James joined the Tigers in the summer of 2002 from Northampton Saints after returning from South Africa where he had travelled with England for the U21 IRB World Championship.

He made his first appearance in Tigers stripes in the Middlesex 7s tournament at Twickenham in August 2002, then joined the first team at their training camp in France, playing in the friendly match against Agen. A regular member of Tigers' league-winning U21 team in 2002/03, James' 12 tries made him the U21's top try scorer that season. The opportunity to progress in the first team was hampered when he broke his leg during a training session at the start of the 2003/04 season.

He returned to the fray in February playing 6 games for Tigers Extras in the Zurich A League, before heading south in the off season to hone his skills in New Zealand's North Island, playing for the Tawa club near Wellington. He returned in time to make his Leicester first team debut at the start of the 2004/05, he was also a member of the Tigers' Extras squad that won the Zurich A League championship that year and retained the title in 2005/06. His performances last season bought him to the attention of the national selectors and James toured to Canada with the England Saxons competing in the Churchill Cup in the summer.

JAMES BUCKLAND			
Position	Hooker	**Tigers Record**	11 + 32 apps
Date of birth	21.09.81		1 try
Height	5'11"		5 pts
Weight	16st 10lb	**Previous Clubs**	
Tigers Debut			Aylesbury, Northampton
11.09.04 v Leeds Tykes		**Rep Hons**	England A

www.leicestertigers.com   33

PLAYER PROFILES

Paul **Burke**

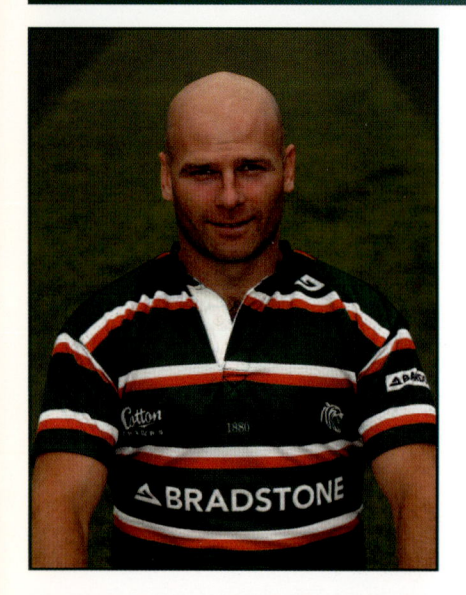

Vastly experienced Paul Burke has racked up well over 2000 points in his 15-season club rugby career which began in the early 1990s for Cork Constitution in Munster. In addition Burke gained 13 caps for Ireland between 1995 and his most recent appearance against Samoa in Apia in June 2003, helping himself to 108 international points in the process.

Paul gained international honours for England at Schools, Under-18, Colts and Under-21 levels, but his Irish-born parents allowed him to declare for Ireland in November 1992, working his way through their Under-21 and A sides until making his debut for the senior team against England at Lansdowne Road in January 1995. Burke was involved in the Ireland squad for the 1995 Rugby World Cup in South Africa.

No stranger to facing the Tigers, Burke has tallied 106 points against Leicester in a dozen appearances for London Irish, Bristol and Harlequins. Whilst playing for 'Quins he appeared in two European finals, the European Shield in 2001 and then winning the Parken Pen Challenge Cup again three years later with victory over Montferrand. Paul has made 26 appearances for Munster in the Celtic League over the past two seasons, also helping them to win the Celtic Cup in 2005.

PAUL BURKE	
Position	Fly-half
Date of birth	1.05.73
Height	5'8"
Weight	13st 3lb
Tigers Debut	
Yet to make Tigers debut.	

Tigers Record	N/A
Previous Clubs	Cork Constitution, London Irish, Munster, Bristol, Cardiff, Harlequins.
Rep Hons	Ireland 13

34   www.leicestertigers.com

PLAYER PROFILES

George **Chuter**

George Chuter joined Tigers in December 2000, vying first with Richard Cockerill then Dorian West as first choice at hooker. After playing for London Division at both U18 and U21 level George joined Saracens and was selected in the first team squad at the age of 19.

He had five years with the club, including winning the Pilkington Cup in 1998, before taking a break from rugby travelling to Australia and the USA. He made his England A debut in 1998 scoring a try in the game against France at Tours, and was included in that summer's tour to Australia and New Zealand, featuring in the match at Invercargill against New Zealand Academies. Impressive club performances in the latter stages of the 2003/04 season earned him selection for the England A side to compete for the Churchill Cup in Canada, where he returned the following year with the successful England XV playing in both matches, including the final against Argentina.

Although selected for the matchday 22 for England against Scotland in the 2006 Six Nations, George had to wait until the summer tour to Australia before making his debut, scoring a memorable try in the second Test in his first start for the senior team. An old boy of Trinity School in Croydon, George played club rugby for Old Mid-Whitgiftians before studying at the West London Institute for a year.

GEORGE CHUTER			
Position	Hooker	**Tigers Record**	81 + 32 apps
Date of birth	9.07.76		15 tries
Height	5'10"		75 pts
Weight	15st 2lb	**Previous Clubs**	
Tigers Debut			Old Mid-Whitgiftians, Saracens
31.03.01 v Gloucester		**Rep Hons**	England (2)

www.leicestertigers.com

PLAYER PROFILES

Martin **Castrogiovanni**

Born in Parana, prop Martin Castrogiovanni played for Atletico Estudiantes in Argentina and appeared for Argentina at Under-19 and Under-21 (in 2001) level before moving to Italy.

After his debut for Calvisano at L'Aquila on 20 October 2001, Martin made 72 appearances for the club in the Italian Super-10, scoring seven tries. He also appeared in 21 Heineken Cup matches including four occasions when he faced his future club, Leicester.

First capped for Italy against New Zealand in Hamilton in June 2002, Martin has gained 35 caps and scored 5 international tries. Against Japan in Tokyo on 4 July 2004 he became only the third prop ever to score a hat-trick of tries in a Test match after Sevaro Walisoliso for Fiji in 1964 and Christian Califano for France in 1996.

An ever-present for Italy during the 2003 World Cup in Australia, Martin has also played in Italy's last 19 Six Nations Championship matches.

MARTIN CASTROGIOVANNI

Position	Prop	Tigers Record	N/A
Date of birth	21.10.81	Previous Clubs	Calvisano
Height	6'1"	Rep Hons	Italy (35)
Weight	17st 5lb		
Tigers Debut			
Yet to make Tigers debut.			

www.leicestertigers.com

PLAYER PROFILES

Matt Cornwell

Matt Cornwell started playing rugby as a seven-year-old with Syston RFC before being invited into Tigers' under-16 squad. He attended Oakham School on a rugby scholarship, and played in both of the school's Daily Mail Cup victories at Twickenham.

He has represented Leicestershire at U16 and U18 levels, and England U18 schools. An ever-present in England's 2005 U21 Six Nations campaign, Matt was named as captain of the England U21 side that competed in the IRB U21 World Cup in Argentina that summer. He led his country again in the 2006 U21 shadow Six Nations when England claimed a grand slam, and for the 2006 U21 World Cup in France. He also captained the Tigers Extras team that took the 2005/06 Guinness A League title with a two-legged victory over Harlequins. His performances on and off the pitch, where he spearheaded the fund-raising for his injured teammate Matt Hampson, led to him being voted as the Tigers Members Young Player of the Season 2005/06.

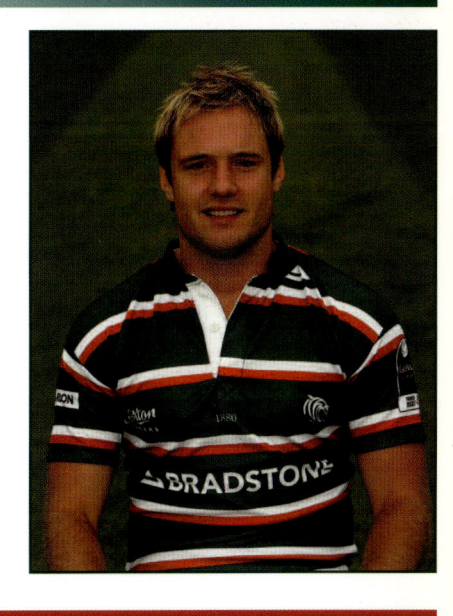

MATT CORNWELL

Position	Centre/Full-back
Date of birth	16.01.85
Height	6'0"
Weight	14st 3lb
Tigers Debut	

2.10.04 v Newcastle Falcons

Tigers Record	9 + 13 apps
	3 tries
	15 pts
Previous Clubs	Syston
Rep Hons	England U21

www.leicestertigers.com

PLAYER PROFILES

Martin Corry

Named as Leicester captain for the 2005/06 season, Martin Corry is now in his 10th season with the club, a spell that has seen success with back-to-back Heineken Cup wins and four Premiership titles.

A versatile player who can cover at lock as well as in the back row, Martin has been selected for two British Lions tours; to New Zealand in 2005, where he took over as captain in the first Test when Brian O'Driscoll was injured, and as late replacement to Australia in 2001 when he put in one of the best performances for the Lions, eventually playing in all three Tests. Corry was also a member of England's 2003 Rugby World Cup-winning squad; again a late selection after putting in some memorable performances during the warm-up games that summer. The trip to Australia was his second World Cup campaign having also played in the 1999.

Martin played in four consecutive Five/Six Nations campaigns, 1999 to 2002 and, following his return from World cup duty, played in all three of the 2004 autumn internationals and the last four of the 2005 Six Nations games, captaining his country for the first time in the match against Italy at Twickenham during that championship. After his return from the Lions he continued as England captain, playing in all their Tests during 2005/06, until rested for this summer's tour to Australia. Having started playing rugby in the mini section at Tunbridge Wells RFC, Martin first represented England at U18 level in 1992 in the team that won the junior grand slam and triple crown. He had a highly successful tenure at Northumbria University, which led to his inclusion in the England Students side in 1995 and, later that year, England A. Martin made his England Test debut in 1997 in Argentina. He was named as the Members' Player of the Season in 1999/2000, and more recently after outstanding performances for club and country was named as both the Zurich Premiership and PRA player of the season 2004/05. He was awarded an MBE in the 2004 New Year's Honours.

MARTIN CORRY

Position	Back-Row
Date of birth	12.10.73
Height	6'5"
Weight	17st 10lb
Tigers Debut	
30.08.97 v Gloucester	

Tigers Record	210 + 12 apps
	20 tries
	100 pts
Previous Clubs	
	Newcastle-Gosforth, Bristol.
Rep Hons	England (45),
	British Lions (6).

www.leicestertigers.com

PLAYER PROFILES

Jordan Crane

Summer signing Jordan Crane made his debut for his former club, Leeds Tykes, in the 9-9 draw at Grenoble in the European Challenge Cup in October 2004 aged just 18. He went on to make 29 appearances for the Tykes in all competitions, scoring five tries, including a hat trick against Valladolid in the European Challenge Cup.

His England U21 debut followed in February 2006, scoring a try against Wales at Worcester, and he was an ever-present in their successful U21 Grand Slam campaign. This was his second successive age group Grand Slam, as he had captained England's U19 side to success the season before. Crane has also captained England at U18 level and took over the leadership role when his new team-mate, Matt Cornwell, was injured during the IRB U21 World Cup in France this summer, fulfilling the promise shown when competing for Colston's College in the final of the Daily Mail U18 competition at Twickenham.

JORDAN CRANE			
Position	Back Row/Lock	Tigers Record	N/A
Date of birth	3.06.86	Previous Clubs	Leeds Tykes
Height	6'3"	Rep Hons	England U21
Weight	16st 2lb		
Tigers Debut			
Yet to make Tigers debut.			

www.leicestertigers.com

39

PLAYER PROFILES

Tom Croft

A former Oakham School pupil, second rower Tom Croft started playing rugby as an 11-year-old joining Newbury RFC, staying with the National Division One outfit for 5 years.

After representing his county at age group level he was selected to captain the South of England U16 side against France. Tom has also represented England U18 schools, and last season was a member of the grand-slam winning England U21 squad, playing alongside team-mate captain Matt Cornwell, whom he also joined for the U21 World Championship in France this summer.

After a successful 2004/05 campaign, in which he was named NIG Academy Player of the Season and was a member of the successful Tigers A League squad, Tom represented Leicester at the Middlesex Sevens before making his first team debut against Gloucester at Welford Road in November 2005. He tasted further success when Tigers Extras retained their A League title in 2005/06.

TOM CROFT

Position	Lock/Back Row
Date of birth	7.11.85
Height	6'5"
Weight	16st 4lb
Tigers Debut	
12.11.05 v Gloucester	

Tigers Record	0 + 2 apps
Previous Clubs	Newbury
Rep Hons	England U19

PLAYER PROFILES

Leo **Cullen**

Lock Leo Cullen joined Tigers in the summer of 2005 from Irish province Leinster. He had played for the Dublin-based side since 1998, making his senior debut for the province in September that year against Edinburgh Reivers at Kelso.

He has gone on to win the Celtic League title with Leinster in 2001 and played Heineken Cup rugby for the province, including four games against Leicester Tigers, the latest occasion being the quarter-final at Lansdowne Road in April 2005. Cullen has gained 18 Ireland caps since his debut in Auckland in June 2002, his most recent coming in the 2005 autumn international against Romania. He has also represented Ireland at Schools, U19, U21 and A level, appearing with Tigers teammate Shane Jennings against France A in Limoges in February.

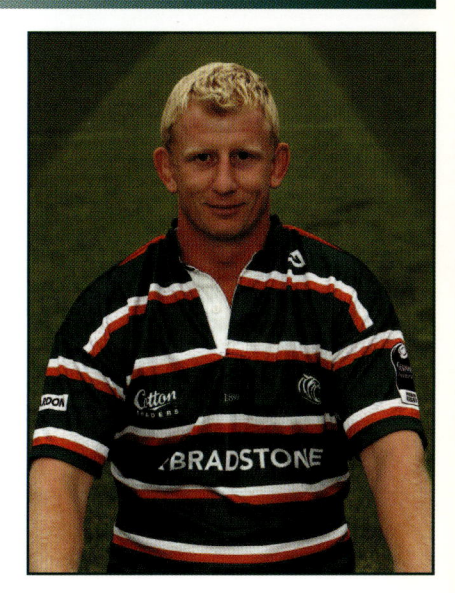

LEO CULLEN

Position	Lock
Date of birth	9.01.78
Height	6'6"
Weight	17st 5lb
Tigers Debut	
3.09.05 v Northampton Saints	

Tigers Record	18 + 10 apps
Previous Clubs	Blackrock College, Leinster.
Rep Hons	Ireland (18)

www.leicestertigers.com   41

PLAYER PROFILES

Brett Deacon

Brett started playing rugby at the age of seven for Wigston RFC, he then moved to Syston when he was 11 and went on to represent Leicestershire, the Midlands and England at U16 and U18 levels.

He was selected for the England U19 squad for the shadow Six Nations 2001/02, and captained them in their game against Wales U19 in January that year. The younger brother of Tigers lock Louis, Brett joined the Tigers Academy as a 16-year-old and has since played for both the Youth and U21 team, and for Tigers' Extras during their successful A League campaigns of 2004/05 and 2005/06. Brett made his first team debut at the start of the 2003/04 campaign, during the Rugby World Cup, although his progress has been hampered due to a series of injuries. He partnered his brother Louis in the second row for his debut, the game against London Irish, when they became only the second pair of brothers to do so after Mark and Paul Grant against Nottingham in March 1994. Brett has since made over 40 appearances for the first team, appearing in almost half of Tigers' games during last season's Guinness Premiership campaign.

BRETT DEACON

Position	Flanker
Date of birth	7.03.82
Height	6'4"
Weight	16st 8lb
Tigers Debut	
13.09.03 v London Irish	

Tigers Record	33 + 9 apps
	2 tries
	10 pts
Previous Clubs	Wigston, Syston
Rep Hons	England U19

42 www.leicestertigers.com

PLAYER PROFILES

Louis Deacon

Since making his Tigers first team debut, Louis has established himself as a highly dependable player at either front or middle jumper, and more recently in the back row. The mainstay of Tigers' lineout during the World Cup campaign at the start of the 2003/04 season, Louis gave such impressive performances that it earned him the accolade of the Player's Player of the Season.

He has now gone on to make over 100 appearances for the club, earning his commemorative 100th cap in the game against Worcester in October 2005. A former pupil of Ratcliffe College, Leicester, Louis started playing rugby as an eight-year-old with Wigston, the same club as both Martin Johnson and his father had played for. He later joined Syston and progressed to play for the County, the Midlands and England at U16 level. Since joining the Tigers Academy in 1997/98 he has appeared in the Tigers' Youth, U21 and Extras teams. He also represented England at U18 and U21 rugby before being selected for the England A team for the Churchill Cup in Canada in 2004. After a try-scoring performance for England A in their victory over France at Bath in February 2005, Louis was selected for his second Churchill Cup campaign last summer, playing in both games in Edmonton, Canada. Deacon was named in the matchday 22 for the first two of last season's autumn internationals, before making his senior England debut against Samoa at Twickenham in November 2005. He next turned out in England colours for the summer tour to Australia, playing in both Tests.

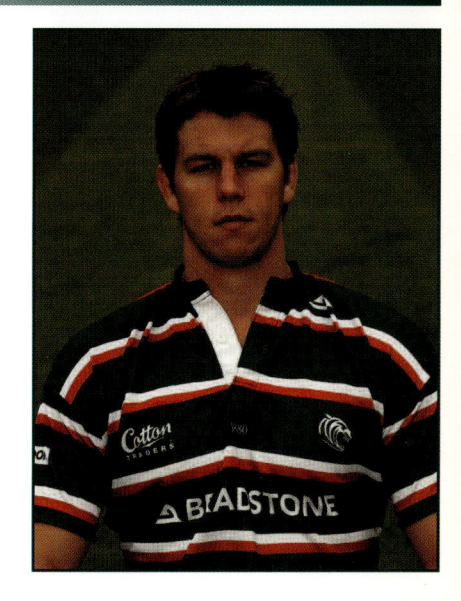

LOUIS DEACON

Position	Lock
Date of birth	7.10.80
Height	6'6"
Weight	17st 13lb
Tigers Debut	
12.08.00 v Cardiff	

Tigers Record	117 + 19 apps
	4 tries
	20 pts
Previous Clubs	Wigston, Syston
Rep Hons	England (3)

www.leicestertigers.com

PLAYER PROFILES

Harry Ellis

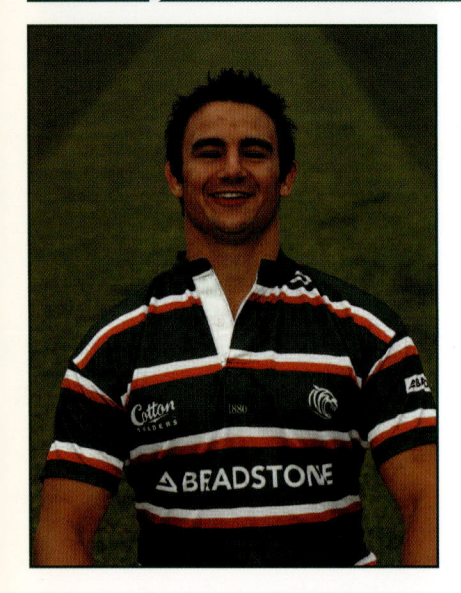

Scrum-half Harry started playing rugby as a six-year-old with South Leicester, then moved to Wigston for a year before joining Tigers' youth team in 1997 after attending a trial. The youngest of three rugby-playing brothers whose father also played for Tigers, Harry studied at Leicester Grammar School and De Montfort University and appeared for the County and Midlands at age group level before going on to represent England 'A', U16, U18, U19 and U21 levels, having appeared in the U18 group whilst only 16 years of age.

He also featured for England in the World Sevens series and was named in the England National Academy training squad announced in September 2003. Harry went on to appear for England A in their game against France in March 2004 and was then selected by Sir Clive Woodward to tour with England to Australia and New Zealand that summer, his first senior tour. He made his England debut in the game against South Africa at Twickenham in November 2004, and played against Australia the following week. He appeared in all Six Nations Championship games in 2005, scoring his debut try in the match against Scotland, was named in the matchday 22 for all three autumn internationals that year, and again was an ever-present during the 2006 Six Nations. Having made his senior club debut in the Orange Cup game in Toulouse in August 2001, Harry went on to score a superb individual try that helped defeat Llanelli in the Heineken Cup semi-final at Nottingham that season which contributed to him being named as the Tigers' Players Young Player of the Year 2001/02.

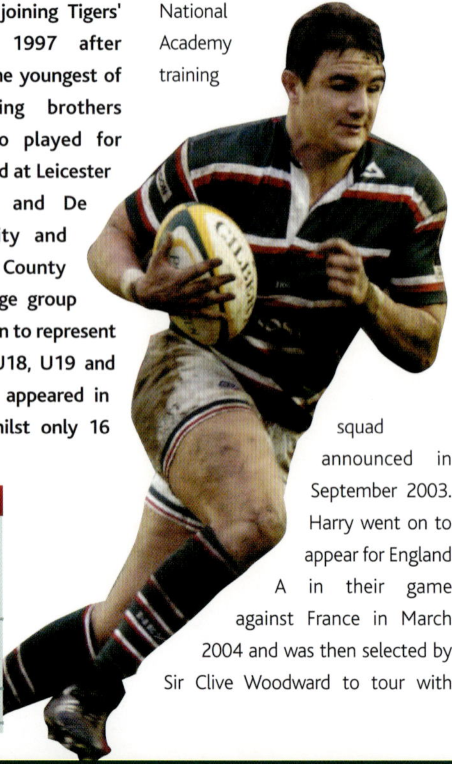

HARRY ELLIS

Position	Scrum-Half
Date of birth	17.05.82
Height	5'10"
Weight	13st 5lb
Tigers Debut	
25.08.01 v Toulouse	
Tigers Record	91 + 30 apps
	26 tries
	130 pts
Previous Clubs	South Leicester, Wigston
Rep Hons	England (13)

44 www.leicestertigers.com

PLAYER PROFILES

Daryl Gibson

Inside centre Daryl Gibson gained 19 New Zealand caps following his debut against Samoa in Albany in June 1999. He played throughout the 1999 Rugby World Cup; his only try for the All Blacks coming against Italy at Huddersfield in that competition.

He also appeared in all five games for the New Zealand Maori on their 1998 tour of Scotland and was called into the New Zealand Barbarians side that played England at Twickenham in December 2003 to celebrate the world champions' homecoming.

Daryl made a team record 78 appearances for the Crusaders in Super-12 rugby from 1996-2002, scoring 14 tries and gaining three winners' medals in 1998, 1999 and 2002. He also played 80 matches for Canterbury following his debut in June 1993, claiming 35 tries and winning the New Zealand Provincial Championship with them in 1997 and 2001. Educated at Christchurch Boys High School and Canterbury University, Gibson played for New Zealand U19 in 1993 and 1994, and New Zealand U21 in 1994, 1995 and 1996. He moved to England, joining Bristol Shoguns in September 2002, making his home debut against Leicester Tigers in the Zurich Premiership on 29 September. A mainstay of the Tigers team during the 2003 World Cup, Gibson has now made over 60 starts for the first XV, although his appearances during 2005/06 campaign were hampered due to injury, at times his experience in the back line was sorely missed.

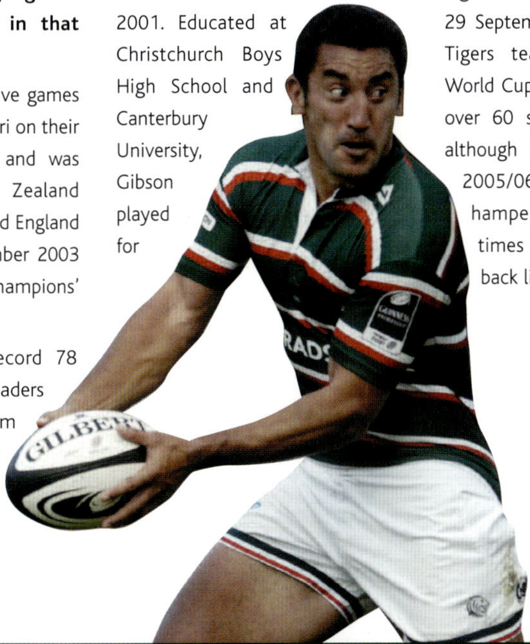

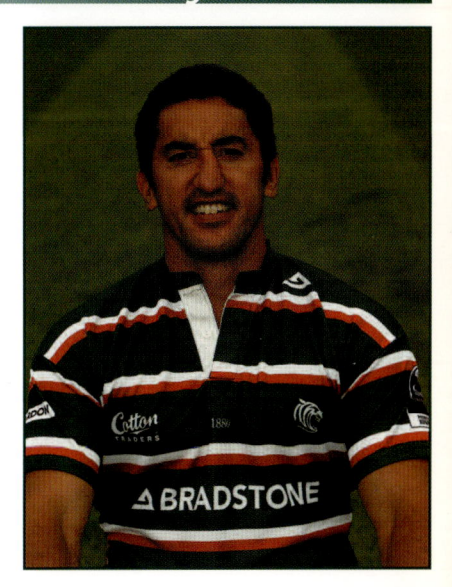

DARYL GIBSON			
Position	Centre	Tigers Record	64 + 3 apps
Date of birth	2.03.75		11 tries
Height	5'11"		55 pts
Weight	15st 4lb	Previous Clubs	Canterbury (NZ), Crusaders (NZ), Bristol Shoguns.
Tigers Debut			
13.09.03 v London Irish		Rep Hons	New Zealand (19)

www.leicestertigers.com 45

PLAYER PROFILES

Andy Goode

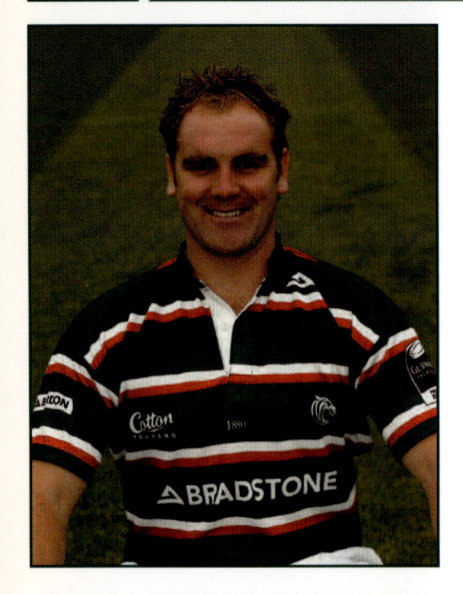

Fly-half Andy Goode rejoined Leicester Tigers in December 2003 after spending almost 18 months with Saracens.

He ended the 2003/04 season as the top Premiership points scorer with 266 in total; his 151 points for Leicester and 115 for Saracens meant he was the top points scorer in each team! In his earlier spell with Leicester, Andy had already picked up two Heineken Cup winners' medals - starting as fly-half against Stade Francais in Paris in 2001, and being a bench replacement against Munster in Cardiff the following year – an inaugural Zurich Championship medal and, despite his youth, played a substantial part in Tigers' record four successive Premiership titles. Andy has represented England at U18 and U21 level and, after an impressive performance in the England A game against France at Bath in February 2005, was called into the senior squad, making his England debut the following month as a replacement in the game against Italy during the Six Nations Championship. He was a member of the successful England XV that competed in the Churchill Cup in Canada in the summer of 2005, and was named in the matchday 22 for all of England's games in the 2006 Six Nations Championship. His most recent appearance in an England shirt came on the summer tour to Australia. His appearances for Leicester have now earned him a commemorative 100 games cap, his 100th start for the club coming in the fixture at Saracens in April 2005. Andy's 1,193 points to date make him fouth on the Tigers all-time top points scoring list behind Dusty Hare, John Liley and Tim Stimpson, whilst he was only the fifth player in Premiership history to pass 1,000 points. His 11 successful conversions in the 83-10 victory over Newcastle in February 2005 at Welford Road is a Leicester league record.

Educated at King Henry VIII School in Coventry, Andy started playing rugby at the age of five, however his sporting talent stretches beyond the rugby field, having been a bowler and opening batsman at school and a top-class swimmer.

ANDY GOODE

Position	Fly-Half
Date of birth	3.04.80
Height	5'11"
Weight	15st
Tigers Debut	
2.10.98 v Cardiff	

Tigers Record	128 + 21 apps
	22 tries
	1,193 pts
Previous Clubs	Nuneaton Colts, Coventry Colts, Saracens
Rep Hons	England (7)

PLAYER PROFILES

James Hamilton

Lock James Hamilton started playing rugby at the age of 15, joining local Coventry club Barker's Butts, the club that launched the careers of Neil Back and Leon Lloyd. He joined the Tigers Academy at the end of 1999 after being spotted by Andy Key and Dusty Hare playing for Warwickshire against Leicestershire.

James was selected for the England U19 team that took part in the U19 World Cup in Chile 2000/01, he has also represented England U21 in the shadow Six Nations in 2002 and 2003. James played regularly for the Tigers Youth team as well as being a member of Leicester's Championship-winning U21 side in 2002/03 and successful Zurich A League squad last season. James is one of three Tigers Academy players who took part in a training programme in Durban, South Africa, in the summer of 2001 whilst he journeyed to New Zealand to play for the Marist Albion club in Christchurch during the 2005 break. Having firmly established himself in the Tigers' first XV squad during 2005/06, James was selected for the Barbarians squad to play Scotland and Georgia in June.

JAMES HAMILTON			
Position	Lock	Tigers Record	19 + 16 apps
Date of birth	17.11.82		4 tries
Height	6'8"		20 pts
Weight	19st 6lb	Previous Clubs	Barker's Butts
Tigers Debut		Rep Hons	England U21
13.09.03 v London Irish			

www.leicestertigers.com

PLAYER PROFILES

Gavin Hickie

Hooker Gavin Hickie joined Leicester Tigers during the summer from Premiership outfit Worcester Warriors. He began his rugby at St Mary's College in Dublin and has played for Ireland Under-21 (in 2001) and Ireland A, winning the Six Nations title in 2002 at that level. Hickie captained Ireland U19 in 1999 and played for them in the Under-19 World Cup in Wales in the summer of that year.

Gavin made 32 appearances for Leinster in the Celtic League between 2001-04 plus a further seven games in the Heineken Cup.

Last season he played in ten matches for Worcester in the Guinness Premiership, and made another start for them in the Powergen Cup.

GAVIN HICKIE

Position	Hooker
Date of birth	24.04.80
Height	5'10"
Weight	15st 10lb
Tigers Debut	Yet to make Tigers debut.
Tigers Record	N/A
Previous Clubs	St Mary's College, Leinster, London Irish, Worcester Warriors.
Rep Hons	Ireland A

www.leicestertigers.com

PLAYER PROFILES

Dan Hipkiss

Having learnt his 'trade' at Hartsmere School and Diss rugby club in Norfolk, Leicester offered Dan a scholarship to Uppingham School and the chance to become involved in the Tigers' Youth set-up. Following in his father's footsteps, (he played for England Schools) Dan has represented England at U16, U17, U18 and U21 levels.

Having overcome a career-threatening injury suffered to his left knee in November 1999, Dan made his first start for the Tigers U21s against Leeds on 9 November 2001, scoring a try on his debut. He was called into the first team squad for summer training in 2002, and scored a stunning solo try on his senior debut in the Orange Cup victory against Biarritz Olympique in Bayonne. Dan became a regular member of the successful Tigers 2002/03 U21 team and was one of five Tigers youngsters called up for the 2003 IRB U21 World Cup. He was included in the England Sevens squad for the IRB Sevens in 2004 and has now participated in 11 World Sevens series events. A member of Tigers' successful Zurich A League squad 2004/05, Dan captained the Leicester side that played in the Middlesex Sevens at Twickenham in August 2005. He has now firmly established himself in the first team squad; his last-gasp try in the Heineken Cup victory at The Ospreys just before Christmas setting the Tigers on course for the knockout stages of the competition.

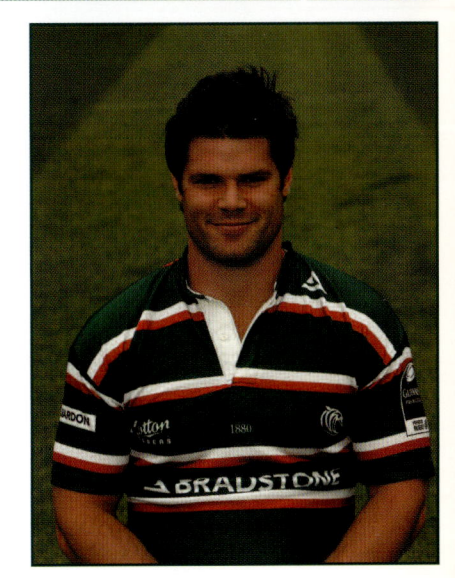

DAN HIPKISS			
Position	Centre	Tigers Record	24 + 12 apps
Date of birth	4.06.82		8 tries
Height	5'10"		40 pts
Weight	14st 3lb	Previous Clubs	Diss
Tigers Debut		Rep Hons	England U21/Sevens
24.10.02 v Biarritz Olympique			

www.leicestertigers.com 49

PLAYER PROFILES

Michael Holford

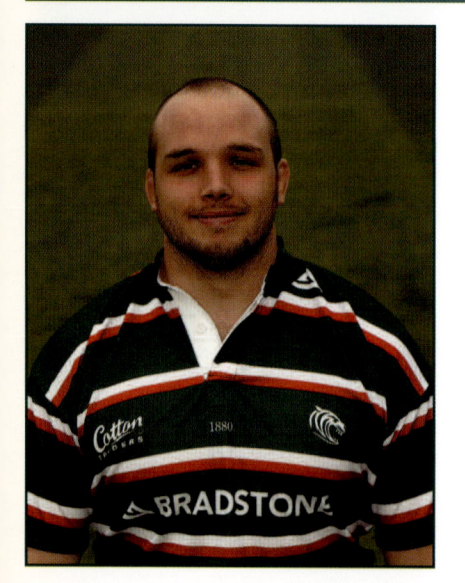

Born in Leicester, Michael attended Oakham School, gaining a sport scholarship to study for his A-Levels in Sports Science and Biology. He started playing rugby at the age of 10 and has since played for the England U18 Schools' team, England U19s, and was one of three young Tigers players to represent England in the IRB U21 World Championship in South Africa in the summer of 2002.

He went on to captain England U21A against their Welsh counterparts in December that year, and play for England U21 in their shadow Six Nations Championship 2003 as well as the FIRA World Cup in England in June that year. After playing for Syston, the talented youngster joined Tigers' Youth set-up in 1998 and has played in the Tigers' U21s, commanding a regular spot in their winning team of 2002/03, and for Tigers Extras, including their successful Zurich A League campaign of 2004/05. Now firmly established in Tigers' first team squad, Holford played in 19 Guinness Premiership games last season, scoring four tries, as well as turning out in both the Powergen and Heineken Cups. Michael was invited to play for the Hong Kong RFU Barbarians in their game against the Penguins marking the 50th anniversary of the Hong Kong RFU in the summer of 2004.

MICHAEL HOLFORD

Position	Prop
Date of birth	11.08.82
Height	5'11"
Weight	16st 1lb
Tigers Debut	
13.10.03 v Leeds Tykes	
Tigers Record	18 + 20 apps
	4 tries
	20 pts
Previous Clubs	Syston
Rep Hons	England U21

www.leicestertigers.com

PLAYER PROFILES

Ian Humphreys

Fly-half Ian Humphreys joined Leicester from the All Ireland League side Belfast Harlequins in the summer of 2005. He has represented Ulster, the province for which his famous brother David also plays, at 21 level, captaining them during the 2002/03 season.

Humphreys has represented Ireland at U19 and U21 level, and captained the Irish side at the Rugby World Cup Sevens tournament in Hong Kong in March 2005, the team finally going out to Samoa in the Plate quarter-finals. He had previously been named player of the tournament for the European Sevens qualifier in Poland. Ian's first

outing in Tigers stripes was at the Middlesex Sevens tournament at Twickenham in August last year. He has since become a regular member of Tigers' successful Guinness A League squad and made six appearances for the first team. Ian represented the Barbarians in November 2004, playing against the Combined Services, and after joining Leicester was again selected for the famous invitational side, this time facing the Royal Navy in April 2006, becoming the 86th Leicester player to represent the Baabaas. The 23-year-old crossed for a late try that sealed a 31-10 victory.

IAN HUMPHREYS

Position	Fly-half	**Tigers Record**	4 + 2 apps
Date of birth	24.04.82		37 pts
Height	5'11"	**Previous Clubs**	Ballymena, Belfast
Weight	13st 1lb		Harlequins, Ulster
Tigers Debut		**Rep Hons**	Ireland U21/Sevens
30.09.05 v Newport Gwent Dragons			

www.leicestertigers.com   51

PLAYER PROFILES

Shane Jennings

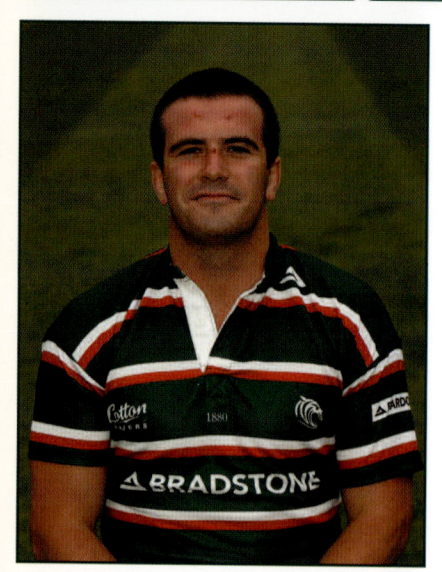

Flanker Shane Jennings joined Tigers in the summer of 2005 from Irish province Leinster where he had played in 10 Heineken Cup games following his debut against Biarritz in 2003, his last appearance in the competition appropriately being against Leicester Tigers in the quarter-finals.

Jennings also made 29 appearances for Leinster in the Celtic League and Cup after making his senior debut for the province against Glasgow at Hughenden in September 2002. He has represented Ireland at Schools, U19, 21 and A level and captained Leinster on several occasions during 2003/04 in the absence of Reggie Corrigan on World Cup duty. After an impressive first outing in Tigers stripes when playing for the club at the Middlesex Sevens at Twickenham, scoring a try in just 32 seconds of the first round, Shane went on to secure his place in Leicester's back row, making 25 starts and coming off the bench on a further four occasions in his first season. Such were his performances that he was named by his teammates as the Tigers Players' Player of the Season 2005/06. Jennings led the Ireland A side to Canada in June for the Churchill Cup where victory over England in the Plate final secured his team third place.

SHANE JENNINGS

Position	Flanker
Date of birth	8.07.81
Height	6'
Weight	16st 2lb
Tigers Debut	3.09.05 v Northampton Saints
Tigers Record	25 + 4 apps
	3 tries
	15 pts
Previous Clubs	St. Mary's College, Leinster
Rep Hons	Ireland A

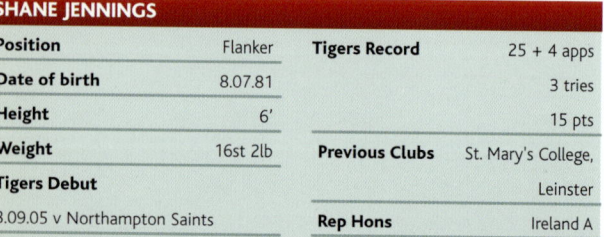

www.leicestertigers.com

PLAYER PROFILES

Ben Kay

An England World Cup winner and one of the Tigers' 2005 British Lions contingent, lock Ben Kay gained his Lions cap playing in the first test against New Zealand in Christchurch. Previously, Ben had given an outstanding performance in the second row for England alongside club colleague Martin Johnson during the 2003 Rugby World Cup, never being replaced in the six games he played during the tournament.

He also featured in all of England's Six Nations games in the intervening two years and has since toured with England to Australia in the summer, playing in the second test in Melbourne.

Ben was educated at Merchant Taylor's School before attending Loughborough University, where he obtained his degree in Sports Science. He has played rugby at Queensland University in Australia, and represented England at U18, U19, Students, U21 and A level as well as appearing for the Barbarians. After showing tremendous form for Tigers during the 2000/01 season Kay was chosen for England to tour Canada and the USA, making his senior debut in the test against Canada at Markham. He was named in the starting line-up for all the Six Nations games in spring 2002; toured with England to Argentina that summer; went on to compete in both the autumn internationals and the 2003 Six Nations, before touring to New Zealand and Australia before the World Cup. After an impressive season he was voted as the Tigers Members' Player of the Year 2001/02. Ben has been named in the starting line up on over 100 occasions for the club, gaining his commemorative cap in the Heineken Cup fixture against the Newport Gwent Dragons at Welford Road on 14 December 2003. A double Heineken Cup winner with Leicester, and a member of the Tigers squad during the last three of their Premiership-winning campaigns, Kay was awarded an MBE in the 2004 New Year's Honours list.

BEN KAY

Position	Lock
Date of birth	14.12.75
Height	6'6"
Weight	17st 9lb
Tigers Debut	
11.09.99 v Northampton	

Tigers Record	148 + 31 apps
	9 tries
	45 pts
Previous Clubs	Waterloo,
	Queensland University (Aus)
Rep Hons	England (41), Lions (1)

www.leicestertigers.com   53

PLAYER PROFILES

Leon Lloyd

Prior to making his debut for the Tigers first team, Leon was a successful try scorer for the Tigers Youth XV and Development XV before a serious car accident sidelined him for six months.

He eventually made his full Tigers debut in 1996 and was part of the squad that won the Madrid Sevens that year. He scored his first memorable try in the Tigers' remarkable Heineken Cup victory at Pau. Leon was selected for England Colts, the Barbarians and England U21 in 1997, two years later he played for England A, and also equalled Rory Underwood's 1985 record of four tries scored in a single domestic Cup tie. In 1999 Leon was included in England's World Cup squad but did not play and in fact had to wait until the following summer to win his first cap in South Africa. He appeared again for England on their tour to Canada and the USA in 2001, unfortunately he suffered a shoulder injury which required surgery and kept him out of the Tigers squad for the start of the 2001/02 season. However, Leon recovered well and returned to the form that saw him score the match-winning try in Tigers' first Heineken Cup Final, only to be cruelly struck down by injury again and denied the chance to repeat his performance when Leicester retained the trophy in May 2002. That injury also ruled him out of the England Sevens squad for the Commonwealth Games in Manchester in which he had been named after his participation in the Brisbane Sevens in February 2002. Leon has now made nearly 250 appearances for Leicester, scoring 82 tries, and 2006/07 will see him celebrate his testimonial season.

LEON LLOYD

Position	Wing/Centre
Date of birth	22.09.77
Height	6'4"
Weight	14st 8lb
Tigers Debut	
8.10.96 v Bridgend	

Tigers Record	222 + 22 apps
	82 tries
	410 pts
Previous Clubs	Barker's Butts
Rep Hons	England (5)

54 www.leicestertigers.com

PLAYER PROFILES

Lewis Moody

A British Lion and World Cup winner, at the time of his debut in 1996 Lewis became the youngest first-team Tiger to feature in a league game.

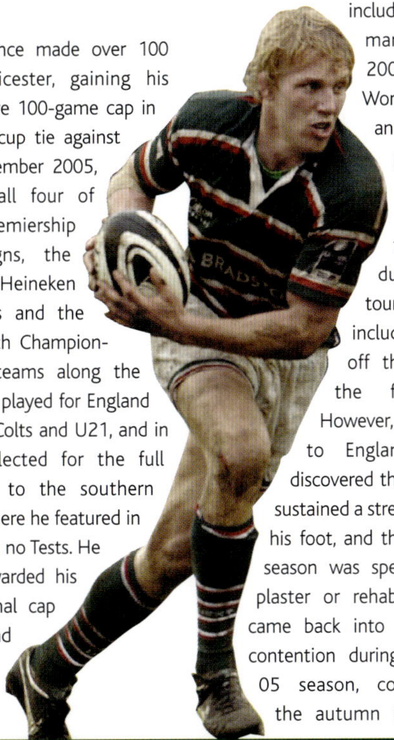

Moody has since made over 100 starts for Leicester, gaining his commemorative 100-game cap in the Heineken cup tie against Wasps in December 2005, featuring in all four of Leicester's Premiership title campaigns, the back-to-back Heineken Cup successes and the inaugural Zurich Championship-winning teams along the way. Lewis has played for England Schools, U18, Colts and U21, and in 1998 was selected for the full England tour to the southern hemisphere where he featured in two games but no Tests. He was finally awarded his full international cap on the England tour to Canada and the USA in 2001. Injury dogged his international and club career over the next couple of seasons, however he recovered well enough to be included in the 30-man England 2003 Rugby World Cup squad and went on to play some part in all seven of the games during the tournament, including coming off the bench in the final itself. However, on his return to England, it was discovered that Lewis had sustained a stress fracture to his foot, and the rest of his season was spent either in plaster or rehabilitation. He came back into international contention during the 2004/05 season, competing in the autumn international games and the Six Nations championship. As a result of performances in those, and for his club, he was named in the British and Irish Lions touring party to New Zealand, playing the last two Tests. On his return, he featured in the starting line-up for every England international until injury forced him out of the second test in Australia in the summer. An all-round sportsman, Lewis competed in athletics, cricket and swimming at school before deciding to concentrate on rugby. He was named Tigers Young Player of the Season 1998/99 and the Zurich Young Player of the Season 2001/02. Along with six of his Tigers colleagues, he was awarded an MBE in the 2004 Queen's New Year's Honours list.

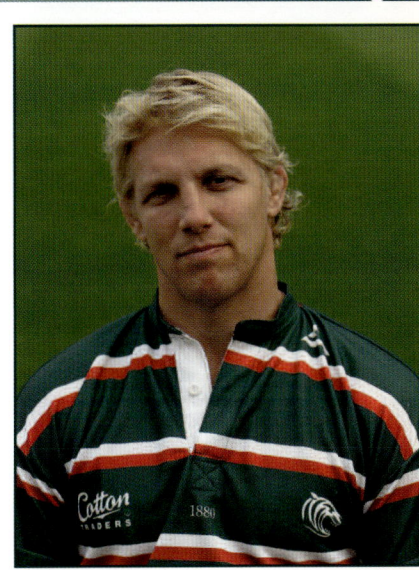

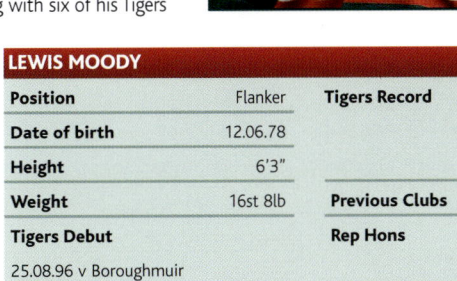

LEWIS MOODY

Position	Flanker
Date of birth	12.06.78
Height	6'3"
Weight	16st 8lb
Tigers Debut	
25.08.96 v Boroughmuir	

Tigers Record	119 + 42 apps
	23 tries
	115 pts
Previous Clubs	Oakham, Bracknell
Rep Hons	England (40),
	British Lions (2)

www.leicestertigers.com 55

PLAYER PROFILES

Alejandro Moreno

Prop Alex Moreno joined Leicester during the summer of 2005 from French club Brive, after making 13 appearances for them in France's Top 16 and the European Challenge Cup. It was not Alex's first visit to Welford Road; he played there for Italy against Tonga during the 1999 World Cup.

That was his debut for Italy having already gained international recognition, winning three caps for Argentina during the 1998 South American Championship. Moreno went on to play for Italy against New Zealand also in the 1999 World Cup, and then appeared twice as a replacement during the 2002 Six Nations Championship. Originally playing his rugby with the San Fernando club in Buenos Aires, Alejandro switched to play for the French side Agen in 1999. He then joined Worcester in the summer of 2001, playing for a season in English National Division One. Two seasons in Perpignan followed, during which time he was a bench replacement for the French Championship final of 2004 in which Perpignan lost to Stade Francais. Since his debut at Northampton, Alejandro has turned out a dozen times for Tigers' first team, packing down on both sides of the scrum, including the trip down to Sixways to play against his old team, Worcester Warriors, in November. A promising player, unfortunately his season was ended prematurely due to injury.

ALEJANDRO MORENO

Position	Prop
Date of birth	26.04.73
Height	6'1"
Weight	17st 5lb
Tigers Debut	
3.09.05 v Northampton Saints	

Tigers Record	11 + 1 apps
Previous Clubs	San Fernando (AR), Agen (FR), Worcester, Perpignan (FR), Brive (FR)
Rep Hons	Argentina (3), Italy (4)

www.leicestertigers.com

PLAYER PROFILES

Frank Murphy

Scrum-half Frank Murphy made four appearances for Ireland U21s during 2002, including a game against Fiji in that season's IRB Under-21 World Cup in Johannesburg.

He joined Munster from University College Cork in the summer of 2003 and made 15 appearances for the province in the Celtic League, scoring one try against Ulster at Thomond Park in March 2004.

He was also named in Munster's Heineken Cup squad last season and featured as a bench replacement in the quarter-final against Perpignan at Lansdowne Road. Educated at Christian Brothers College, Frank has also previously played for Ireland Schools.

FRANK MURPHY

Position	Scrum-Half
Date of birth	2.12.81
Height	5'9"
Weight	13st
Tigers Debut	
Yet to make Tigers debut.	

Tigers Record	N/A
Previous Clubs	University College Cork, Munster
Rep Hons	Ireland U21

www.leicestertigers.com 57

PLAYER PROFILES

Geordan Murphy

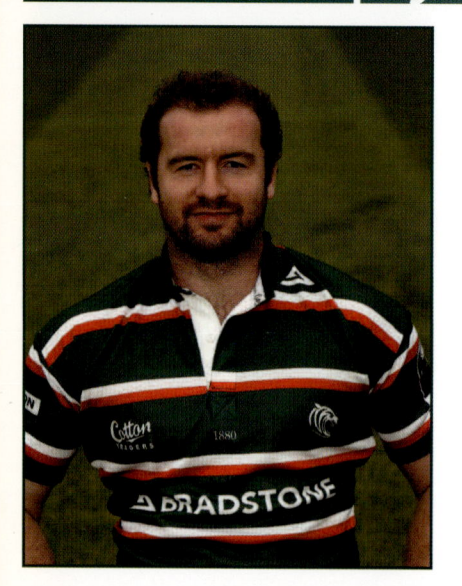

One of eight Tigers players named by Sir Clive Woodward for the British and Irish Lions tour to New Zealand in the summer of 2005, Geordan played in seven games including the 3rd Test in Auckland. Born in Dublin, the youngest of six children who all played rugby, Geordan was educated at Newbridge College, Naas before attending De Montfort University in Leicester.

He first represented his country playing at U19 level and in June 2000, after appearing for Ireland A and an Ireland XV, he made his full Ireland debut against the United States, scoring twice. He played during the 2002 Six Nations tournament and toured with Ireland that summer, but missed the start of Tigers' 2002/03 campaign after undergoing surgery. He returned to fitness in time to participate in the autumn internationals, and his form for his country in the 2003 Six Nations, where he was an ever-present, earned him the accolade of being named Irish Player of the Season by the Irish Rugby Writers. He was also voted Tigers Supporters Player of the Season the same year. Murphy was tipped to be one of the outstanding players at the Rugby World Cup until fate dealt him a cruel blow: he broke his left leg in a seemingly innocuous tackle in Ireland's last warm-up game against Scotland at Murrayfield. He returned to club action earlier than anticipated and was almost immediately back into international action, playing for Ireland during the Six Nations and touring with them to South Africa in June 2004. He appeared in all of Ireland's international Tests leading up to the Lions tour, and was then an ever-present in the Ireland starting line-up until the summer tour to Australia and New Zealand.

A member of Leicester's successful Heineken Cup-winning teams of 2001 and 2002, scoring a try in the victory over Munster when Tigers retained the trophy, Murphy has won four Premiership titles with the club 1998/99 to 2001/02 as well as the inaugural Zurich Championship in 2001/02.

GEORDAN MURPHY

Position	Full-back/Wing
Date of birth	19.04.78
Height	6'1"
Weight	13st 3lb
Tigers Debut	14.11.97 v Rotherham
Tigers Record	170 + 15 apps
	73 tries
	571 pts
Previous Clubs	Naas, Auckland GS (NZ)
Rep Hons	Ireland (41) Lions (1).

PLAYER PROFILES

Johne **Murphy**

Full back/wing Johne Murphy joined Tigers having impressed during a loan spell with the club at the start of the 2005/06 season.

Hailing from Naas near Dublin, Johne attended the same school as his Leicester namesake Geordan and, like Geordan, attributes some of his kicking skills to his experience in Gaelic football. Johne first came to the attention of the Leicester coaching staff while playing in a game against Tigers Academy in Ireland the previous season. Having scored a try on his debut Guinness A League game, Murphy went on to make five appearances for the Tigers Development team during their successful 2005/06 campaign before major knee surgery ruled him out of the rest of the season.

JOHNE MURPHY

Position	Full-back/Wing	Previous Clubs	Lansdowne
Date of birth	10.11.84		Cill Dara
Height	6'1"		
Weight	14st 6lb		
Tigers Debut			
Yet to make Tigers Debut			

www.leicestertigers.com

PLAYER PROFILES

Ian Nimmo

Lock Ian Nimmo joined Tigers from Scottish club Heriots during the summer of 2005 after helping the club to second place in the SRU BT Premiership Division One that season.

He has played for Scotland at U18, U19 and U21 levels; his U19 honours include the 2004 IRB World Championship in Durban, South Africa. His U21 international debut followed when Scotland lost only narrowly 12-8 to France in Bourgoin in February. He was an ever-present in the No.4 shirt for Scotland U21 in their shadow Six Nations Championship last season, and again represented them at the IRB U21 World Championships in France during the summer. Since joining Leicester, Ian has been a regular member of the successful Tigers Extras squad that claimed the 2005/06 Guinness A League title.

IAN NIMMO

Position	Lock	Tigers Record	N/A
Date of birth	25.07.85	Previous Clubs	Heriots
Height	6'7"	Rep Hons	Scotland U21
Weight	18st 12lb		
Tigers Debut			
Yet to make Tigers debut.			

www.leicestertigers.com

PLAYER PROFILES

Seru Rabeni

A former teacher, centre Seru Rabeni played for the Fijian first division side Lautoka whilst at college, before moving on to the capital's club, Suva. Seru is also an accomplished Sevens player, making his debut in Dubai in 1998, playing in two Hong Kong Sevens tournaments and appearing for Fiji in the 2002 Commonwealth Games in Manchester.

He played at both U21 and U23 level for Fiji before making his senior Test debut in May 2000 against Japan in Tokyo during the Epson Cup tournament. He has since toured with Fiji to New Zealand in 2002, and the same year played Wales at the Millennium Stadium. The following year he toured with the national side to South America and started all four of Fiji's pool games in the 2003 World Cup. He has also played for the unified team, the Pacific Islanders. In 2001 Seru took up a three-year degree course at Otago University, New Zealand, and the following year played seven games for Otago in the National Provincial Championship before gaining a Super 12 contract with Highlanders for whom he played a dozen games over the 2003 and 2004 seasons. Following his Tigers debut in September 2004, Seru became only the ninth player in the 124-year history of the Tigers to score tries in each of his first three starts, he went on to score eight tries in his first 10 appearances. His progress was hampered after knee surgery kept him on the sidelines for most of last season, but he returned in time to play for Fiji in the Pacific Five Nations during the summer.

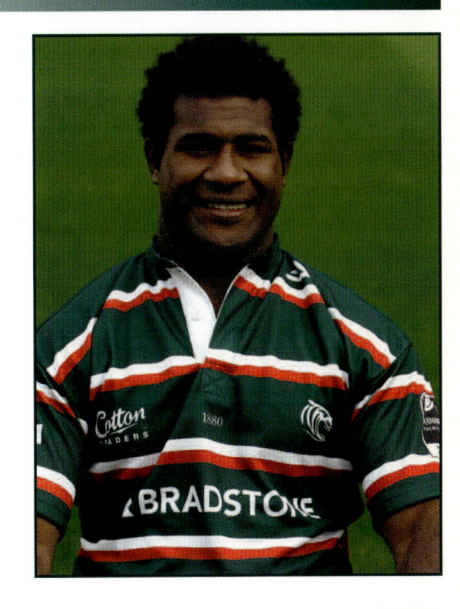

SERU RABENI

Position	Centre/Wing
Date of birth	27.12.78
Height	6'2"
Weight	16st 5lb
Tigers Debut	5.09.04 v Sale Sharks

Tigers Record	14 + 4 apps
	8 tries
	40 pts
Previous Clubs	Lautoka (FJ), Suva (FJ), Otago (NZ), Highlanders (NZ)
Rep Hons	Fiji (20), Pacific Islanders (3)

www.leicestertigers.com 61

PLAYER PROFILES

Graham Rowntree

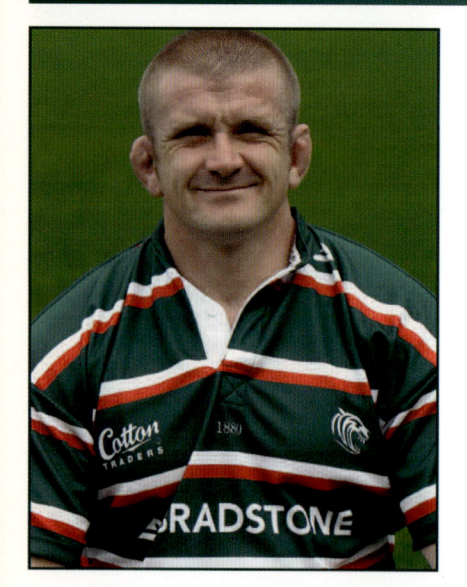

Since joining Tigers' Youth set-up in 1988, and making his full debut against Oxford University in 1990, Graham has gone on to make almost 400 first-team appearances for the club, placing him sixth on the Tigers' all-time list.

Graham also became only the 2nd player from any club to make 200 appearances in the English top division and was the first Leicester player to receive the ERC Elite award for appearing in 50 Heineken Cup games. Season 2004/05 saw him receive the Tigers' Members Award for Outstanding Service, the second time he had received the accolade. He has appeared in three Heineken Cup finals for the club, winning two; four Pilkington Cup finals, also winning two; and has been a member of five championship wining squads. In 1993 he made his England A, Barbarians and Midlands debuts, and in 1995 he gained his first full England cap against Scotland in the Five Nations tournament. He was a prominent figure in the next two Five Nations tournaments, the 1995 and 1999 World Cups, and also in the Lions tour to South Africa in 1997, playing six games but no Tests. After the World Cup, Graham was not capped for almost two years until a series of imperious performances for his club forced him back into international contention. He was selected for the England squad to tour Canada and the USA in 2001; participated in all that season's autumn internationals and capped in each of the following Six Nations games. An ever-present in the 2003 Six Nations Championship, he toured with England to New Zealand and Australia that summer, putting in a memorable performance against the All Blacks. He was very unlucky to miss out on selection for the World Cup squad, however he was selected for England in all three of the autumn international series and the first four Six Nations games in 2005. He was one of eight Tigers players named by Sir Clive Woodward for the British and Irish Lions tour to New Zealand that summer, and finally gained his first Lions cap in the second Test, eight years after his original Lions selection. His latest outing in international colours came when he was selected to tour Australia with England in June, playing in both Tests.

GRAHAM ROWNTREE			
Position	Prop	Tigers Record	361 + 36 apps
Date of birth	18.04.71		18 tries
Height	6'		87 pts
Weight	17st 3lb	Previous Clubs	Nuneaton Colts
Tigers Debut		Rep Hons	England (54), Lions (2)
23.10.90 v Oxford University			

PLAYER PROFILES

Matt Smith

Matt, son of former club captain and coach Ian "Dosser" Smith, started playing rugby at Oakham School at the age of 11. He represented the school in their Daily Mail Cup Final victory, 30-28 over Barnard Castle at Twickenham in 2003.

Invited into the junior academy at U16 level, Matt has also participated in Tigers' apprenticeship scheme. A regular for the Tigers' Development XV, he has made 16 appearances for Leicester in the Guinness A League over the past couple of seasons. Although Matt has mostly played at full back, he has also started at centre and fly half. He played in both legs of the 2006 Guinness A League Final, when Leicester retained their trophy beating NEC Harlequins 58-51 on aggregate. Matt was also part of the first team pre-season to tour to France and also started the match with Toulon at Welford Road.

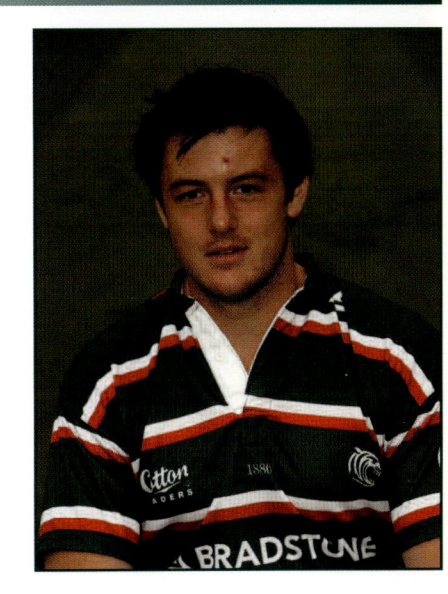

MATT SMITH	
Position	Full Back/Centre
Date of birth	15.11.85
Height	6'4"
Weight	15st 2lb
Tigers Debut	
17.03.06 v Barbarians	

Tigers Record	1 app

www.leicestertigers.com 63

PLAYER PROFILES

Ollie Smith

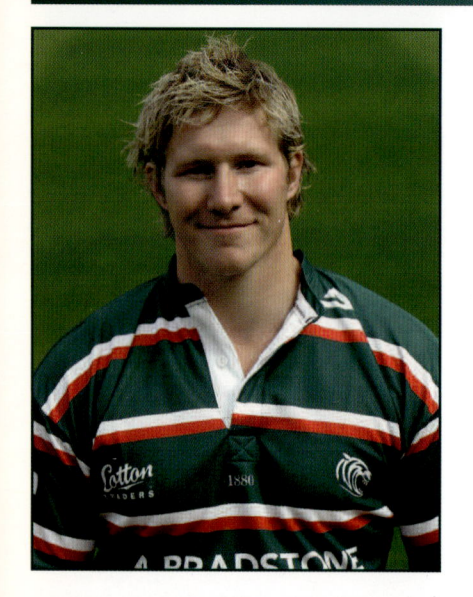

Centre Ollie Smith started playing junior rugby with Old Bosworthians and then switched to Market Bosworth at U14 level. He joined Tigers in 1999 after attending a trial and went on to surpass Lewis Moody's record for the being youngest Tigers player to appear in a league game. Success in the Heineken Cup final at Cardiff in 2002 also made him the only teenager to hold a Heineken Cup winner's medal.

Ollie had played for England at U18, U19 and U21 levels before finally making his senior debut, getting on as a replacement in the Six Nations game against Italy at Twickenham in March 2003. Named in Clive Woodward's extended World Cup squad during the summer of 2003, Smith made his first start for England in the game against France in Marseilles. His performance during a season curtailed by injury earned him a nomination for Young Player of the Season 2002/03 by the Professional Rugby Players Association. He had previously been voted the 2000/01 and 2001/02 Tigers' Members' Young Player of the Season, as well as the Players' Young Player of the Season in 2000/01.

Ollie forced his way back into international contention with an outstanding performance for England A against France A, scoring a try in the game at Bath in February 2005, then played in the final two Six Nations games that year. He was selected to tour with the British and Irish Lions party to New Zealand in the summer, playing in five games and scoring two tries.

Last season Ollie earned his commemorative Tigers 100 cap in the Heineken Cup game against Clermont Auvergne at Welford Road in October.

OLLIE SMITH

Position	Centre/Wing
Date of birth	14.08.82
Height	6'1"
Weight	14st 7lb
Tigers Debut	16.09.00 v London Irish
Tigers Record	122 + 20 apps
	31 tries
	155 pts
Previous Clubs	Old Bosworthians, Market Bosworth
Rep Hons	England (5)

64 www.leicestertigers.com

PLAYER PROFILES

Alesana Tuilagi

Alesana Tuilagi joined Leicester from Italian club Parma, for whom he had played the previous two seasons after joining his brother Henry in Europe.

Alesana was equal second-top try scorer in Italy in the 2003/04 season, his 12 tries helping his club to the semi-finals of both the Italian Super 10 Championship and the Parker Pen Shield. Now in his second spell at the Tigers, Alesana had previously made 11 appearances for the Under-21 team during the 2000/01 season, playing alongside future first teamers Sam Vesty and Harry Ellis. A member of the successful 2004/05 Zurich A League squad, Alesana set a Zurich A League record by scoring five tries in the game against Leeds in September 2004. Now firmly established in the Tigers first XV, making 24 appearances and scoring seven tries last season, the strong-running wing is fast becoming a crowd favourite. Alesana made his international debut for Samoa in their World Cup qualifier against Fiji in June 2002, and in his five international appearances during the summer of 2005 he scored five tries, four in a single game against Tonga in Apia. Unfortunately his appearance for Samoa at Twickenham last season was marred when he was red carded along with Leicester teammate Lewis Moody for an altercation in the 77th minute.

ALESANA TUILAGI

Position	Wing
Date of birth	24.02.81
Height	6'1"
Weight	17st 7lb
Tigers Debut	
11.09.04 v Leeds Tykes	

Tigers Record	24 + 19 apps
	17 tries
	85 pts
Previous Clubs	Parma (IT)
Rep Hons	Samoa (10)

www.leicestertigers.com 65

PLAYER PROFILES

Anitelea Tuilagi

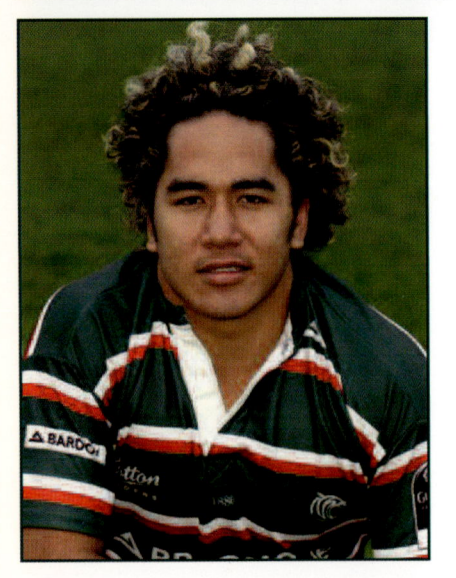

Utility back Anitelea Tuilagi became the fourth member of the Tuilagi family to play at Leicester since Freddie made the move from St Helens rugby league club in June 2000.

As with his elder brothers, he has represented his country on eight occasions to date, scoring four Test tries - the first on his Test debut against Tonga in July 2005. Over the summer he scored a further three Test tries during the Pacific Five Nations, one in the game against Japan in New Plymouth, New Zealand, and a brace versus Tonga in the game played in Gosford, Australia. Anitelea has also played seven games for the Tigers Development XV in the Guinness A League over the past two seasons, scoring three tries. He is currently on a season-long loan deal with Leeds Tykes.

ANITELEA TUILAGI

Position	Utility Back
Date of birth	5.06.86
Height	6'1"
Weight	15st 2lb
Tigers Debut	
12.11.05 vs. Gloucester	

Tigers Record	0+1 app.
Previous Clubs	Fogapoa, Samoa
Rep Hons	Samoa (8)

66 www.leicestertigers.com

PLAYER PROFILES

Henry Tuilagi

Henry Tuilagi made a real impact in the back row after joining his elder brother Fereti at Leicester. Henry made 24 first-team appearances in his first season, scoring a try on his debut in the opening game against London Irish, and went on to consolidate his position both in the team and as a favourite of the fans.

His 2004/05 season was cut short however when he suffered a broken leg in the final home Premiership match against London Wasps in April, the recovery from which restricted him to just three first team appearances last season. Henry previously played for Italian club Parma, where his younger brother Alesana had joined him for a season. The No 8 was first included in the Samoa squad for the 2000 Pacific Rim Championship but had to wait another two years for his test debut against Fiji in Apia, Samoa in June 2002. Both Fereti and Alesana joined him in the international team later in the month when the three brothers played together in the World Cup qualifier against Fiji at Nadi. Henry now has four international caps. He was also capped for Samoa at Rugby League in 1999.

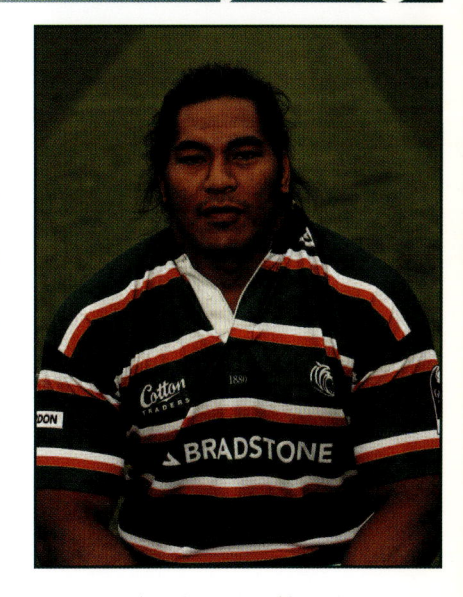

HENRY TUILAGI			
Position	Back Row	**Tigers Record**	24 + 23 apps
Date of birth	12.08.76		8 tries
Height	6'1"		40 pts
Weight	18st 8lb	**Previous Clubs**	
Tigers Debut		Marist St Joseph's (SAM), Parma (IT)	
13.09.03 v London Irish		**Rep Hons**	Samoa (4)

www.leicestertigers.com

PLAYER PROFILES

Tom **Varndell**

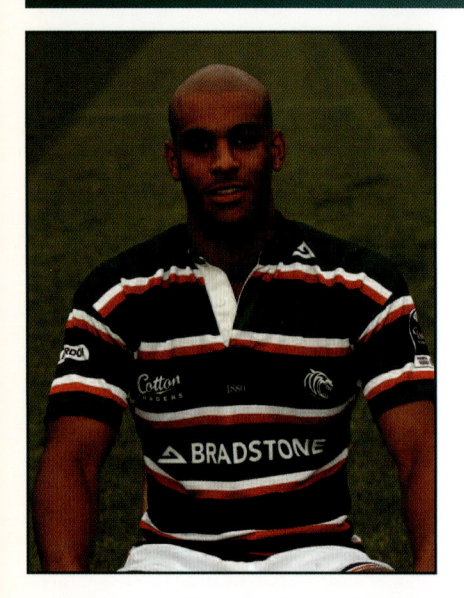

Winger Tom Varndell, a graduate of Colston College, returned to Leicester Tigers in the summer of 2004 having previously spent two years at the Tigers Academy under the guidance of Dusty Hare. The speedy youngster made an impressive start in the Zurich Premiership, scoring a hat-trick in his second outing at Worcester in November 2004.

An ever-present in England's U21 squad during the 2004/05 shadow Six Nations, he also toured with them to Argentina that summer, competing in the IRB U21 World Cup. Tom has also tasted success with the England Sevens squad, winning a silver medal at the Commonwealth Games in Melbourne in March 2006, and the following month was a member of the England team that took the Hong Kong Sevens title. Varndell finished the 2005/06 season as the top try scorer in the Guinness Premiership, claiming 14 tries in 21 outings in the competition, including a hat-trick in the victory over former champions Wasps at Welford Road in April. He was also the Tigers' top try scorer overall, running in 21 tries in all tournaments during the season, the best total since Simon Povoas scored 25 tries in 1989/90. His talent was recognised when he was named as the Tigers Young Player of the Season and the Premiership's Land Rover Discovery of the Season. Tom made his debut for the England senior team against Samoa at Twickenham in November last year, and toured to Australia with England this summer, scoring two tries in his three international appearances to date.

TOM VARNDELL

Position	Wing
Date of birth	16.09.85
Height	6'3"
Weight	15st
Tigers Debut	
6.11.04 v Gloucester	

Tigers Record	31 + 7 apps
	29 tries
	145 pts
Previous Clubs	N/A
Rep Hons	England (3)

68 www.leicestertigers.com

PLAYER PROFILES

Sam Vesty

Sam started playing rugby at age 10 having been inspired by his father Phil (who used to play prop for the Tigers). After graduating through the Tigers' U21 team and Tigers Extras, Sam was rewarded with a first-team debut, coming on as a second-half replacement in the Orange Cup game against Biarritz Olympique, making him the fourth generation of his family to play for Leicester.

Having already represented his country at U18 level, Sam was one of three Tigers youngsters in the England squad that competed in the IRB U21 World Championship in South Africa during the summer of 2002.

Propelled into the Tigers' first team for the 2002/03 season due to injuries, Sam acquitted himself well in the pivotal role of fly half, picking up both the Supporters' and Players' awards for Young Player of the Season. During the 2004/05 Sam switched to full-back to accommodate the return of Andy Goode; his form was such that he was selected for the England XV for the Churchill Cup in Canada during that summer. His switch to full-back suited Tigers' style of play, and his safe hands and ability to spot gaps, as well as the flexibility of moving into the fly-half position, built his reputation during the 2005/06 season when he was voted by members as the Tigers Player of the Season. He again toured to Canada in the summer with England A and was selected for all three games in the Churchill Cup. Sam's sporting talent stretches beyond the rugby field on to the cricket pitches where he has played for the Leicestershire 2nd XI and Leicestershire U19, as well as playing tennis at county level.

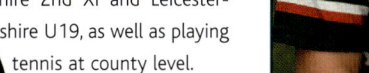

SAM VESTY

Position	Utility Back
Date of birth	26.11.81
Height	6'
Weight	14st 3lb
Tigers Debut	
24.08.02 v Biarritz Olympique	

Tigers Record	67 + 25 apps
	7 tries
	111 pts
Previous Clubs	N/A
Rep Hons	England XV

www.leicestertigers.com 69

PLAYER PROFILES

Julian White

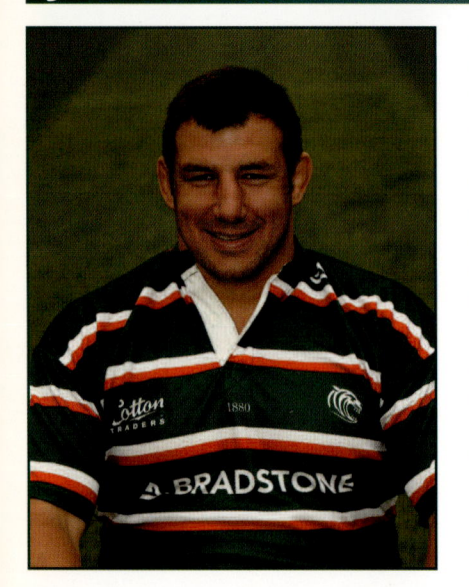

After signing for the Tigers in the summer of 2003, prop Julian White's Leicester debut was held over as he was in Australia on duty with England at the Rugby World Cup. Having made his international debut at Loftus Versfeld in Pretoria in June 2000, Julian then toured with England to North America in 2001.

A knee injury sustained during the 2003 Six Nations curtailed further international appearances but he did regain his fitness in time to be included in the final World Cup warm-up games against France and Wales. His performances ensured his place on the plane to Australia.

Since then Julian has played in the 2004 Six Nations Championship; toured with England to New Zealand and Australia in the summer of 2004; was an ever-present for that year's autumn internationals and played the first game of the 2005 Six Nations campaign before succumbing to injury. His form was such that he was named among the Leicester contingent for the 2005 summer tour to New Zealand by the British and Irish Lions, playing in all three Tests at tighthead. He was rested for last season's autumn internationals, but returned to the squad for all 2006 Six Nations games and toured with England to Australia in the summer. White is one of a select band of four England capped players who have appeared in the Southern Hemisphere's Super-12 tournament, appearing for the Crusaders against Natal at Christchurch in 1997 whilst in New Zealand playing for Hawke's Bay, with whom he appeared in the NZ Provincial Championship. Returning to the UK, White played for Bridgend in 1998/99 before switching to Saracens for two seasons. He joined Bristol at the start of 2002/03. Along with his England teammates Julian was awarded an MBE in the 2004 New Year's Honours.

JULIAN WHITE

Position	Prop
Date of birth	14.05.73
Height	6'1"
Weight	18st
Tigers Debut	
29.11.03 v Bath	

Tigers Record	49 + 6 apps
	2 tries
	10 pts
Previous Clubs	Dannevirke RSC (NZ), Hawke's Bay (NZ), Crusaders (NZ), Bridgend, Saracens, Bristol
Rep Hons	England (35) Lions (3)

www.leicestertigers.com

PLAYER PROFILES

David Young

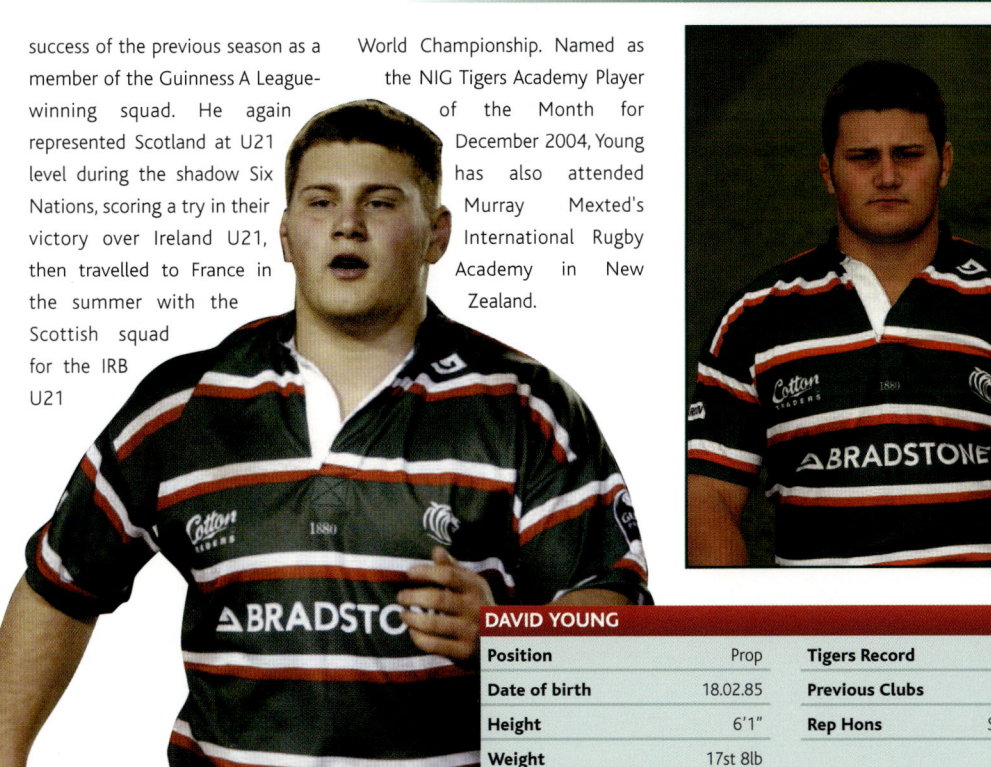

Prop David Young joined Leicester Tigers' academy in 2004 and was elevated to the first-team squad last season following solid performances for Tigers Extras during their successful Zurich A League campaign.

Young played for Scotland U19 at the IRB U19 World Cup in Durban, South Africa in 2004 and for Scotland U21 during last season's shadow Six Nations. Having made his first-team debut in the Powergen Cup game against Northampton at Welford Road in December, David repeated the success of the previous season as a member of the Guinness A League-winning squad. He again represented Scotland at U21 level during the shadow Six Nations, scoring a try in their victory over Ireland U21, then travelled to France in the summer with the Scottish squad for the IRB U21 World Championship. Named as the NIG Tigers Academy Player of the Month for December 2004, Young has also attended Murray Mexted's International Rugby Academy in New Zealand.

DAVID YOUNG

Position	Prop
Date of birth	18.02.85
Height	6'1"
Weight	17st 8lb
Tigers Debut	
3.12.05 v Northampton Saints	

Tigers Record	0 + 1 apps
Previous Clubs	N/A
Rep Hons	Scotland U21

www.leicestertigers.com

COACHES PROFILES

72 www.leicestertigers.com

COACHES PROFILES

COACHES PROFILES

Pat Howard

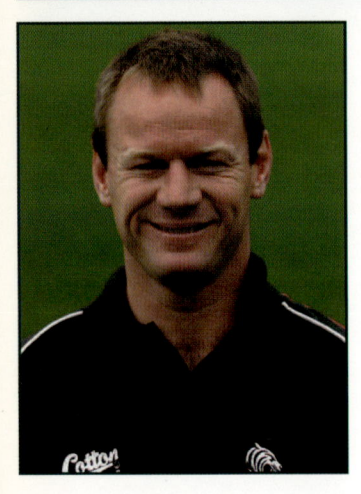

HEAD COACH

This is Pat's second spell with Tigers, having enjoyed a hugely successful time here as a player between 1998 and 2001. Pat played 94 matches during one of the most memorable periods in the club's history, scoring 10 tries and winning three Premiership titles and a Heineken Cup.

A former Wallaby fly-half or inside centre, Pat was born in Sydney on November 14, 1973 and played 20 tests for Australia between 1993 and 1997.

After leaving Tigers at the end of the 2000/01 season, Pat returned to his country of birth where he joined Super 12 outfit, the ACT Brumbies. He then enjoyed a spell with French club Montferrand, ahead of his return to Leicester where he initially took on the position of backline coach. Pat is now in his second season of his current role as head coach, having taken over from John Wells in 2005.

Neil Back

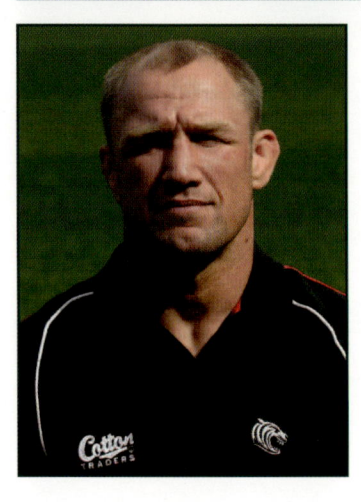

TECHNICAL DIRECTOR

Neil Back was one of England's outstanding players during their victorious 2003 Rugby World Cup campaign, starting six of the seven games in the tournament and scoring two tries along the way. It was his third successive World Cup, having previously been involved in '95 and '99. He also toured with the British & Irish Lions squad three times in a row - to South Africa in 1997, Australia in 2001 and New Zealand in 2005.

He captained his country to victory on four occasions during his 66-test career, including the Cook Cup match against Australia during 2001/02, with the last occasion being the day of his 50th England cap. During his time with the national side, Neil scored 16 tries and a drop goal, before retiring from international rugby during the 2004 Six Nations.

Neil took on coaching responsibilities within Tigers whilst still serving as a player during the 2003/04 season. He then retired from first-class rugby at the end of 2004/05, after 339 matches and a staggering 125 tries for the Leicester first team. He now combines his role as head coach of the academy, with responsibility for the first team defence and the development team forwards.

COACHES PROFILES

Richard Cockerill

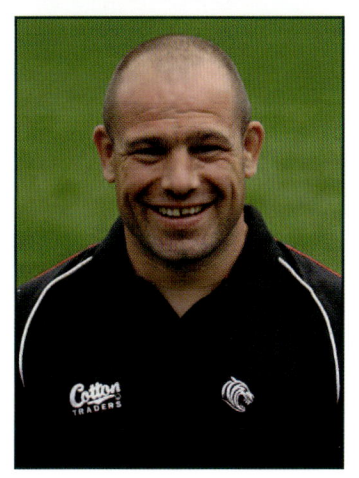

FORWARDS COACH

Like former team-mate and current head coach, Pat Howard, this is Richard's second stint with Leicester Tigers. Richard was a member of the famous 'ABC Club' and an instrumental part of a very successful Tigers set-up during his first period at Welford Road.

He left at the end of Tigers' double-winning season of 2001/02 to join French club Montferrand, where he played for two years, guiding them through to the final of the Parker Pen Cup against Harlequins.

Richard, known as one of the game's most spirited players, hails from Rugby and was educated at Harris Church of England School and played for Warwickshire Schools. He went on to represent England at U21 and A level before making his Test debut in 1997. He played in the '98 and '99 Five Nations and the '99 World Cup, only missing out on two possible selections for the England 22 during his Test career.

Richard has also been invited to play for the Barbarians, joining them on their 2001 summer tour of the UK, and then captaining the side that came to Welford Road for the Neil Back Testimonial game in March 2003.

Jo Hollis

FIRST TEAM MANAGER

Jo was born and raised in Hong Kong, being educated there and at Abbotsholme School before obtaining a degree in Sports Science and Education at London University. Prior to joining Leicester Tigers in 1997, Jo was responsible for anti-terrorist training and administration during her time as security manager at Cathay Pacific Airways.

As first team manger, Jo takes a great deal of pressure off the players and coaching staff by looking after every aspect of off-field organisation and administration. Her responsibilities range from new player introductions to game logistics; from managing players' diaries to travel and player administration, as well as providing general support for all first team players and coaches.

COACHES PROFILES

Dr Mukul Agarwal

TEAM DOCTOR

Mukul was Team Doctor and Sports Physician for the Great Britain team which finished second in the medal table at the 2004 Paralympics in Athens. He has also worked for organising committees at the Athens Olympics, as well as taking on a similar role at the Manchester Commonwealth Games. In 2005, Mukul worked with the Australian squad at the U-19 Rugby World Championships in South Africa, having previously been highly involved with the 2003 Champions Trophy for the top eight women's hockey teams in the world. He was Head of Medical Services and Club Doctor at Sydney University Rugby Club and has also held roles at the Olympic Medical Institute and the English Institute of Sport.

He has extensive experience in adventure, research and youth development projects with able-bodied and disabled team members in a variety of terrains, such as the High Himalayas, Africa and the Americas. Most recently, Mukul traveled across Nicaragua with the 11 disabled participants involved in the ground-breaking and critically acclaimed series, Beyond Boundaries, broadcast on BBC2.

John Dams

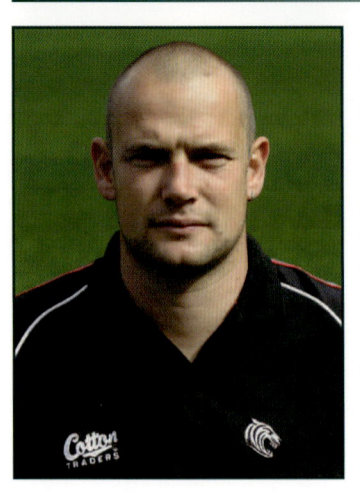

ATHLETIC PERFORMANCE COACH

John was born in Lower Hutt, in Wellington, New Zealand, and studied physical education at Otago University in Dunedin. He ran his own business in Dunedin for two years, then moved to Wellington where again had his own business, before spending a year-and-a-half working for the Wellington Rugby Union.

In his time in that role, John worked with the Wellington Lions - the National Provincial Championship outfit that boasted the likes of All Blacks Tana Umaga and Jerry Collins - and the Wellington cricket team, before moving to Leicester in 2004.

Recently retired from the game of rugby, John played for the Otago Colts Development side and their Sevens team.

COACHES PROFILES

Jamie Hamilton

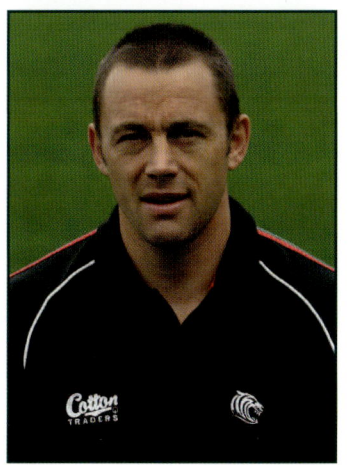

SPECIALIST SCRUM-HALF COACH & VIDEO ANALYST

A former pupil of Gleanon School in Sydney, Australia and Stonefield House in Lincoln, Jamie played 162 games for Tigers between 1990 and 2001/02, despite taking 12 months out to play for London Scottish for the 1996/97 season. An experienced Sevens player, his expertise earned him selection in the England squads for both the Hong Kong Sevens and the International Rugby Board World Sevens in 2001.

Jamie's talents in the shortened version of the game also resulted in him playing in the Tigers squads which won the Middlesex Sevens in 1995 and the Madrid Sevens in 1997. The long-serving scrum-half is one of only seven Tigers players to gain five league winners' medals with the club. Jamie, who also enjoyed a playing spell in Christchurch, New Zealand, featured in both of Tigers' Heineken Cup successes in 2000/01 and 2001/02. He rates that first European triumph as the best moment of his Tigers playing career.

Dusty Hare

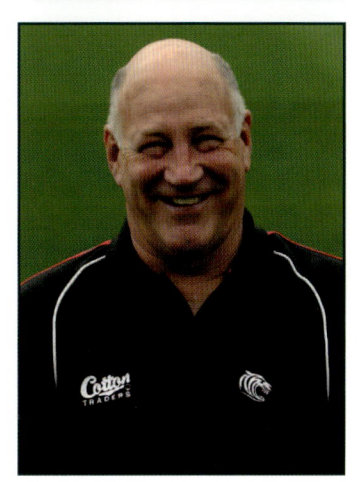

CHIEF SCOUT

Dusty was a professional cricketer from 1971-76, before seeing the light and moving to rugby union. He represented Tigers between 1976 and 1989, playing 394 games for the club. By the time he retired, Dusty was the world's highest points-scorer, achieving 7,137 points in total, with 4,507 scored for Tigers alone. He was capped 25 times for England and was a British and Irish Lions tourist in 1983.

He served on the Barbarian Committee between 1989 and 1992, and was awarded an MBE in 1989. In 1993, Dusty took on the role of director of rugby at Nottingham, before coming back to Tigers in 1994 as development co-ordinator.

Before becoming full-time at Tigers, Dusty was a farmer. He was also awarded an honorary Bachelor of Arts degree from Leicester University in 1990.

COACHES PROFILES

Julie Hayton

REHABILITATION COACH

Welsh-born Julie grew up in Wigan and she studied in Manchester, where she completed a sports rehabilitation degree, after previously obtaining another degree in physical therapy.

Julie has been with Leicester Tigers since 2001, but she has worked with a lot of the senior players for longer. She used to be in a private practice, which saw her serve as Tigers' masseuse for 18 months before joining the set-up on a full-time basis.

Julie works closely with the physiotherapists and strength and conditioning staff to ensure that players are eased in properly from injuries. She was instrumental in Tigers adapting a 'prehab' routine to prevent players from picking up injuries, whilst she also specialises in soft-tissue injuries.

Andy Key

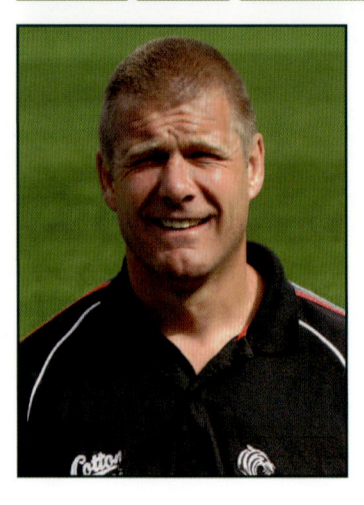

HEAD OF RUGBY DEVELOPMENT

Andy, who is known to all as Kiwi, was born in Market Harborough, educated at Welland Park High School, Market Harborough Grammar School and Leicester Polytechnic.

He played for Tigers between 1975 and 1981 and again from 1987-92. In between these two periods he played for Bedford and Nottingham. Andy's father, Maurice, played for Tigers in the late '50s while his two brothers, Richard and Lance, have both been professional footballers.

Andy spent 15 years in total at BSS Group Plc before joining Tigers as full-time general operations manager. He has since been appointed as Head of Rugby Development at the club, a role which includes the positions of assistant first team backs coach and academy manager. His current position also focuses on ensuring the successful elite development of future first team players.

COACHES PROFILES

Ollie **Richardson**

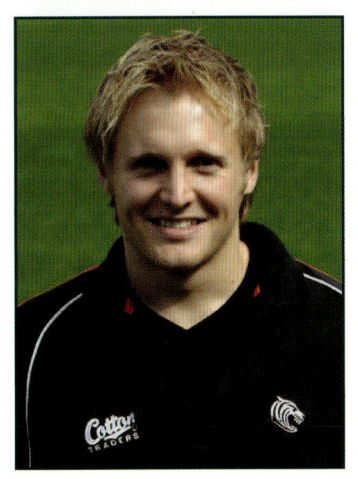

ATHLETIC PERFORMANCE COACH

Ollie - who joined Tigers in 2004/05 - is a graduate of the University of Bath's Coach Education and Sports Performance programme and also holds a Sports Science degree. His main duty involves looking after the training needs of the Tigers first team squad, along with fellow strength and conditioning coaches Craig White and John Dams. Ollie is also responsible for the Tigers development team on match days.

Having played rugby for Leicestershire and Bath University, Ollie then began work as a strength and conditioning coach in athletics, rugby and swimming. Having spent a year running a personal training business in London, he travelled to Christchurch, New Zealand for a year, where he worked as a strength and conditioning coach for New Zealand swimming, and a Christchurch rugby club side, before returning to Leicester to join Tigers.

Cliff **Shephard**

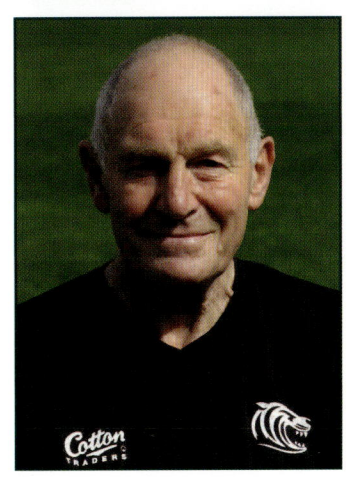

FIRST TEAM KIT-MAN

Cliff was born in Wigston and educated at Wigston HS. He played wing for the Leicester Schools team and had a final England Schools trial. He captained the Leicestershire Alliance Colts and also represented the county and the RAF.

He made his Tigers debut in 1955 against Coventry, going on to appear 140 times for the club's first XV, scoring 36 tries. Cliff became the LFC first team secretary in 1996 after looking after the Extras in the same capacity for a few years. Before his retirement, Cliff was a sales representative with Bass Breweries.

COACHES PROFILES

Paul Stanton

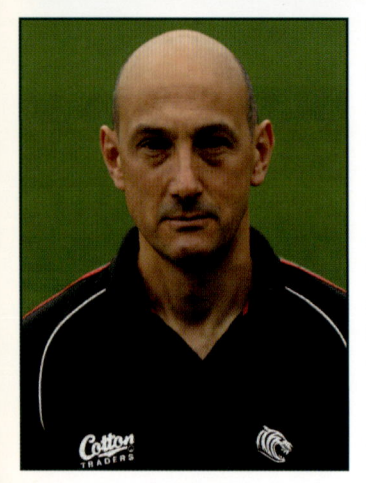

HEAD PHYSIOTHERAPIST

Paul was born in Walsall, West Midlands, and studied at the University Hospital of Wales, qualifying in 1981.

He worked in Walsall for two years after completing his studies, before moving to Leicester in 1983. He began working at the Leicester General Hospital, then had a stint at the Leicester Royal Infirmary and also at BUPA.

Paul began working for Leicester Tigers on a part-time basis in 1996 and become a full-time member of staff in June 2004. His duties include looking after the first team squad along with Jackie Limna.

Craig White

HEAD CONDITIONER

Craig White joined Tigers in April 2006 as the club's new head conditioner.

Craig, who hails from Wigan, played rugby league for Great Britain as an amateur but chose not to sign professional terms. From then on in, his focus has been firmly directed towards the fitness and conditioning side of the game.

In the early stages of his career, Craig was involved with a number of rugby clubs across both the 13 and 15-man codes. Craig began by working as an assistant at Waterloo, during which time he combined his club duties with international commitments, working as an assistant conditioning coach with the Irish national team. Craig's success within that role saw him progress to a full-time position which led to a three-and-a-half-year stint living in Dublin.

Craig then moved to work in football, taking up a role with Premiership side Bolton Wanderers, before returning to rugby union with London Wasps. In summer 2005, Craig was chosen by Sir Clive Woodward to take part in the British and Irish Lions tour to New Zealand.

COACHES PROFILES

www.leicestertigers.com   81

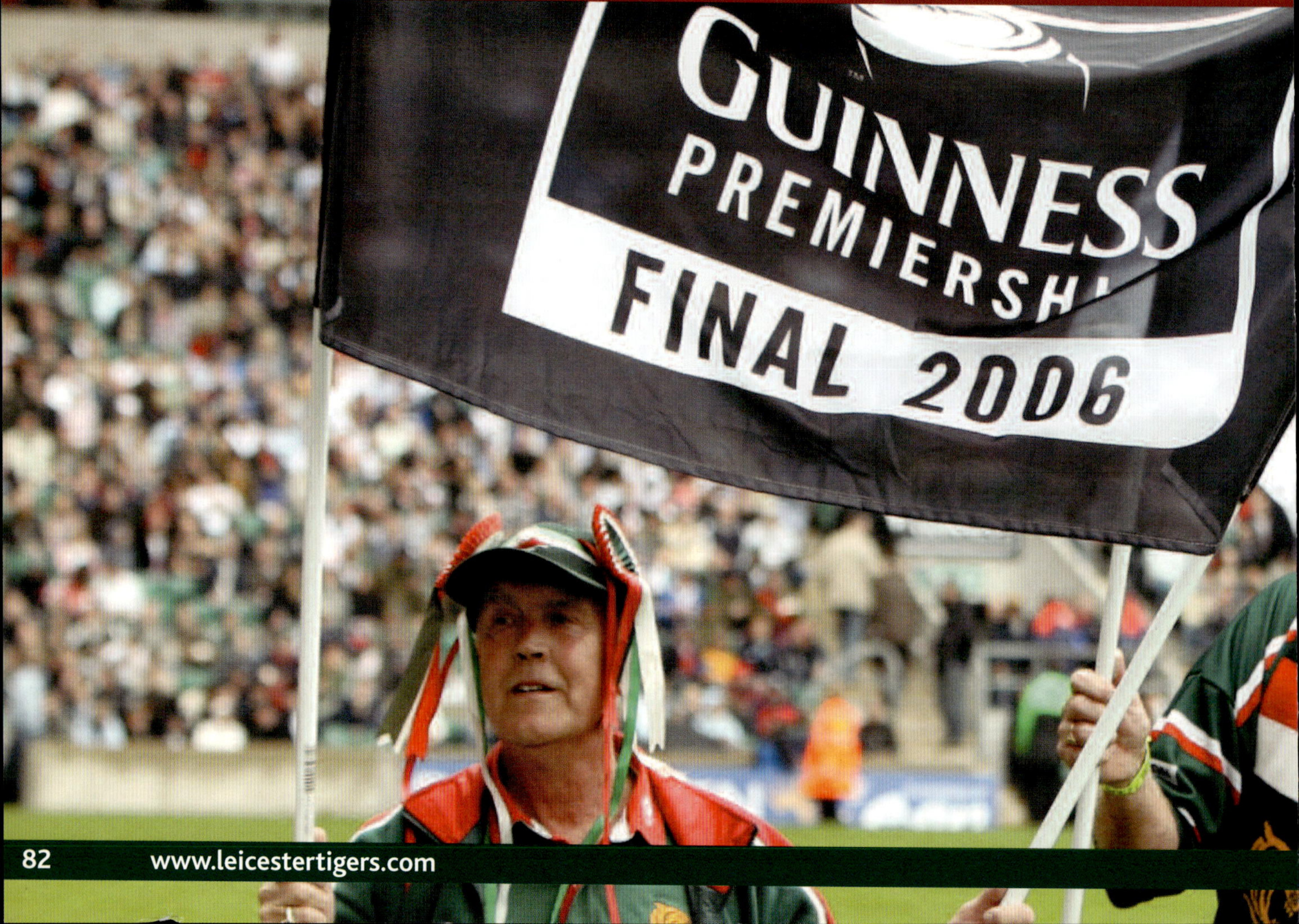
GUINNESS
PREMIERSH
FINAL 2006

SEASON REVIEW 2005/06

www.leicestertigers.com

83

SEASON REVIEW 2005/06

The 2005/06 season will go down in Tigers history as one of genuine highs and lows. A number of exhilarating performances to reach the latter stages of all three domestic and European competitions, only to finish the campaign empty handed.

Tigers began the season in fine form, scoring five tries as they hammered East Midlands rivals Northampton Saints 32-0 in their opening Guinness Premiership fixture. Next stop the Causeway Stadium, High Wycombe, where the visitors fought out a tough 29-29 draw against defending champions Wasps. The fine start continued back at Welford Road, with a second successive home bonus-point victory, this time with Bath soundly beaten 40-26. Things were about to get much harder though, with a trip to Headingley – a place that Leicester had never won. The bogey was finally laid to rest with a 28-20 win as Pat Howard's youthful selection paid off.

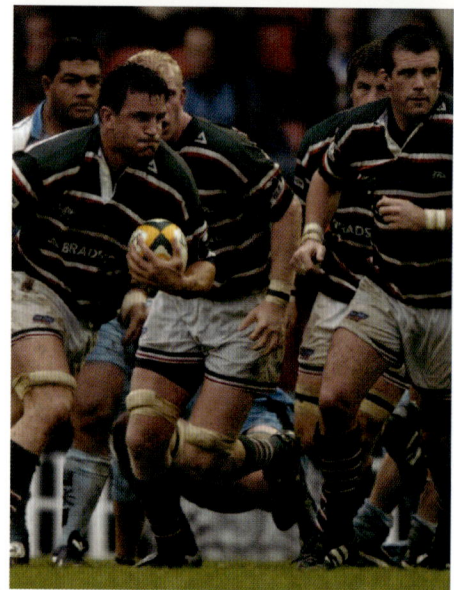

September 30 saw Tigers slip to their first defeat of the season, as they went down 24-15 at Newport Gwent Dragons in the Powergen Cup group stages, but victory over Worcester the following week kept them in with a chance of qualifying for the knockout stages, if Northampton could be overcome in December. A 16-16 draw at home to Newcastle kept Leicester in second place in the Premiership, although the suspension of Julian White following his red card was a serious blow.

SEASON REVIEW 2005/06

All eyes turned to Europe as the former champions got off to a flying start in their Heineken Cup campaign. Having been drawn in the 'group of death', Tigers thrashed Clermont Auvergne 57-23 with a free-flowing display at Welford Road.

Unfortunately, Leicester were unable to carry that form to Paris, were they suffered a dismal 12-6 loss to Stade Francais in late October. The traditional Leicester spirit once again came to the fore though, as Tigers recorded four wins on the trot, including a vital Heineken Cup double over the Ospreys. They beat the Celtic League champions 30-12 at Welford Road but were on the verge of defeat at the Liberty Stadium, before Danny Hipkiss' stunning injury-time try left the whole of Leicester smiling.

Tigers were soon brought back down to earth as they produced their worst performance of the season in their defeat at Bristol, making January the make-or-break month. Narrow victories over London Irish and Saracens provided the build-up to the final two Heineken Cup group matches. Expectation was high and nerves were fraught, but Leicester kept their cool to deliver two memorable victories. Despite trailing 22-16 with less than 20 minutes remaining in the home fixture with Stade Francais, Tigers rallied superbly to register a stunning 29-22 victory thanks to late tries from Louis Deacon and that man Hipkiss. A place in the last eight was then secured with a

SEASON REVIEW 2005/06

40-27 win at Clermont in a fixture that saw Graham Rowntree start his 50th Heineken Cup match and Tom Varndell run in four tries.

The jubilation of qualifying for the knockout stages of the Heineken Cup couldn't hide the disappointment of the next month-and-a-half of the domestic campaign though. After registering only one win in their next four Premiership games throughout much of the Six Nations, Tigers suffered a major shock to the system when they were knocked out of the Powergen Cup at the semi-final stage. Leicester racked up three tries at the Millennium Stadium but still fell 22-17 to perennial rivals Wasps.

The annual fixture with the Barbarians provided its usual feast of entertainment in mid-March, although the same probably couldn't be said of Tigers' dogged 19-12 win at Bath in the Guinness Premiership.

Despite the psychological boost of victory at the Rec, Tigers suffered their biggest set-back of the season when they lost 15-12 to the same opponents in the Heineken Cup quarter-final at the Walkers Stadium. The disappointment of that exit could well have derailed a lesser side, but the players showed fantastic character to bounce back in superb fashion by producing some hugely adventurous and entertaining rugby in a 24-19 win at Franklin's Gardens. That sense of adventure continued in the following week's fixture with reigning champions Wasps, in a match that would finish as a 20-19 nail-biter.

Leicester then guaranteed a top-four finish with another one-point victory at Saracens on April 28. Tigers created a number of try-scoring chances but had to settle for a 13-12 win at Vicarage Road. The relief at the final whistle was clear for all to see, after what seemed like an hour of injury time threatened to snatch defeat from the jaws of victory.

With play-off qualification already assured, Leicester's destiny was in their own hands - something which seemed highly unlikely when the side languished in fifth place at the end of February. Tigers went into their final home game of the regular league season knowing a win would secure a second-place finish and a home semi-final. This was duly achieved with a comprehensive 32-3 defeat of the West Country side. Another five-pointer from Varndell saw him finish top of the Guinness Premiership try-scoring charts with 14 tries. London Irish were comprehensively dispatched 40-8 in the semi-final at Welford Road the following week, but the season ended in disappointment as Tigers failed to re-capture that form at Twickenham where they missed out on the Premiership title following a 45-20 defeat at the hands of Sale Sharks.

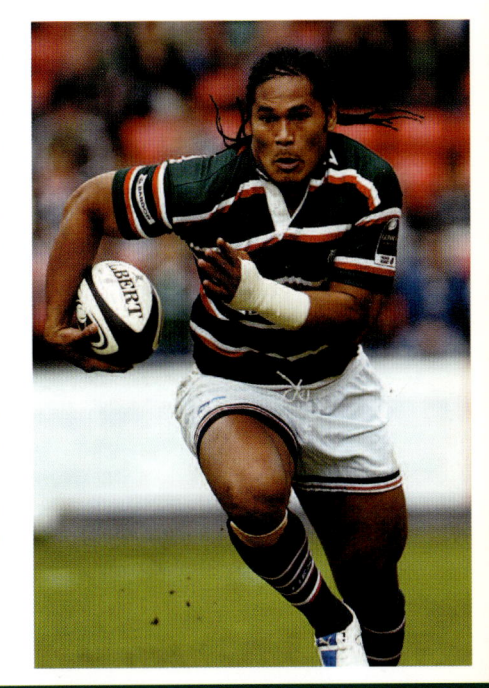

www.leicestertigers.com 87

SEASON REVIEW 2005/06

Leicester Tigers 32
Northampton Saints 0

Guinness Premiership
Welford Road
Att: 16,815
Referee: Roy Maybank
Saturday September 3 2005

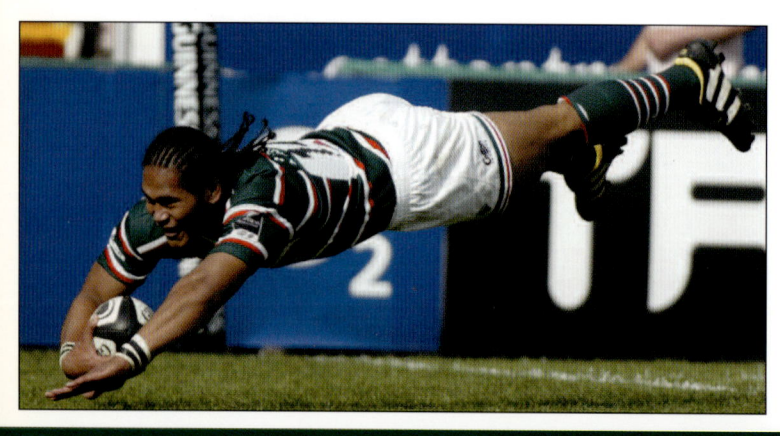

Leicester Tigers began their 2005/06 Guinness Premiership campaign with a comprehensive 32-0 win over East Midlands rivals Northampton Saints at a packed Welford Road, with the industrious home side picking up a four-try bonus point in the process.

Tigers' five tries were scored by second row James Hamilton, loose-head prop Michael Holford, right-wing Alesana Tuilagi, outside centre Dan Hipkiss, who clinched the bonus-point score in the 43rd minute, and left-wing Tom Varndell, who put an end to the scoring in injury-time.

New club captain Martin Corry led his team out to thunderous applause from the Welford Road faithful, before Hamilton opened the scoring in the 13th minute. The young second row marked his 14th appearance for the club with his second career try as he crashed over from a close-range line-out.

From a Tigers scrum, Holford then pounced on the ball to score his first-ever senior Tigers try, which the Premiership's leading scorer for 2004/05, Andy Goode, converted. Tuilagi then rubbed salt into Northampton's wounds when he sprinted away for try number three just over two minutes later, to put Leicester 17-0 ahead at the break.

After half-time, Hipkiss linked well with Sam Vesty and Tuilagi to sprint over for a converted try, before Goode added a penalty.

Tigers then finished the game in style when Bradstone Man of the Match Hamilton took another impressive line-out ball and supplied Varndell with the chance to dive over for the final score.

88 www.leicestertigers.com

SEASON REVIEW 2005/06

TIGER TIMELINE

			SCORE	MIN
T		Hamilton	5-0	15
YC		Smith		27
S		Budgen Rae		29
T+C		Holford + Goode	12-0	33
T		A.Tuilagi	17-0	36
S		Rae Budgen		40
HALF TIME 17-0				
S		Boome Rae		41
T+C		Hipkiss + Goode	24-0	44
S		Abraham Corry		49
S		Lloyd Hipkiss		49
S		Kay Cullen		56
S		Hipkiss Gibson		58
S		Lewitt Fox		59
S		Budgen Smith		59
S		White Holford		60
P		Goode	27-0	64
S		Healey Ellis		67
S		Broadfoot Goode		68
S		Taukafa Chuter		71
S		Lamont Rudd		72
S		Richmond Hartley		78
S		Holford Moreno		79
T		Varndell	32-0	85
FULL TIME 32-0				

Key
Player coming on
Player going off

LEICESTER TIGERS

- 15 S.Vesty
- 14 A.Tuilagi
- 11 T.Varndell
- 13 D.Hipkiss
- 12 D.Gibson
- 10 A.Goode
- 9 H.Ellis
- 8 M.Corry (c)
- 7 S.Jennings
- 6 W.Johnson
- 5 L.Cullen
- 4 J.Hamilton
- 3 A.Moreno
- 2 G.Chuter
- 1 M.Holford

NORTHAMPTON SAINTS

- 1 T.Smith
- 2 D.Hartley
- 3 B.Sturgess
- 4 M.Lord
- 5 D.Browne
- 7 D.Fox
- 6 A.Rae
- 8 D.Browne
- 9 M.Robinson
- 10 C.Spencer
- 12 S.Mallon
- 13 J.Clarke
- 11 B.Cohen
- 14 J.Rudd
- 15 B.Reihana (c)

REPLACEMENTS

- 16 E.Taukafa
- 17 B.Kay
- 18 J.White
- 19 L.Abraham
- 20 A.Healey
- 21 R.Broadfoot
- 22 L.Lloyd

"I'm really happy with some of the younger guys that stepped in and showed that they're well and truly up to this level."
Pat Howard

REPLACEMENTS

- 16 D.Richmond
- 17 C.Budgen
- 18 S.Boome
- 19 B.Lewitt
- 20 J.Howard
- 21 R.Davies
- 22 S.Lamont

TIGERS MILESTONES

Martin Corry led Tigers out for the first competitive game of the new season. Corry took over the captaincy from Martin Johnson, who retired at the end of the last campaign.

www.leicestertigers.com 89

SEASON REVIEW 2005/06

London Wasps 29
Leicester Tigers 29

Guinness Premiership
Causeway Stadium
Att: 8,459
Referee: Dave Pearson
Saturday September 10 2005

Leicester Tigers and London Wasps played out a 29-29 draw in their Guinness Premiership fixture at the Causeway Stadium, with fly-half Andy Goode - who drew the scores level in the 75th minute with a penalty - very nearly winning the game with a late drop-goal attempt.

A draw was perhaps evident early on, with the scores tied at 23-23 after an intriguing first 40 minutes. By half-time, the match had already produced a total of four tries, four conversions and six penalties, with both sides taking their try-scoring chances and goal-kickers Goode and Mark van Gisbergen sporting 100-per-cent kicking records.

Tigers had crept into the lead in the third minute through a Goode penalty, before the home side stole the ascendancy through a converted Tom Rees try.

The visitors then went ahead again through Tom Varndell, who ran in an unopposed try which Goode converted.

Goode and Van Gisbergen traded a host of penalties to take the score to 16-16, before Wasps stormed into the lead with Rees' second try of the day.

Van Gisbergen's conversion put his team ahead 23-16, but Tigers hit back just over five minutes later when England scrum-half Harry Ellis scored a try which Goode converted to make it 23-23 at the break.

The second half was less eventful, with both sides failing to cross the whitewash. Goode and Van Gisbergen struck two penalties a piece and, despite a late drop-goal effort from the Tigers outside-half, the match ended all-square.

90 www.leicestertigers.com

SEASON REVIEW 2005/06

TIGER TIMELINE

			SCORE	MIN
🏃	P	Goode	0-3	3
🏃	T+C	Rees + Van Gisbergen	7-3	5
🏃	T+C	Varndell + Goode	7-10	9
🏃	P	Goode	7-13	12
🏃	P	Van Gisbergen	10-13	17
🏃	P	Van Gisbergen	13-13	24
🏃	P	Goode	13-16	27
🟨	YC	Jennings		28
🏃	P	Van Gisbergen	16-16	29
🏃	T+C	Rees + Van Gisbergen	23-16	30
🏃	S	Healey Murphy		32
🏃	T+C	Ellis & Goode	23-23	36
🏃	S	Cornwell Ellis		38

HALF TIME 23-23

🏃	S	White Holford		41
🏃	S	Murphy Healey		41
🏃	S	Ellis Cornwell		41
🏃	S	Gotting Ibanez		44
🏃	P	Goode	23-26	45
🏃	P	Van Gisbergen	26-26	48
🏃	S	Hart Rees		48
🏃	S	Bracken J.Dawson		49
🏃	S	L.Deacon Cullen		50
🏃	S	M.Dawson Reddan		52
🏃	P	Van Gisbergen	29-26	63
🏃	S	Abraham B.Deacon		66
🏃	S	Healey Varndell		70
🏃	S	Lock Shaw		72
🏃	P	Goode	29-29	76
🏃	S	Broadfoot Gibson		77
🏃	S	Hoadley Abbott		79
🏃	S	J.Dawson Bracken		82

FULL TIME 29-29

Key
Player coming on
Player going off

LEICESTER TIGERS

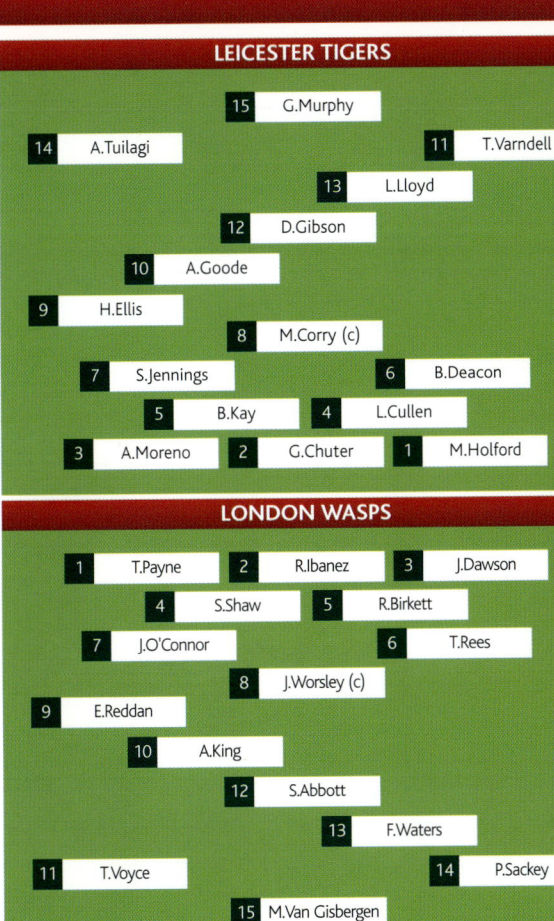

- 15 G.Murphy
- 14 A.Tuilagi
- 11 T.Varndell
- 13 L.Lloyd
- 12 D.Gibson
- 10 A.Goode
- 9 H.Ellis
- 8 M.Corry (c)
- 7 S.Jennings
- 6 B.Deacon
- 5 B.Kay
- 4 L.Cullen
- 3 A.Moreno
- 2 G.Chuter
- 1 M.Holford

LONDON WASPS

- 1 T.Payne
- 2 R.Ibanez
- 3 J.Dawson
- 4 S.Shaw
- 5 R.Birkett
- 7 J.O'Connor
- 6 T.Rees
- 8 J.Worsley (c)
- 9 E.Reddan
- 10 A.King
- 12 S.Abbott
- 13 F.Waters
- 11 T.Voyce
- 14 P.Sackey
- 15 M.Van Gisbergen

REPLACEMENTS

16	E.Taukafa
17	J.White
18	L.Deacon
19	L.Abraham
20	A.Healey
21	R.Broadfoot
22	M.Cornwell

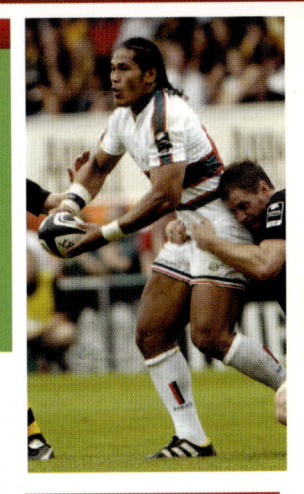

"Obviously, two points are better than none, but it just sticks in the throat that we could've sneaked a victory."
Martin Corry

REPLACEMENTS

16	B.Gotting
17	P.Bracken
18	J.Hart
19	M.Lock
20	M.Dawson
21	J.Brooks
22	R.Hoadley

TIGERS MILESTONES

Tigers' England scrum-half Harry Ellis made his 100th appearance for the club, nine years after joining the youth set-up in 1997.

www.leicestertigers.com 91

SEASON REVIEW 2005/06

Leicester Tigers recorded their second successive home win in the 2005/06 Guinness Premiership, as they saw off a competitive Bath outfit at Welford Road.

Tigers regained the league's top spot via a 40-26 victory, which was their first over their West Country rivals since February 2003.

Pat Howard's side also secured a second try-scoring bonus point in three games, thanks to Shane Jennings' injury-time score.

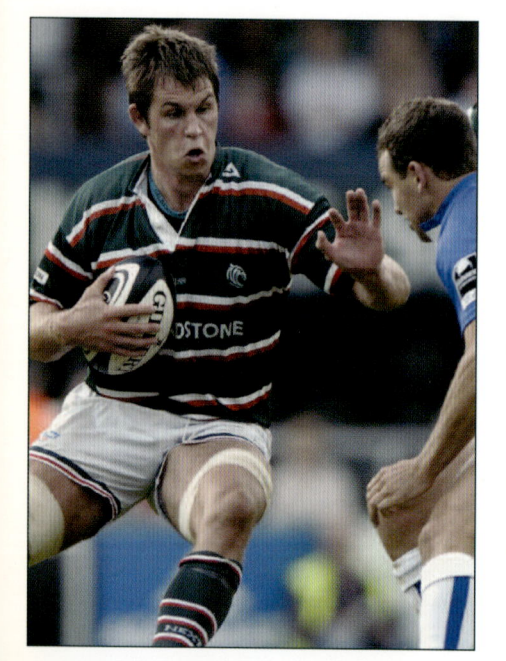

The former Leinster open-side touched down in the 87th minute to register Tigers' fourth try, after a Geordan Murphy score had been sandwiched by two Tom Varndell efforts.

Most of the 16,815 capacity crowd had barely settled into their seats when Varndell celebrated his 20th birthday in style as he sped away for his team's first points of the day. The England U-21 star crossed the visitors' line after only 28 seconds of play to give Tigers the perfect start to the much-talked-about fixture. Andy Goode converted to give Leicester an early 7-0 lead, before Bath's Olly Barkley narrowed the gap to a single point with two well-taken penalties.

Varndell was then at the thick of the action again as his pass supplied Lions tourist Murphy, who coolly finished off the impressive move. Goode added the extras, as well as an earlier penalty, to take the score to 17-6 in Tigers' favour.

Bath centre Andy Higgins ran in an interception try which Barkley converted, before fly-half Andy Dunne scored a drop goal to leave Tigers just a point ahead at 17-16. The visitors then shocked the Welford Road crowd as they took the lead for the first time in the match, courtesy of a David Bory try which Barkley converted.

However, Tigers maintained their composure as three Goode penalties and a conversion, together with Varndell's second try, guaranteed victory, before Jennings added the final touch.

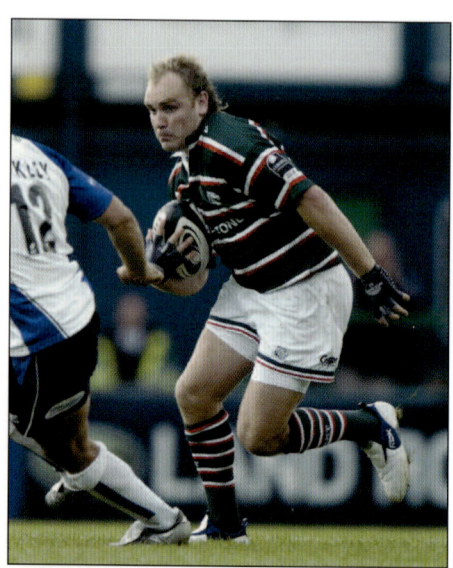

Leicester Tigers 40
Bath 26

Guinness Premiership
Welford Road
Att: 16,815
Referee: Chris White
Saturday September 17 2005

SEASON REVIEW 2005/06

TIGER TIMELINE

			SCORE	MIN
🏃	T+C	Varndell + Goode	7-0	1
🏃	P	Barkley	7-3	13
🏃	P	Barkley	7-6	13
🏃	P	Goode	10-6	22
🏃	T+C	Murphy + Goode	17-6	25
🏃	S	Finau Welsh		26
🏃	T+C	Higgins + Barkley	17-13	36
🏃	DG	Dunne	17-16	39

HALF TIME 17-16

🏃	S	Hudson Borthwick		41
🏃	S	Borthwick Hudson		42
🏃	S	Hamilton Kay		53
🏃	S	Bell Stevens		54
🏃	S	Scaysbrook Delve		54
🏃	T+C	Bory + Barkley	17-23	55
🏃	S	Smith Lloyd		57
🏃	S	A.Tuilagi Healey		57
🏃	P	Goode	20-23	59
🏃	S	Walshe Wood		60
🏃	T+C	Varndell + Goode	27-23	63
🏃	P	Goode	30-23	66
🏃	S	Hudson Borthwick		66
🏃	S	Borthwick Hudson		68
🏃	S	Holford Moreno		70
🏃	P	Goode	33-23	72
🏃	S	Taukafa Chuter		72
🏃	P	Barkley	33-26	80
🏃	T+C	Jennings + Goode	40-26	80

FULL TIME 40-26

Key
Player coming on
Player going off

LEICESTER TIGERS

- 15 G.Murphy
- 14 T.Varndell
- 11 A.Healey
- 13 L.Lloyd
- 12 D.Gibson
- 10 A.Goode
- 9 H.Ellis
- 8 M.Corry (c)
- 7 S.Jennings
- 6 W.Johnson
- 5 B.Kay
- 4 L.Deacon
- 3 J.White
- 2 G.Chuter
- 1 A.Moreno

BATH

- 1 D.Barnes
- 2 L.Mears
- 3 M.Stevens
- 4 S.Borthwick (c)
- 5 D.Grewcock
- 7 G.Delve
- 6 A.Beattie
- 8 Z.Feau'nati
- 9 M.Wood
- 10 A.Dunne
- 12 O.Barkley
- 13 A.Higgins
- 11 F.Welsh
- 14 D.Bory
- 15 M.Perry

REPLACEMENTS

- 16 E.Taukafa
- 17 M.Holford
- 18 J.Hamilton
- 19 W.Skinner
- 20 R.Broadfoot
- 21 O.Smith
- 22 A.Tuilagi

"I thought Daryl Gibson was fabulous today. He had a superb game all around the ground and probably played his best game ever for the club."
Pat Howard

REPLACEMENTS

- 16 P.Dixon
- 17 D.Bell
- 18 J.Scaysbrook
- 19 J.Hudson
- 20 N.Walshe
- 21 S.Finau
- 22 R.Davis

TIGERS MILESTONES

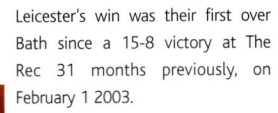

Leicester's win was their first over Bath since a 15-8 victory at The Rec 31 months previously, on February 1 2003.

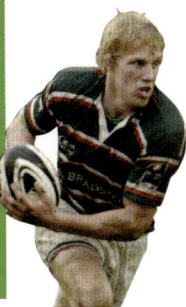

www.leicestertigers.com

SEASON REVIEW 2005/06

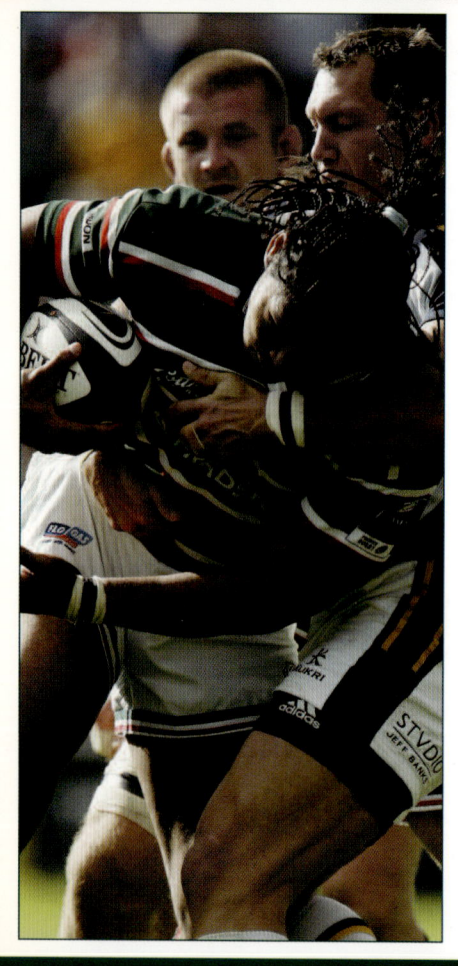

Leeds Tykes 20
Leicester Tigers 28

Guinness Premiership
Headingley
Att: 7,143
Referee: Rob Debney
Sunday September 25 2005

Leicester Tigers laid their Headingley bogey to rest with a courageous 28-20 Guinness Premiership win over Leeds Tykes. Captain Louis Deacon, a try-scorer in injury-time, led from the front to secure Tigers' first-ever win at the ground.

Leicester were ahead by just one point before Deacon snapped up a stray line-out throw from Leeds on their own line and powered over amidst huge celebrations. England U-21 outside-half Ross Broadfoot coolly struck the conversion from the left-hand touchline to put Tigers two scores ahead with minimal time left on the clock.

Leon Lloyd had opened the scoring for Tigers with a try in the 13th minute, before Andre Snyman crossed for Leeds, with Italian international Roland De Marigny converting. Leicester vice-captain Matt Cornwell then sliced through a gap in the Leeds defensive line, with the 20-year-old's momentum helping him over the whitewash for his first try for the club.

Broadfoot's conversion gave the visitors a 12-7 advantage at the break, but Leeds struck back at the start of the second half, as a Chris Murphy try was converted by De Marigny, who then added his first penalty of the match.

Broadfoot slotted three points for Tigers to reduce the gap to 17-15, but De Marigny restored Leeds' five-point advantage.

Leicester's persistence paid off as two late penalties from Broadfoot gave them a one-point lead, before Deacon's last-gasp effort gave the visitors enough breathing space to withstand Leeds' final onslaught.

94   www.leicestertigers.com

SEASON REVIEW 2005/06

TIGER TIMELINE

			SCORE	MIN
T		Lloyd	0-5	14
T+C		Snyman + De Marigny	7-5	18
T+C		Cornwell + Broadfoot	7-12	40

HALF TIME 7-12

	YC	L.Deacon		41
	S	Gerber **Shelley**		44
	T+C	Murphy + De Marigny	14-12	45
	P	De Marigny	17-12	53
	S	Chuter **Taukafa**		53
	S	Jennings **Johnson**		53
	P	Broadfoot	17-15	57
	P	De Marigny	20-15	61
	S	Cullen **Hamilton**		61
	S	Hooper **Murphy**		61
	S	Thomas **Crane**		61
	P	Broadfoot	20-18	68
	S	Varndell **Lloyd**		68
	P	Broadfoot	20-21	72
	S	Hipkiss **Smith**		72
	S	Rawlinson **Bulloch**		77
	T+C	L.Deacon + Broadfoot	20-28	80

FULL TIME 20-28

Key
Player coming on
Player going off

LEICESTER TIGERS

- 15 G.Murphy
- 14 A.Tuilagi
- 11 L.Lloyd
- 13 O.Smith
- 12 M.Cornwell
- 10 R.Broadfoot
- 9 A.Healey
- 8 W.Johnson
- 7 W.Skinner
- 6 B.Deacon
- 5 J.Hamilton
- 4 L.Deacon (c)
- 3 M.Holford
- 2 E.Taukafa
- 1 G.Rowntree

LEEDS TYKES

- 1 M.Shelley
- 2 G.Bulloch
- 3 G.Kerr
- 4 C.Murphy
- 5 T.Palmer
- 7 R.Parks
- 6 J.Dunbar
- 8 J.Crane
- 9 J.Marshall
- 10 R.De Marigny
- 12 A.Snyman
- 13 C.Jones
- 11 T.Biggs
- 14 D.Rees
- 15 I.Balshaw (c)

REPLACEMENTS

- 16 G.Chuter
- 17 D.Young
- 18 L.Cullen
- 19 S.Jennings
- 20 H.Ellis
- 21 D.Hipkiss
- 22 T.Varndell

"I'm very, very proud of the entire 22 as I thought they were incredibly courageous. They deserve all the credit for what was an outstanding performance."
Pat Howard

REPLACEMENTS

- 16 R.Gerber
- 17 R.Rawlinson
- 18 S.Hooper
- 19 N.Thomas
- 20 D.Care
- 21 T.Stimpson
- 22 G.Ross

TIGERS MILESTONES

Tigers recorded their first Premiership away victory since January 2, as they won at Headingley for the first time in five attempts.

www.leicestertigers.com

SEASON REVIEW 2005/06

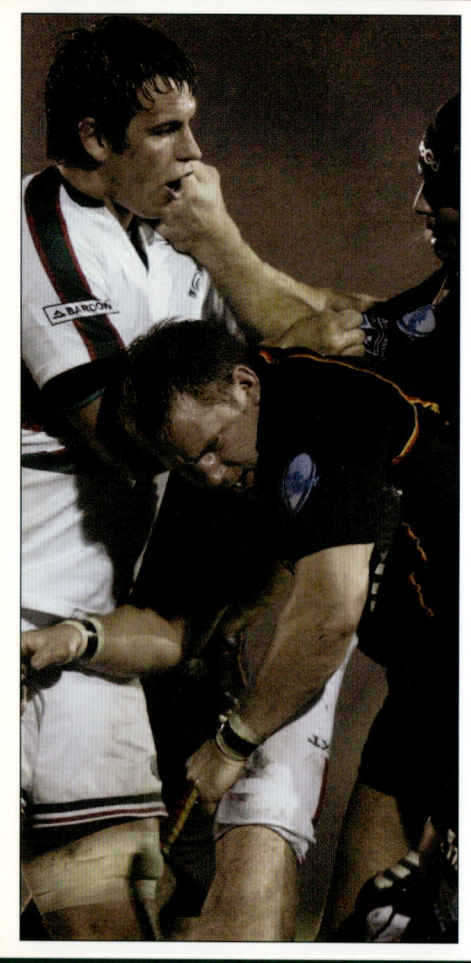

Newport Gwent Dragons 24
Leicester Tigers 15

Powergen Cup
Rodney Parade
Att: 6,327
Referee: Nigel Owens
Friday September 30 2005

Leicester Tigers' 2005/06 Powergen Cup campaign got off to a disappointing start at a soaking Rodney Parade as they suffered a 24-15 defeat at the hands of the Newport Gwent Dragons.

The Dragons held an 18-10 half-time lead, having outscored Tigers by two tries to one in the first 40 minutes. Newport Gwent outside-half Craig Warlow and left-wing Ben Breeze scored for the Welsh region, as Paul Turner's side looked for their first victory over Tigers in three attempts.

Leicester replied through Ireland A flanker Shane Jennings who crossed for his second try in three games, with England fly-half Andy Goode adding a conversion and a penalty.

Tigers head coach Pat Howard rang the changes in the second half but Warlow's 72nd minute penalty extended his side's advantage.

Leicester's last throw of the dice saw the introduction of fleet-footed fly-half Ian Humphreys, who desperately attempted to inject some spark in the dying minutes.

A late long-range run-in from Leon Lloyd saw the visitors edge nearer to their Celtic opponents, but Ireland Sevens international Humphreys missed the conversion from the left-hand touchline to leave the score 24-15 in the home team's favour.

96   www.leicestertigers.com

SEASON REVIEW 2005/06

TIGER TIMELINE

		SCORE	MIN
T	Warlow	5-0	10
T+C	Breeze + Warlow	12-0	15
T+C	Jennings + Goode	12-7	29
P	Warlow	15-7	40
P	Goode	15-10	40
P	Warlow	18-10	40

HALF TIME 18-10

			MIN
DG	Warlow	21-10	44
S	Cullen Hamilton		49
S	Healey Cornwell		49
S	Maddocks Black		60
S	Ringer Forster		60
S	Lloyd Varndell		62
S	Skinner B.Deacon		63
S	Bryan Hall		69
S	Taukafa Chuter		71
P	Warlow	24-10	74
S	Humphreys Goode		76
S	Tuipulotu Luscombe		79
T	Lloyd	24-15	80

FULL TIME 24-15

Key
Player coming on
Player going off

LEICESTER TIGERS

- 15 M.Cornwell
- 14 A.Tuilagi
- 11 T.Varndell
- 13 O.Smith
- 12 D.Gibson
- 10 A.Goode
- 9 H.Ellis
- 8 W.Johnson
- 7 S.Jennings
- 6 B.Deacon
- 5 J.Hamilton
- 4 L.Deacon (c)
- 3 J.White
- 2 G.Chuter
- 1 G.Rowntree

NEWPORT GWENT DRAGONS

- 1 A.Black
- 2 A.Brown
- 3 R.Thomas
- 4 I.Gough
- 5 P.Sidoli
- 7 J.Forster (c)
- 6 A.Hall
- 8 M.Owen
- 9 G.Baber
- 10 C.Warlow
- 12 C.Sweeney
- 13 H.Luscombe
- 11 B.Breeze
- 14 G.Wyatt
- 15 K.Morgan

REPLACEMENTS

16	E.Taukafa
17	M.Holford
18	L.Cullen
19	W.Skinner
20	A.Healey
21	I.Humphreys
22	L.Lloyd

"We played very poorly and had a bad day at the office but if the Welsh teams turn up for it like the Dragons did tonight, the competition has a great future."
Pat Howard

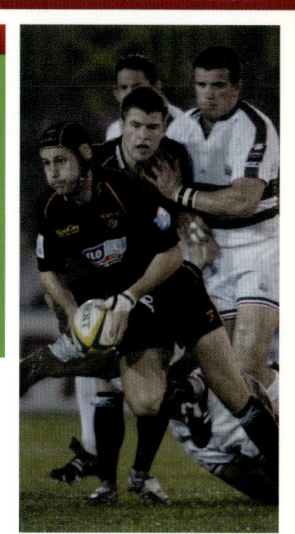

REPLACEMENTS

16	L.Jones
17	D.Maddocks
18	R.Bryan
19	J.Ringer
20	S.Tuipulotu
21	J.Bryant
22	J.Ireland

TIGERS MILESTONES

Tigers' loss was their first against the Newport Gwent Dragons, having won both previous encounters in the 2003/04 Heineken Cup.

www.leicestertigers.com   97

SEASON REVIEW 2005/06

Leicester Tigers bounced back from their shock Powergen Cup defeat to Welsh side Newport Gwent Dragons with an emphatic 42-16 Pool D triumph over Worcester Warriors.

A strong start to the match and a 15-point second-half blitz in as many minutes laid the platform for Tigers' victory.

First-half tries from hooker George Chuter and wing Leon Lloyd, coupled with the kicking of debutant starter Ian Humphreys, had Tigers sitting pretty. Worcester refused to lie down however and clawed their way back into the game shortly before the end of the first 40 minutes.

Chuter's sixth-minute try from a rolling maul put Tigers 7-0 ahead, after Humphreys had added the conversion. The young Irishman kicked a penalty in between two Shane Drahm efforts for the visitors, before Lloyd hacked through to score from a testing up and under by Humphreys.

Worcester added to their tally with another Drahm penalty and a converted try from Ben Hinshelwood to leave Tigers with a slender 20-16 lead at the break.

Leicester began the second half with England fly-half Andy Goode replacing Humphreys, who had impressed in his first-ever senior Tigers start. The 25-year-old Churchill Cup winner made an instant impact as he slotted a 47th minute penalty.

Captain and Bradstone Man of the Match Austin Healey then scored a try which Goode converted, before Harry Ellis went over for Tigers' fourth score of the afternoon.

Goode missed the touchline conversion, before try-scoring sensation Tom Varndell replaced powerhouse Alesana Tuilagi on the wing.

Varndell wasted little time in joining Tigers' try-scoring quartet, as he finished off a clever move in the left-hand corner.

Leicester Tigers 42
Worcester Warriors 16

Powergen Cup
Welford Road
Att: 8,642
Referee: Ashley Rowden
Saturday October 8 2005

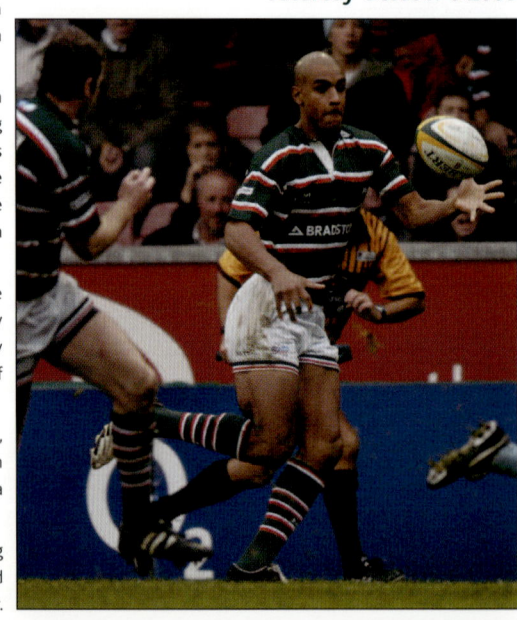

SEASON REVIEW 2005/06

TIGER TIMELINE

			SCORE	MIN
✈	T+C	Chuter + Humphreys	7-0	7
🏃	P	Drahm	7-3	10
🏃	P	Humphreys	10-3	16
✈	T+C	Lloyd + Humphreys	17-3	24
🏃	P	Drahm	17-6	27
YC		Lombard		28
🏃	P	Humphreys	20-6	29
YC		Hipkiss		33
🏃	P	Drahm	20-9	34
	S	L.Deacon Kay		40
✈	T+C	Hinshelwood + Drahm	20-16	40

HALF TIME 20-16

	S	Goode Humphreys		41
🏃	P	Goode	23-16	48
✈	T+C	Healey + Goode	30-16	53
✈	T	Ellis	35-16	55
	S	Ellis Healey		55
	S	Blaze O'Donoghue		55
✈	S	B.Deacon Skinner		57
	S	Buckland Chuter		63
	S	Lennard Tucker		63
	S	Powell Gomarsall		67
	S	Varndell A.Tuilagi		68
🏃	S	Hickey Vaili		68
	S	Holford Rowntree		71
✈	T+C	Varndell + Goode	42-16	73
	S	Healey Ellis		75

FULL TIME 42-16

Key
Player coming on
Player going off

LEICESTER TIGERS

15	G.Murphy		
14	L.Lloyd	11	A.Tuilagi
	13	D.Hipkiss	
	12	S.Vesty	
	10	I.Humphreys	
9	A.Healey		
	8	M.Corry (c)	
7	S.Jennings	6	W.Skinner
	5	L.Cullen	4	B.Kay
3	J.White	2	G.Chuter	1	G.Rowntree

WORCESTER WARRIORS

1	S.Sparks	2	C.Fortey	3	T.Taumoepeau
	4	T.Collier	5	E.O'Donoghue	
7	J.Tu'amoheloa		6	S.Vaili	
	8	K.Horstmann		
9	A.Gomarsall			
	10	S.Drahm		
	12	T.Lombard		
	13	B.Hinshelwood (c)		
11	U.Oduoza		14	M.Tucker
	15	J.Hylton		

REPLACEMENTS

16	J.Buckland
17	M.Holford
18	L.Deacon
19	B.Deacon
20	H.Ellis
21	T.Varndell
22	A.Goode

"I thought Martin Corry was outstanding, while even some of the old dogs like Austin Healey played really, really well today!"
Pat Howard

REPLACEMENTS

16	M.Mullan
17	A.Keylock
18	R.Blaze
19	D.Hickey
20	M.Powell
21	S.Robinson
22	J.Lennard

TIGERS MILESTONES

Tigers first played Worcester in March 1895 but had to wait until December 2002 for their next encounter. This victory meant Leicester had won each of the five matches between the two sides.

www.leicestertigers.com 99

SEASON REVIEW 2005/06

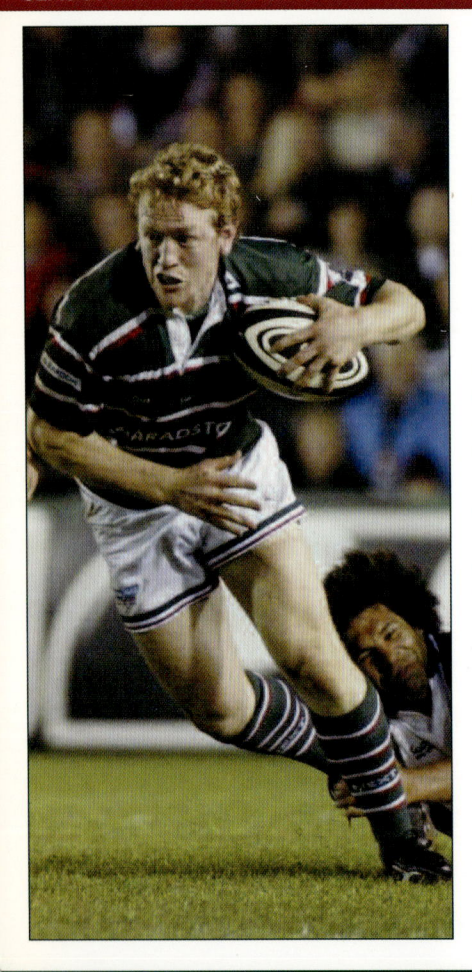

Leicester Tigers 16
Newcastle Falcons 16

Leicester Tigers and Newcastle Falcons played out a 16-16 draw in a drama-filled Guinness Premiership encounter at Welford Road. Newcastle became the first team to claim any league points at Tigers' home ground since Leicester drew 16-16 with Bath back in October 2004.

The scores were tied at 6-6 when Tigers' Louis Deacon was forced to leave the field through injury. Andy Goode kicked two first-half penalties in the 10th and 13th minutes, while Jonny Wilkinson succeeded with an early drop-goal and a penalty in the 29th minute. Australian full-back Matt Burke then added a second Falcons penalty to give his side a 9-6 half-time lead.

Both teams were then reduced in numbers, with Tigers' Julian White and Newcastle's Andy Perry receiving red cards for their part in an unsavoury melee. The dismissals led to uncontested scrums, before Tigers scored the first try of the match when James Hamilton touched down after some good work by the Leicester forwards. Goode added the conversion to give Tigers a four-point advantage.

Minutes later Goode extended the hosts' lead when he slotted a penalty that took the score to 16-9. However, Newcastle continued to come back at Tigers and prop Robbie Morris eventually found himself over the whitewash in the 74th minute.

Burke slotted the tricky conversion from the left-hand touchline to set up a heart-stopping five-minute finale, in which the former Wallaby missed a long-range penalty, before an injury-time Goode drop-goal also failed to find its mark.

Guinness Premiership
Welford Road
Att: 16,815
Referee: Tony Spreadbury
Friday October 14 2005

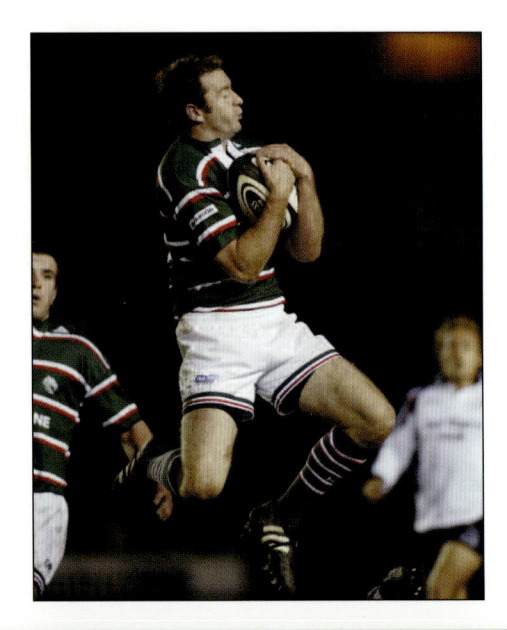

SEASON REVIEW 2005/06

TIGER TIMELINE

			SCORE	MIN
🏉	DG	J.Wilkinson	0-3	5
🏉	P	Goode	3-3	12
🏉	P	Goode	6-3	14
↔	S	Morris Rowntree		30
🏃	P	J.Wilkinson	6-6	31
↔	S	Cullen L.Deacon		36
🟨	YC	Goode		40
🟨	YC	Long		40
🟥	RC	White		40
🟥	RC	Perry		40
↔	S	Thompson Harris		40
🏉	P	Burke	6-9	40

HALF TIME 6-9

↔	S	Harris Thompson		48
🏃	T+C	Hamilton + Goode	13-9	49
↔	S	Vesty Murphy		54
↔	S	McCarthy Finegan		56
↔	S	Gross Ward		56
🏉	P	Goode	16-9	58
↔	S	Noon May		61
↔	S	Thompson Long		68
↔	S	Healey Ellis		70
↔	S	A.Tuilagi Varndell		70
🏃	T+C	Morris + Burke	16-16	74

FULL TIME 16-16

Key
Player coming on
Player going off

LEICESTER TIGERS

- 15 G.Murphy
- 14 L.Lloyd
- 11 T.Varndell
- 13 O.Smith
- 12 D.Hipkiss
- 10 A.Goode
- 9 H.Ellis
- 8 M.Corry (c)
- 7 S.Jennings
- 6 L.Abraham
- 5 J.Hamilton
- 4 L.Deacon
- 3 J.White
- 2 G.Chuter
- 1 G.Rowntree

REPLACEMENTS

16	J.Buckland
17	D.Morris
18	L.Cullen
19	W.Skinner
20	A.Healey
21	S.Vesty
22	A.Tuilagi

"It was a disappointing result, but when you go down to 14 men, it normally becomes a farce out there."
Pat Howard

NEWCASTLE FALCONS

- 1 M.Ward
- 2 A.Long
- 3 R.Morris
- 4 A.Perry
- 5 G.Parling
- 7 C.Harris
- 6 O.Finegan
- 8 C.Charvis (c)
- 9 H.Charlton
- 10 J.Wilkinson
- 12 M.Mayerhofler
- 13 M.Tait
- 11 A.Elliott
- 14 T.May
- 15 M.Burke

REPLACEMENTS

16	T.Paoletti
17	M.Thompson
18	L.Gross
19	M.McCarthy
20	J.Noon
21	J.Grindal
22	D.Walder

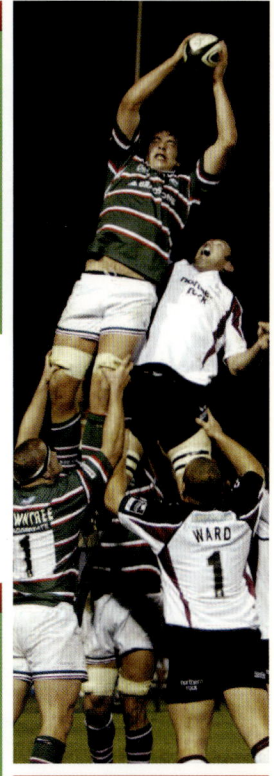

TIGERS MILESTONES

Tigers prop Graham Rowntree joined Martin Johnson as only the second player to start 200 league games for the club.

www.leicestertigers.com   101

SEASON REVIEW 2005/06

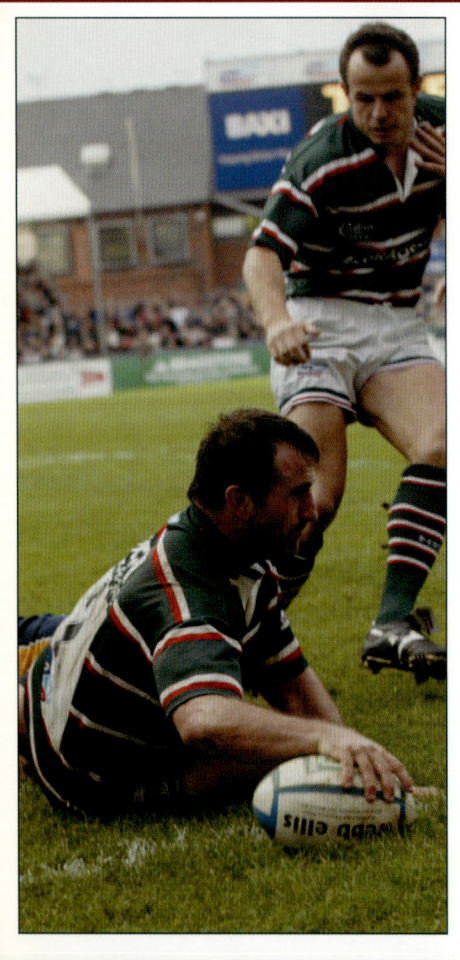

Leicester Tigers 57
Clermont Auvergne 23

Leicester Tigers romped to a 57-23 Pool 3 win over Clermont Auvergne at Welford Road, as they ended their French Heineken Cup bogey with an impressive six-tries-to-two victory.

A sensational first-half performance laid the platform for the double Heineken Cup champions, with tries from Harry Ellis and Leon Lloyd, two Andy Goode conversions and a further five penalty goals from the Tigers No 10 giving them a 29-9 lead at the break.

Leicester scored four more tries in the second half, with Goode's boot taking his team past the 50-point barrier. The former Saracens outside-half recorded 32 points, as he notched up a try, six conversions and five penalties.

Goode exchanged a brace of penalties with Clermont full-back Jean-Baptiste Dambielle before adding a further three points shortly before Tigers opened their try-scoring account through England scrum-half Harry Ellis. Goode added the conversion and then stretched Tigers' lead to 22-6 with penalty goals. Lloyd then sped over four minutes later, with Goode converting to give Leicester a 20-point advantage at half-time.

The second half was barely under way when Tom Varndell registered his side's third try, before George Chuter responded to a mini-Clermont fightback, as he capped an industrious afternoon with a try in the right-hand corner.

Replacement half-back Austin Healey then freed Varndell down the left flank, with the latter using his pace to set-up Geordan Murphy for try No. 6.

Heineken Cup
Welford Road
Att: 16,815
Referee: Alan Lewis
Saturday October 22 2005

SEASON REVIEW 2005/06

TIGER TIMELINE

			SCORE	MIN
🏃	P	Dambielle	0-3	3
🏃	P	Goode	3-3	6
🏃	P	Goode	6-3	15
🏃	P	Dambielle	6-6	19
🏃	P	Goode	9-6	21
🏃	T+C	Ellis + Goode	16-6	23
🏃	P	Goode	19-6	28
🏃	P	Goode	22-6	31
🟨	YC	Dambielle		31
🏃	P	McMullen	22-9	33
	T+C	Lloyd + Goode	29-9	35

HALF TIME 29-9

	T+C	Varndell & Goode	36-9	44
	T+C	Marsh & Dambielle	36-16	48
	P	Goode	43-16	50
	S	Kay Hamilton		51
	S	Vesty Gibson		51
	S	Kiole Dambielle		53
	T+C	Scelzo & McMullen	43-23	56
	S	A.Tuilagi Lloyd		56
	S	Shvelidze Emmanuelli		56
	S	Vermeulen Audebert		56
	S	Holford Morris		59
	S	Healey Ellis		59
	T+C	Chuter & Goode	50-23	62
	S	Buckland Chuter		67
	S	Johnson Jennings		67
	T+C	Murphy & Goode	57-23	70
	S	Vigouroux Barrier		70
🟨	YC	Kay		73
	S	Emmanuelli Scelzo		77

FULL TIME 57-23

LEICESTER TIGERS

- 15 G.Murphy
- 14 L.Lloyd
- 11 T.Varndell
- 13 O.Smith
- 12 D.Gibson
- 10 A.Goode
- 9 H.Ellis
- 8 M.Corry (c)
- 7 S.Jennings
- 6 L.Moody
- 5 L.Cullen
- 4 J.Hamilton
- 3 D.Morris
- 2 G.Chuter
- 1 A.Moreno

CLERMONT AUVERGNE

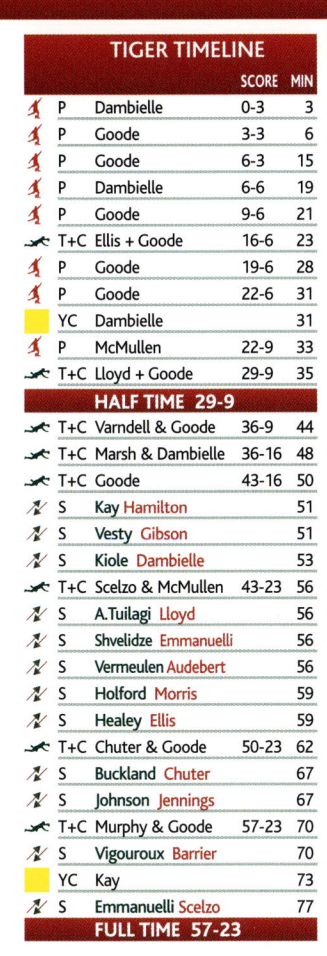

- 1 L.Emmanuelli
- 2 M.Ledesma
- 3 Arocena
- 4 M.Scelzo
- 5 D.Barrier
- 7 A.Audebert
- 6 J.Cudmore
- 8 S.Broomhall
- 9 J.Moreau
- 10 C.McMullen
- 12 T.Marsh
- 13 G.Canale
- 11 B.Paulse
- 14 A.Rougerie (c)
- 15 J.Dambielle

REPLACEMENTS

16	J.Buckland
17	M.Holford
18	B.Kay
19	W.Johnson
20	A.Healey
21	S.Vesty
22	A.Tuilagi

"I thought the scrum was fantastic, the two second rows played out of their skin, the back row played very, very well, and the pack as a whole set the platform for the win."
Pat Howard

REPLACEMENTS

16	B.Miguel
17	G.Shvelidze
18	P.Vigouroux
19	E.Vermeulen
20	P.Garcia
21	S.Kiole
22	J.Malzieu

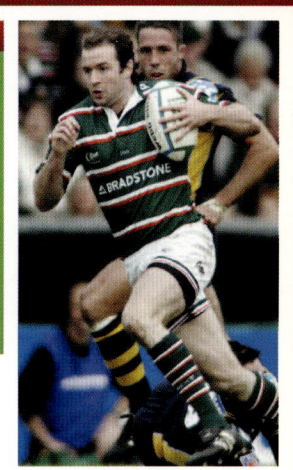

TIGERS MILESTONES

Ollie Smith made his 100th start for Tigers, who recorded their first win in six matches against French opposition.

www.leicestertigers.com 103

SEASON REVIEW 2005/06

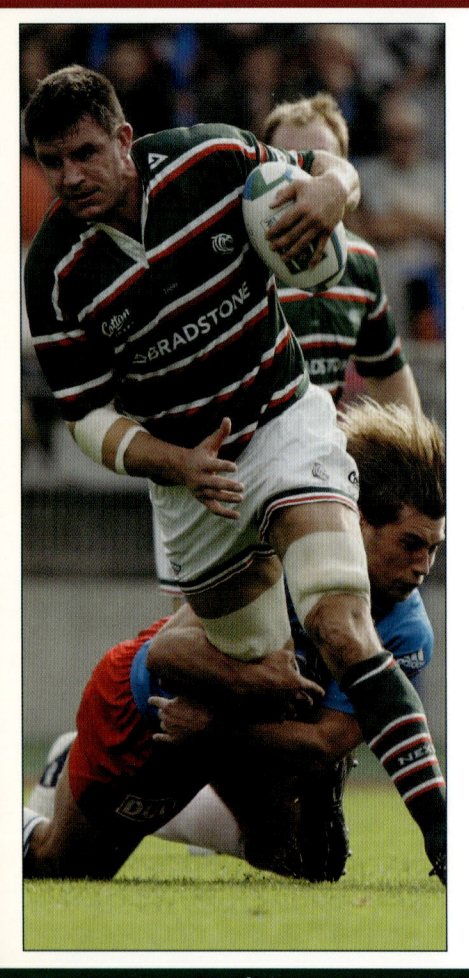

Stade Français 12
Leicester Tigers 6

Leicester Tigers suffered a gut-wrenching 12-6 loss to Stade Français in the pool stages of the Heineken Cup at Stade Charlety in Paris.

It was a disappointing defeat for Pat Howard's troops, who fought hard for every scrap of possession but in the end they were unable to come away with a win.

After their free-flowing six-tries-to-two destruction of Clermont Auvergne in the last round, Tigers fans witnessed a more stagnated blood-and-guts encounter in Paris.

The match began with Stade scrum-half Jerome Fillol missing two penalties, before No 10 Alain Penaud also missed a kick at goal for the hosts. Andy Goode then missed his first attempt at goal with a long-range effort which had the distance but not the direction.

Fillol finally redeemed himself in the 25th minute when his shot from in front of the posts gave Stade a 3-0 lead.

Goode then ensured the sides entered the break on level terms, as he made his second penalty kick from Stade's 10-metre line look ridiculously simple.

The second half began with a ferocious Tigers onslaught, as Goode immediately put his team on the attack with an accurate kick into Stade's 22. However, Stade took advantage of the visitors' failure to turn pressure into points, with Fillol scoring two penalties to give his side a 9-3 lead.

Fillol then added his fourth successful penalty of the day to give his side a nine-point advantage which put Tigers out of bonus-point range for losing by seven points or less.

However, Tigers continued to battle and ultimately won a penalty which Goode converted to give his side an all-important bonus point.

Heineken Cup
Stade Charlety
Att: 19,700
Referee: Donal Courtney
Saturday October 29 2005

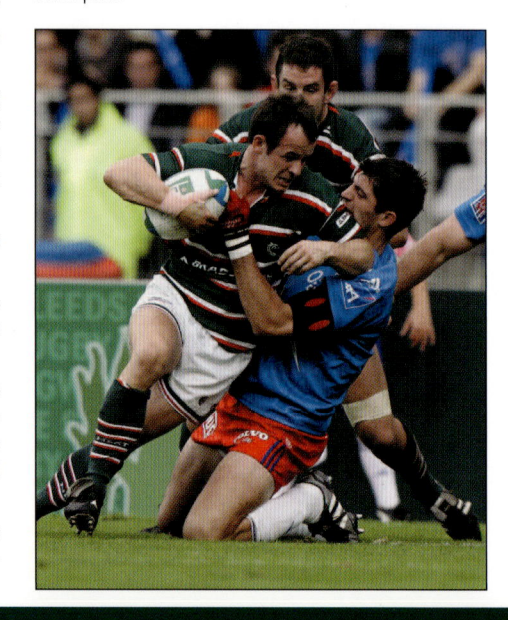

104 www.leicestertigers.com

SEASON REVIEW 2005/06

TIGER TIMELINE

			SCORE	MIN
🏃	P	Fillol	3-0	24
🏃	S	Johnson Corry		31
🏃	S	Corry Johnson		37
🏃	P	Goode	3-3	40

HALF TIME 3-3

🏃	S	Kay Hamilton		50
🏃	S	Hipkiss Gibson		57
🏃	P	Fillol	6-3	58
🏃	S	Healey Ellis		61
🏃	P	Fillol	9-3	64
🏃	P	Fillol	12-3	68
🏃	P	Goode	12-6	75
🏃	S	Blin Szarzewski		75
🏃	S	Johnson Jennings		75
🟨	YC	Kay		78
🏃	S	Rabadan Marchois		81

FULL TIME 12-6

Key
Player coming on
Player going off

LEICESTER TIGERS

- 15 G.Murphy
- 14 A.Tuilagi
- 11 T.Varndell
- 13 O.Smith
- 12 D.Gibson
- 10 A.Goode
- 9 H.Ellis
- 8 M.Corry (c)
- 7 S.Jennings
- 6 L.Moody
- 5 L.Cullen
- 4 J.Hamilton
- 3 D.Morris
- 2 G.Chuter
- 1 A.Moreno

STADE FRANCAIS

- 1 R.Roncero
- 2 D.Szarzewski
- 3 P.De Villiers (c)
- 4 A.Marchois
- 5 M.James
- 7 R.Martin
- 6 S.Parisse
- 8 S.Sowerby
- 9 J.Fillol
- 10 A.Penaud
- 12 B.Liebenberg
- 13 G.Messina
- 11 Mirco Bergamasco
- 14 L.Borges
- 15 O.Sarramea

REPLACEMENTS

16	J.Buckland
17	M.Holford
18	B.Kay
19	W.Johnson
20	A.Healey
21	R.Broadfoot
22	D.Hipkiss

"I was proud of the guys defensively in terms of their work-rate and their competition around the breakdown, but at the same stage we missed one or two try-scoring opportunities."
Pat Howard

REPLACEMENTS

16	M.Blin
17	Y.Montes
18	P.Rabadan
19	Mauro
20	Bergamasco
21	A.Pichot
22	J.Saubade

TIGERS MILESTONES

The Stade Charlety in Paris became the 25th different Heineken Cup ground that Tigers have played on since they first entered the competition in 1997.

www.leicestertigers.com   105

SEASON REVIEW 2005/06

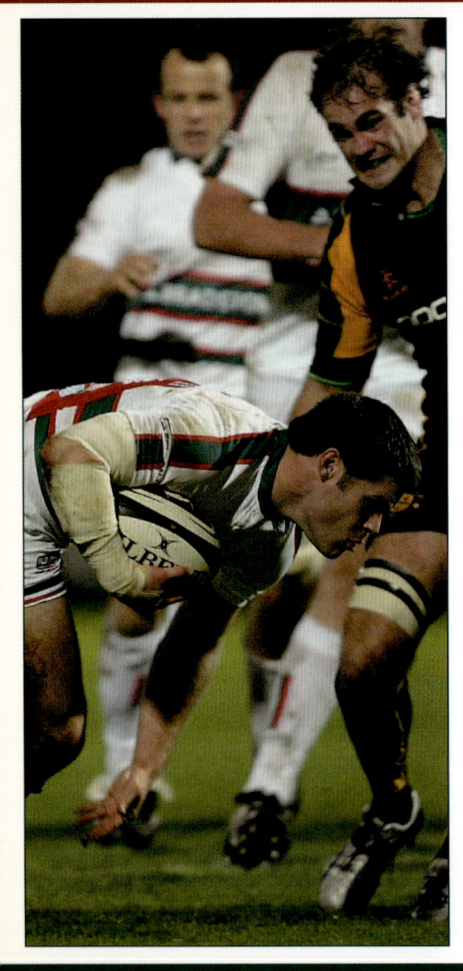

Worcester Warriors 15
Leicester Tigers 11

Leicester Tigers suffered a disappointing 15-11 Guinness Premiership loss to Worcester Warriors at a noisy Sixways, as the home side recorded their first-ever win over Tigers. Leicester scored the only try of a hard-fought match but returned home with only a losing bonus point.

The match began with some serious pressure from the home team, before Tigers fly-half Ross Broadfoot kicked a penalty goal to give the visitors a 3-0 lead.

Worcester put that initial disappointment behind them almost immediately however, as former Springboks back Thinus Delport's clever angled run earned a penalty, which Shane Drahm converted.

Tigers captain Austin Healey led from the front on the night and he put his side back on the attack soon afterwards, before an Andy Gomarsall box kick eventually resulted in another Worcester penalty. Drahm again made no mistake to give the Warriors a 6-3 lead.

Open-side flanker Will Skinner then touched down for an unconverted try to put Tigers 8-6 ahead, although Worcester fought back as Drahm added a brace of penalties to give his side a 12-8 lead, with Tigers second row Ben Kay serving time in the sin-bin.

Drahm then succeeded with his fifth penalty goal of the half to put the Warriors seven points clear at the break.

Despite a strong second half, Tigers could only manage a penalty from Andy Goode, meaning Pat Howard's team dropped two places to fourth in the Guinness Premiership standings.

Guinness Premiership
Sixways
Att: 9,776
Referee: Roy Maybank
Friday November 4 2005

106 www.leicestertigers.com

SEASON REVIEW 2005/06

TIGER TIMELINE

			SCORE	MIN
🏃	P	Broadfoot	0-3	3
🏃	P	Drahm	3-3	6
🏃	P	Drahm	6-3	10
🏃	T	Skinner	6-8	16
🏃	P	Drahm	9-8	22
🟨	YC	Kay		30
🏃	P	Drahm	12-8	37
🏃	P	Drahm	15-8	40

HALF TIME 15-8

🟨	YC	Hamilton		46
↔	S	Goode Broadfoot		50
↔	S	Cullen Hamilton		56
↔	S	Morris Holford		63
↔	S	Smith Lloyd		63
🏃	P	Goode	15-11	69
↔	S	Vaili Tu'amoheloa		70

FULL TIME 15-11

Key
Player coming on
Player going off

LEICESTER TIGERS

- 15 S.Vesty
- 14 A.Tuilagi
- 11 T.Varndell
- 13 L.Lloyd
- 12 D.Hipkiss
- 10 R.Broadfoot
- 9 A.Healey (c)
- 8 W.Johnson
- 7 W.Skinner
- 6 B.Deacon
- 5 B.Kay
- 4 J.Hamilton
- 3 A.Moreno
- 2 G.Chuter
- 1 M.Holford

REPLACEMENTS

16	J.Buckland
17	D.Morris
18	L.Cullen
19	T.Croft
20	N.Cole
21	O.Smith
22	A.Goode

"We didn't play anywhere near the level we can do. We defended well, but for two weeks on the trot now we haven't conceded any tries but we've failed to come away with a win."
Pat Howard

WORCESTER WARRIORS

- 1 T.Windo (c)
- 2 C.Fortey
- 3 T.Taumoepeau
- 4 P.Murphy
- 5 C.Gillies
- 7 J.Tu'amoheloa
- 6 K.Horstmann
- 8 D.Hickey
- 9 A.Gomarsall
- 10 S.Drahm
- 12 T.Lombard
- 13 B.Hinshelwood
- 11 T.Delport
- 14 A.Havili
- 15 N.Le Roux

REPLACEMENTS

16	M.MacDonald
17	L.Fortey
18	R.Blaze
19	S.Vaili
20	M.Powell
21	J.Brown
22	M.Tucker

TIGERS MILESTONES

Austin Healey captained the side from scrum-half, as he marked his 150th league appearance since his Tigers debut in 1996.

www.leicestertigers.com 107

SEASON REVIEW 2005/06

Leicester Tigers 25
Gloucester 20

Guinness Premiership
Welford Road   Att: 16,815
Referee: Tony Spreadbury
Saturday November 12 2005

A superb first-half effort from the Leicester Tigers pack helped Pat Howard's side to a 25-20 Guinness Premiership win over a determined Gloucester outfit at Welford Road.

Tries either side of the break from Tom Varndell saw Tigers record a three-tries-to-two victory against a spirited Cherry and Whites side, who pushed the home team right until the very end.

Second row Ben Kay walked off with the Bradstone Man of the Match Award, while fly-half Andy Goode weighed in with 10 points.

Gloucester's Ludovic Mercier gave his side a 3-0 lead after four minutes, before an excellent Tigers forward move resulted in a converted try for prop Michael Holford.

Leicester kept the pressure on their opponents, as debutant Tom Croft showed a great deal of skill and composure to free left-wing Varndell, who made the short dash to the try-line look like a Sunday afternoon stroll.

Mercier pulled back three points with his second penalty goal of the day before Goode added his own three-pointer just over 10 minutes later.

Gloucester's only real chance of the first period came just as the half was drawing to a close. James Simpson-Daniel beat a host of defenders, before putting his centre partner, Anthony Allen, away for a try which Mercier converted, leaving Tigers with a 15-13 lead at the break.

After a bright start to the second half by Gloucester, Varndell scored his second try of the day which was converted by Goode to make it 22-13.

Tigers went in search of a fourth try and that all-important bonus point shortly afterwards, but they found themselves up against a resilient Cherry and Whites defensive line.

Goode added a penalty before Olly Morgan went over for Gloucester, with Mercier's conversion leaving the final score 25-20 in Tigers' favour.

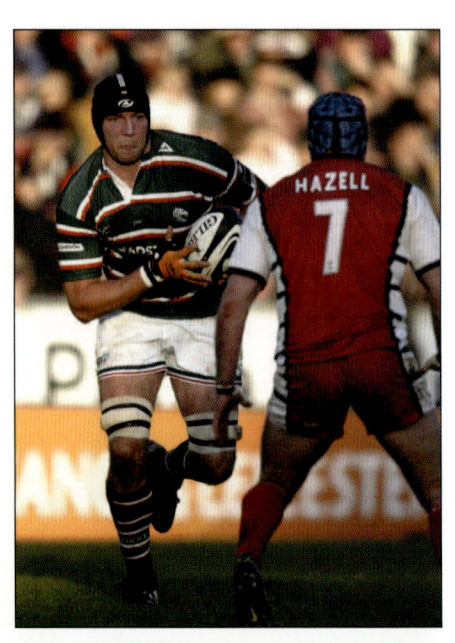

108   www.leicestertigers.com

SEASON REVIEW 2005/06

TIGER TIMELINE

			SCORE	MIN
🏃	P	Mercier	0-3	3
🏃	T+C	Holford + Goode	7-3	8
🏃	T	Varndell	12-3	20
🏃	P	Mercier	12-6	28
🏃	P	Goode	15-6	38
🏃	T+C	Allen + Mercier	15-13	40

HALF TIME 15-13

🏃	S	Boer Balding		45
🏃	T+C	Varndell +Goode	22-13	46
🏃	S	Moreno Holford		46
🏃	S	Hamilton Cullen		49
🏃	P	Goode	25-13	58
🏃	S	Johnson Jennings		58
🏃	S	Fanolua Allen		58
🏃	S	A Tuilagi Hipkiss		62
🏃	S	Cornwell Buxton		66
🏃	S	Thomas Richards		70
🏃	S	Cole Healey		73
🏃	T+C	Morgan & Mercier	25-20	74

FULL TIME 25-20

Key
Player coming on
Player going off

LEICESTER TIGERS

- 15 S.Vesty
- 14 L.Lloyd
- 11 T.Varndell
- 13 O.Smith
- 12 D.Hipkiss
- 10 A.Goode
- 9 A.Healey (c)
- 8 B.Deacon
- 7 S.Jennings
- 6 T.Croft
- 5 B.Kay
- 4 L.Cullen
- 3 D.Morris
- 2 G.Chuter
- 1 M.Holford

GLOUCESTER

- 1 P.Collazo
- 2 M.Davies
- 3 G.Powell
- 4 A.Eustace
- 5 P.Buxton (c)
- 7 A.Hazell
- 6 A.Balding
- 8 J.Forrester
- 9 P.Richards
- 10 L.Mercier
- 12 A.Allen
- 13 J.Simpson-Daniel
- 11 R.Thirlby
- 14 M.Foster
- 15 O.Morgan

REPLACEMENTS

16	J.Buckland
17	A.Moreno
18	J.Hamilton
19	W.Johnson
20	N.Cole
21	R.Broadfoot
22	Anitele'a Tuilagi

"Considering the problems we've got with international call-ups and injuries, I thought everybody stood up exceptionally well and dug in when we had to right at the end." **Richard Cockerill**

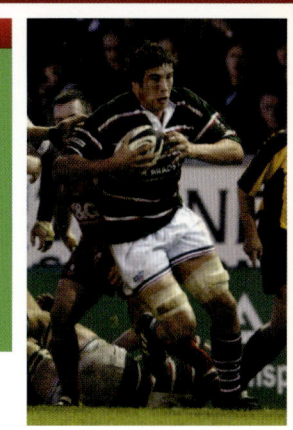

REPLACEMENTS

16	J.Parkes
17	T.Sigley
18	M.Cornwell
19	J.Boer
20	H.Thomas
21	T.Fanolua
22	B.Davies

TIGERS MILESTONES

Anthony Allen's try for Gloucester was the first five-pointer Tigers had conceded in 224 minutes of rugby.

www.leicestertigers.com 109

SEASON REVIEW 2005/06

Sale Sharks 24
Leicester Tigers 16

Leicester Tigers' Friday night hoodoo continued at Edgeley Park where they were beaten 24-16 by Guinness Premiership leaders Sale Sharks. On Will Johnson's 200th appearance for the club, Tigers were unable to overcome their determined opponents despite throwing everything at them in the final few minutes of the match.

With Sam Vesty, Dan Hipkiss and Tom Varndell particularly threatening for Tigers, the home side produced a brilliant defensive display to deny Tigers victory.

Sale went ahead through a Daniel Larrechea penalty just five minutes into the game, with Tom Croft sent to the sin-bin for throwing a punch.

The home side then extended their lead courtesy of two further Larrachea penalties, before Ross Broadfoot finally got the visitors off the mark in the 23rd minute with a successful kick at goal.

Just after the half-hour mark, Broadfoot again reduced the deficit, but a try from Welsh centre Mark Taylor and a conversion from fly-half Valentin Courrent gave Sale a 16-9 lead at the break.

Sale strengthened their grip on the match immediately after the re-start, as a Magnus Lund try took the score to 21-9.

Another Courrent penalty extended the lead to 15 points, before Tigers replacements Matt Cornwell and Andy Goode combined to give their side hope. Cornwell's timely score was converted by the England fly-half to reduce the gap to 24-16.

Although they created a number of further try-scoring opportunities, Tigers were unable to capitalise as Sale held on for the win.

Guinness Premiership
Edgeley Park
Att: 10,641
Referee: Sean Davey
Friday November 18 2005

SEASON REVIEW 2005/06

TIGER TIMELINE

			SCORE	MIN
	YC	Croft		5
	P	Larrechea	3-0	6
	P	Larrechea	6-0	14
	P	Larrechea	9-0	18
	P	Broadfoot	9-3	21
	P	Broadfoot	9-6	31
	T+C	Taylor + Courrent	16-6	35
	P	Broadfoot	16-9	38

HALF TIME 16-9

	S	Cornwell Hipkiss		41
	T	Lund	21-9	42
	S	Anglesea Taione		49
	S	Goode Broadfoot		52
	P	Courrent	24-9	53
	S	Turner Coutts		56
	S	Hamilton Cullen		56
	S	Johnson B.Deacon		56
	S	Buckland Chuter		58
	S	Holford Morris		58
	YC	Bonner-Evans		66
	S	Foden Larrechea		68
	S	Wigglesworth Martens		72
	YC	Stewart		73
	T+C	Cornwell +Goode	24-16	74
	S	Coutts Bonner-Evans		76

FULL TIME 24-16

Key
Player coming on
Player going off

LEICESTER TIGERS

- 15 S.Vesty
- 14 L.Lloyd
- 11 T.Varndell
- 13 O.Smith
- 12 D.Hipkiss
- 10 R.Broadfoot
- 9 A.Healey (c)
- 8 B.Deacon
- 7 W.Skinner
- 6 T.Croft
- 5 B.Kay
- 4 L.Cullen
- 3 D.Morris
- 2 G.Chuter
- 1 A.Moreno

SALE SHARKS

- 1 B.Coutts
- 2 A.Titterrell
- 3 B.Stewart
- 4 C.Day
- 5 D.Schofield
- 7 M.Lund
- 6 E.Taione
- 8 N.Bonner-Evans
- 9 S.Martens
- 10 V.Courrent
- 12 R.Todd
- 13 M.Taylor
- 11 J.Robinson (c)
- 14 O.Ripol Fortuny
- 15 D.Larrechea

REPLACEMENTS

- 16 J.Buckland
- 17 M.Holford
- 18 J.Hamilton
- 19 W.Johnson
- 20 N.Cole
- 21 M.Cornwell
- 22 A.Goode

"We made enough breaks to win about five games, so to come away with nothing from the match is very, very disappointing."
Pat Howard

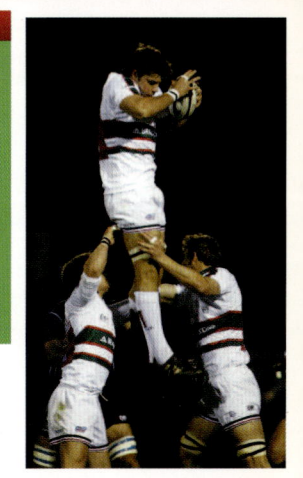

REPLACEMENTS

- 16 N.Briggs
- 17 S.Turner
- 18 P.Anglesea
- 19 D.Tait
- 20 R.Wigglesworth
- 21 B.Foden
- 22 C.Mayor

TIGERS MILESTONES

Will Johnson made his 200th appearance for Tigers, whilst Matt Cornwell scored his second try in his fifth game for the club.

www.leicestertigers.com 111

SEASON REVIEW 2005/06

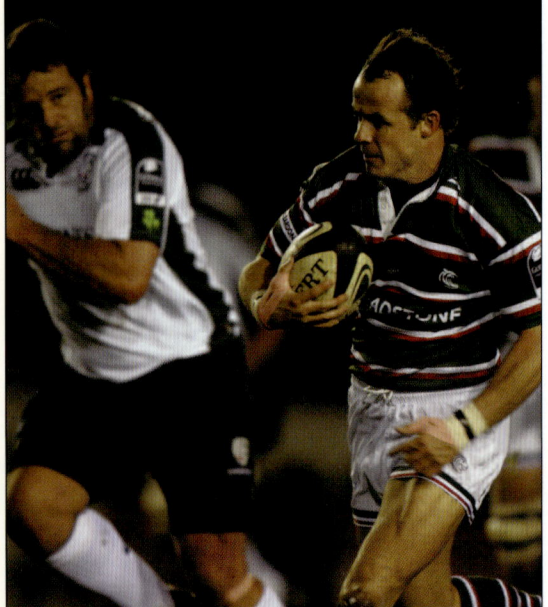

Leicester Tigers 35
London Irish 3

Guinness Premiership
Welford Road
Att: 16,815
Referee: Roy Maybank
Friday November 25 2005

An under-strength Leicester Tigers team romped to a 35-3 Guinness Premiership win over London Irish at Welford Road, recording a crucial four-try bonus point in the process.

The match marked the comeback of Fijian back Seru Rabeni, who returned after a lengthy injury lay-off. Fittingly, Rabeni played a pivotal part in the last-ditch attack which secured an all-important bonus-point try for Tigers.

After Barry Everitt had put Irish in front with a penalty in the first minute of the game, Tigers took the lead somewhat against the run of play when Bradstone Man of the Match and captain Austin Healey charged down an attempted clearance kick just inside the Exiles half, before racing away to touch the ball down under the posts. Goode added the straight-forward conversion and a first penalty to make the score 10-3 to the home side.

The hosts extended their lead when Ben Kay scored an unconverted try, before Goode stretched his side's advantage with another penalty minutes later to ensure Tigers held an 18-3 half-time lead.

After the break, George Chuter crashed over for a try which Goode converted.

With Tigers now beginning to dominate the match, the Welford Road crowd was urging the team to score the bonus-point fourth try.

This duly came when prop Michael Holford touched down with just minutes left following some excellent work by the forwards. Goode again converted to ensure Irish returned home with a 35-3 hammering.

SEASON REVIEW 2005/06

TIGER TIMELINE

			SCORE	MIN
	P	Everitt	0-3	3
	T+C	Healey + Goode	7-3	8
	P	Goode	10-3	22
	T	Kay	15-3	28
	P	Goode	18-3	33

HALF TIME 18-3

	S	Horak Catt		41
	S	Leguizamon Murphy		47
	T+C	Chuter + Goode	25-3	49
	S	Collins Hatley		51
	S	Hodgson Willis		52
	S	Abraham Jennings		54
	YC	Johnson		57
	S	Skuse Rautenbach		59
	S	Rabeni Lloyd		60
	S	Buckland Chuter		61
	S	Holford Morris		61
	S	Cole Healey		61
	S	Broadfoot Cornwell		61
	P	Goode	28-3	64
	S	Russell Coetzee		65
	S	Strudwick Roche		65
	YC	Russell		69
	T+C	Holford + Goode	35-3	79
	S	Morris Moreno		80

FULL TIME 35-3

Key
Player coming on
Player going off

LEICESTER TIGERS

15 S.Vesty
14 L.Lloyd 11 O.Smith
13 D.Hipkiss
12 M.Cornwell
10 A.Goode
9 A.Healey (c)
8 B.Deacon
7 S.Jennings 6 W.Johnson
5 B.Kay 4 J.Hamilton
3 D.Morris 2 G.Chuter 1 A.Moreno

LONDON IRISH

1 N.Hatley 2 D.Coetzee 3 F.Rautenbach
4 B.Casey 5 N.Kennedy
7 D.Danaher 6 K.Roche
8 P.Murphy
9 B.Willis
10 B.Everitt
12 M.Catt (c)
13 R.Penney
11 J.Bishop 14 S.Staniforth
15 R.Flutey

REPLACEMENTS

16	J.Buckland
17	M.Holford
18	T.Croft
19	L.Abraham
20	N.Cole
21	R.Broadfoot
22	S.Rabeni

"We used 21 guys and it took all of them to get that bonus point. We had to work very hard and credit goes to London Irish for that."
Pat Howard

REPLACEMENTS

16	M.Collins
17	R.Russell
18	R.Skuse
19	R.Strudwick
20	J.Leguizamon
21	P.Hodgson
22	M.Horak

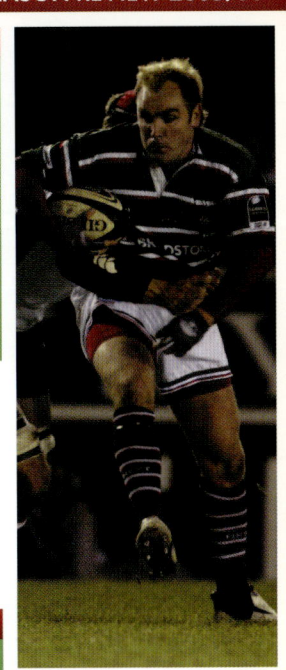

TIGERS MILESTONES

Tigers' victory was their fifth successive win against London Irish, and their 19th in 20 home matches against the Exiles since 1923.

www.leicestertigers.com 113

SEASON REVIEW 2005/06

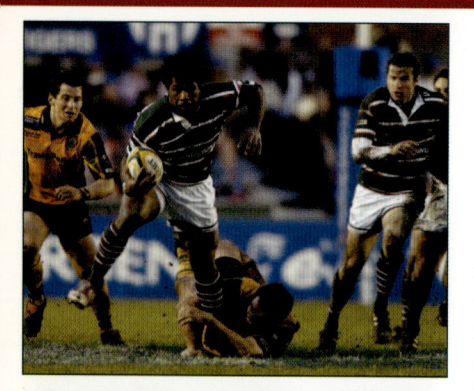

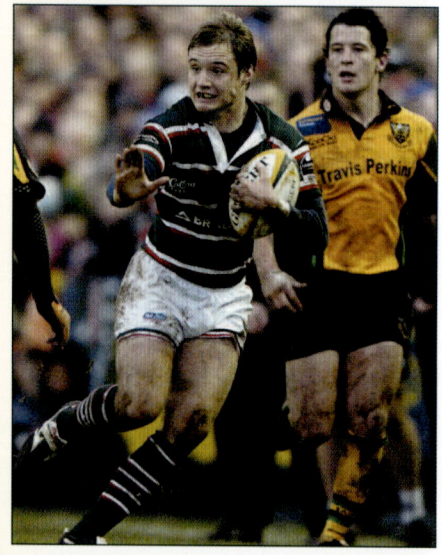

Leicester Tigers 29
Northampton Saints 16

Powergen Cup
Welford Road
Att: 11,072
Referee: Chris White
Saturday December 3 2005

Leicester Tigers recovered from a half-time deficit to record a 29-16 victory over East Midlands rivals Northampton Saints in the Powergen Cup pool stages. The win saw Pat Howard's men through to the semi-finals of the newly-revamped tournament at the Millennium Stadium in March 2006.

It was a tough day at the office for Tigers, who trailed 11-7 at half-time, but their four-try victory puts them into the last four of the cup for the first time in three years.

Saints took the lead just four minutes into the match when New Zealand scrum-half Mark Robinson touched down on the right for an unconverted try.

Tigers then conceded a penalty after 20 minutes, which Saints captain Bruce Reihana converted from 40 metres out on the left. The visitors extended their lead shortly afterwards, with Reihana again on target with a penalty kick to make the score 11-0.

Minutes before the interval, Andy Goode converted Leon Lloyd's try to bridge the half-time gap.

Tigers started the second period brightly as Ben Kay crashed over from a rolling maul to give his side the lead for the first time in the match.

Saints soon replied via John Rudd's unconverted try, before Shane Jennings scored for Tigers after Martin Corry had blocked an attempted clearance kick on the edge of the Northampton 22.

Lloyd's second try secured the bonus point just after the hour mark, with Goode converting to make the score 26-16 to the home side. Soon afterwards, Northampton conceded a penalty which Goode coolly kicked to put his side 29-16 ahead.

Despite some late flourishes by Saints, the Tigers defence held firm under pressure and keep their search for Powergen Cup glory very much alive.

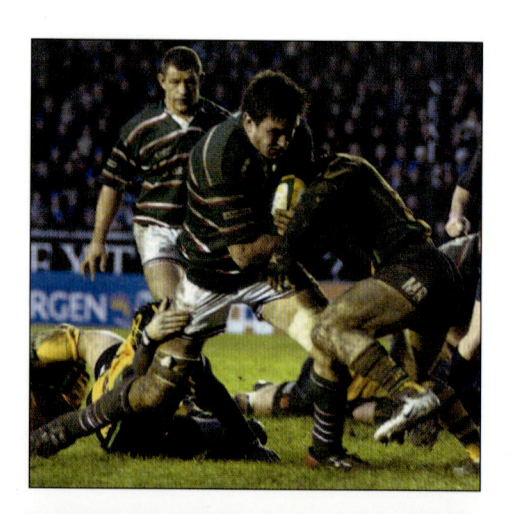

114 www.leicestertigers.com

SEASON REVIEW 2005/06

TIGER TIMELINE

			SCORE	MIN
T		Robinson	0-5	5
P		Reihana	0-8	8
P		Reihana	0-11	38
T+C		Lloyd + Goode	7-11	40

HALF TIME 7-11

T+C		Kay + Goode	14-11	45
S		Rabeni Vesty		46
T		Rudd	14-16	48
S		Hartley Thompson		48
T		Jennings	19-16	55
S		Fox Harding		58
S		Abraham Jennings		60
S		Hamilton L.Deacon		66
T+C		Lloyd + Goode	26-16	70
S		Seely Gerard		71
S		Howard Robinson		71
S		Noon Barnard		72
S		Cole Ellis		73
S		Hipkiss Cornwell		73
S		Buckland Chuter		74
S		Young Moreno		76
P		Goode	29-16	78

FULL TIME 29-16

Key
Player coming on
Player going off

LEICESTER TIGERS

- 15 S.Vesty
- 14 L.Lloyd
- 11 G.Murphy
- 13 O.Smith
- 12 M.Cornwell
- 10 A.Goode
- 9 H.Ellis
- 8 M.Corry (c)
- 7 S.Jennings
- 6 B.Deacon
- 5 B.Kay
- 4 L.Deacon
- 3 A.Moreno
- 2 G.Chuter
- 1 M.Holford

NORTHAMPTON SAINTS

- 1 C.Budgen
- 2 S.Thompson
- 3 P.Barnard
- 4 Damien Browne
- 5 D.Gerard
- 7 S.Harding
- 6 B.Lewitt
- 8 Daniel Browne
- 9 M.Robinson
- 10 C.Spencer
- 12 R.Davies
- 13 B.Cohen
- 11 J.Rudd
- 14 S.Lamont
- 15 B.Reihana (c)

REPLACEMENTS

- 16 J.Buckland
- 17 D.Young
- 18 J.Hamilton
- 19 L.Abraham
- 20 N.Cole
- 21 D.Hipkiss
- 22 S.Rabeni

"We were far from clinical, but we were good in certain areas and there are plenty of positives to take from the match as that's a far better Northampton team than the one we played earlier in the season." **Pat Howard**

REPLACEMENTS

- 16 D.Hartley
- 17 C.Noon
- 18 G.Seely
- 19 D.Fox
- 20 J.Howard
- 21 L.Myring
- 22 S.Mallon

TIGERS MILESTONES

Tigers beat Northampton for the second time at Welford Road this season, following their 32-0 Guinness Premiership victory back on September 3.

www.leicestertigers.com

SEASON REVIEW 2005/06

Leicester Tigers 30
Ospreys 12

Heineken Cup
Welford Road
Att: 16,815
Referee: Joel Jutge
Sunday December 11 2005

Leicester Tigers completed a four-try bonus-point victory over the Ospreys at Welford Road to consolidate their position at the top of Pool Three in the Heineken Cup.

Tigers produced a determined performance to come back from a 12-6 half-time deficit to secure an 18-point victory over the reigning Celtic League champions.

It was Leicester who took the lead through an Andy Goode penalty after 20 minutes, but the Ospreys replied with a try scored by Sonny Parker and converted by Shaun Connor.

A second penalty was then awarded to the hosts, with Goode again making no mistake as he reduced the gap to just a point at 7-6.

The Ospreys increased their lead when full-back Adrian Cashmore cruised over for an unconverted try to leave the score at 12-6 after the opening 40 minutes.

After the break, a period of Tigers dominance was rewarded when Brett Deacon crashed over for an unconverted try.

Welford Road erupted five minutes later when Harry Ellis scythed through the Ospreys defence from 20 metres out, eventually diving over for a fantastic try which Goode converted to give the home side a deserved 18-12 lead.

Tigers extended their advantage in the 71st minute when the ball broke to the right corner, where hooker George Chuter was on hand to touch down for a converted try to send Tigers 25-12 ahead.

As the home side searched for the fourth bonus-point try, a fantastic rolling maul by the Tigers forwards allowed Austin Healey to dart over the line to guarantee a vital five points.

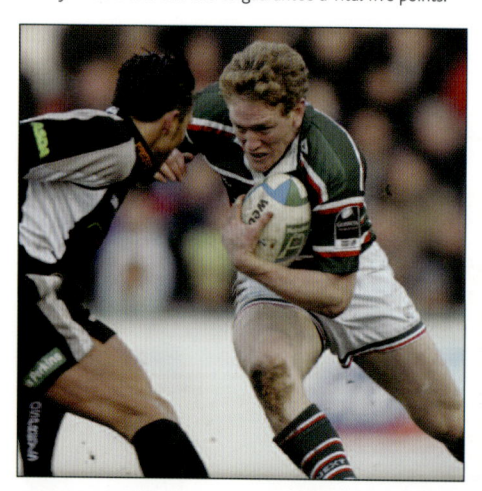

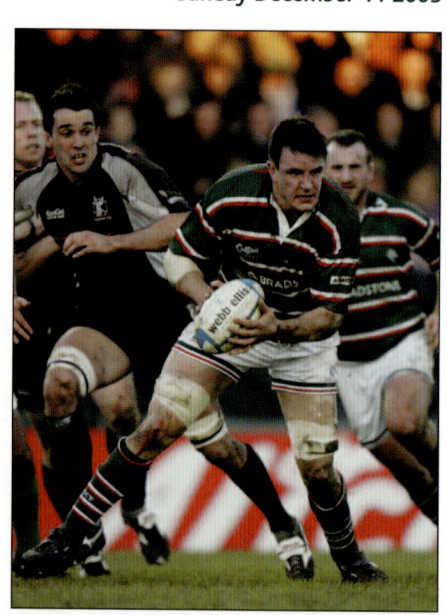

116   www.leicestertigers.com

SEASON REVIEW 2005/06

TIGER TIMELINE

			SCORE	MIN
	S	M.Jones Connor		6
	S	Connor M.Jones		12
	P	Goode	3-0	21
	T+C	Parker + Connor	3-7	25
	P	Goode	6-7	34
	T	Cashmore	6-12	40

HALF TIME 6-12

	S	Healey Lloyd		51
	T	B.Deacon	11-12	54
	T+C	Ellis + Goode	18-12	61
	S	Bennett B.Williams		66
	S	S.Williams Cashmore		66
	S	Holford Morris		70
	S	Millward A.Jones		70
	T+C	Chuter + Goode	25-12	72
	S	Hipkiss Ellis		76
	S	M.Jones Connor		76
	T	Healey	30-12	80
	S	Buckland Chuter		81
	S	Abraham Jennings		81
	S	Broadfoot Goode		81

FULL TIME 30-12

Key
Player coming on
Player going off

LEICESTER TIGERS

- 15 S.Vesty
- 14 L.Lloyd
- 11 G.Murphy
- 13 O.Smith
- 12 M.Cornwell
- 10 A.Goode
- 9 H.Ellis
- 8 M.Corry (c)
- 7 S.Jennings
- 6 B.Deacon
- 5 B.Kay
- 4 L.Deacon
- 3 D.Morris
- 2 G.Chuter
- 1 A.Moreno

OSPREYS

- 1 D.Jones
- 2 B.Williams (c)
- 3 A.Jones
- 4 A.Newman
- 5 I.Evans
- 7 S.Tandy
- 6 J.Bater
- 8 J.Thomas
- 9 J.Spice
- 10 S.Connor
- 12 G.Henson
- 13 S.Parker
- 11 R.Mustoe
- 14 S.Terblanche
- 15 A.Cashmore

REPLACEMENTS

16	J.Buckland
17	M.Holford
18	L.Cullen
19	L.Abraham
20	A.Healey
21	R.Broadfoot
22	D.Hipkiss

"Today was a good win but next week's encounter is another match altogether and I don't think it will have too much bearing on the return fixture. I know we will be in for a tough match."
Pat Howard

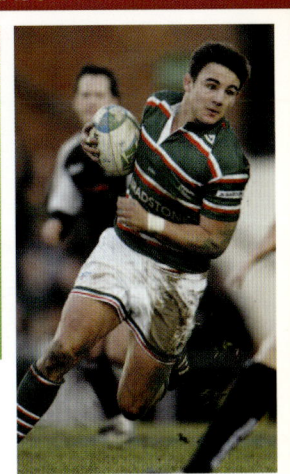

REPLACEMENTS

16	H.Bennett
17	A.Millward
18	L.Bateman
19	L.Beach
20	M.Jones
21	A.Bishop
22	S.Williams

TIGERS MILESTONES

Andy Goode joined Harold Day, Bob Barker, Dusty Hare, John Liley, Jez Harris and Tim Stimpson as he became only the seventh player in Tigers' history to score over 1,000 points for the club.

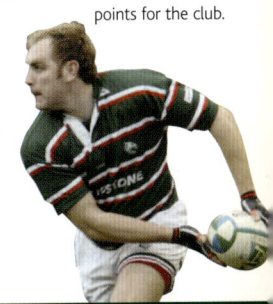

www.leicestertigers.com 117

SEASON REVIEW 2005/06

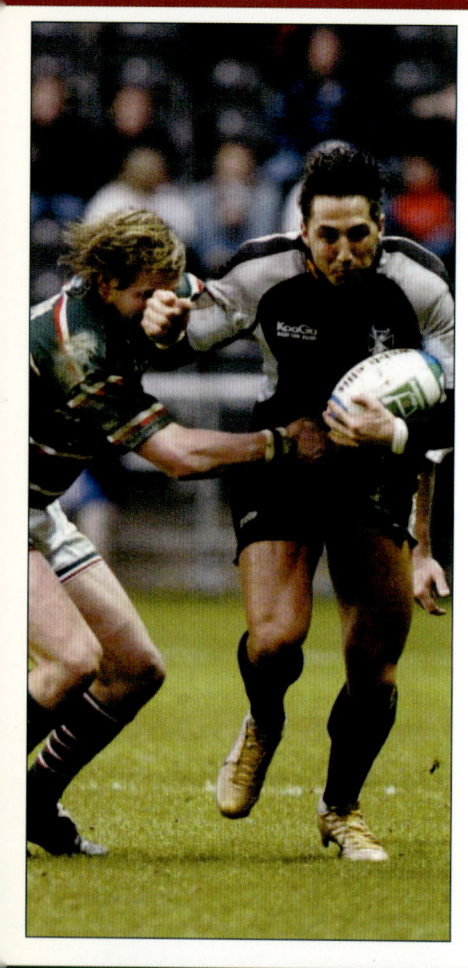

Ospreys 15
Leicester Tigers 17

Heineken Cup
Liberty Stadium
Att: 11,448
Referee: Alain Rolland
Sunday December 18 2005

Tigers snatched a sensational 17-15 Heineken Cup victory over the Ospreys thanks to a last-gasp Dan Hipkiss try which Andy Goode converted with the final kick of the game.

Reduced to 13 players at one stage and behind by seven points at half-time, Tigers snatched victory from the jaws of defeat to leave them top of the 'Pool of Death' by a single point from Stade Français.

A match which marked Austin Healey's 50th European appearance for the club had little else in the way of interest during a scrappy first half which saw Ospreys take a 10-3 lead courtesy of a Shaun Connor penalty and a converted try from captain Barry Williams.

With Tigers only having a Goode penalty to show for their efforts, they went further behind when Connor darted over for a second Ospreys try just minutes after the re-start.

Ollie Smith and Louis Deacon were then sent to the sin-bin within minutes of each other, leaving their Tigers team-mates having to defend scrum after scrum on their own line.

However, after heroic defence kept their opponents at bay, the visitors bridged the gap courtesy of Leon Lloyd's 19th Heineken Cup try, which Goode converted.

With just minutes of the game left, Tom Varndell's pace launched Tigers into the Ospreys half and after numerous phases inside the hosts' territory, the ball came to Hipkiss who ran in the match-winning try. Goode's pressure conversion then secured the points for a mightily relieved Tigers side.

118   www.leicestertigers.com

SEASON REVIEW 2005/06

TIGER TIMELINE

			SCORE	MIN
▲	P	Connor	3-0	14
	S	Rowntree Moreno		18
▲	P	Goode	3-3	24
	S	Moreno Rowntree		33
	S	Rowntree Moreno		35
	S	Healey Ellis		36
▶	T+C	B.Williams + Connor	10-3	40

HALF TIME 10-3

	S	Moreno Rowntree		41
	S	Hipkiss Cornwell		47
▬	YC	Smith		49
▶	T	Connor	15-3	50
	S	Rowntree Morris		51
	S	L.Deacon Kay		54
▬	YC	L.Deacon		56
▶	T+C	Lloyd + Goode	15-10	64
	S	Abraham B.Deacon		68
	S	A.Bishop Connor		72
	S	Vesty Murphy		75
	S	Bateman I.Evans		80
▶	T+C	Hipkiss + Goode	15-17	85

FULL TIME 15-17

Key
Player coming on
Player going off

LEICESTER TIGERS

15 G.Murphy
14 L.Lloyd   11 T.Varndell
         13 O.Smith
         12 M.Cornwell
         10 A.Goode
9 H.Ellis
         8 M.Corry (c)
7 S.Jennings   6 B.Deacon
    5 B.Kay   4 L.Cullen
3 A.Moreno 2 G.Chuter 1 D.Morris

OSPREYS

1 D.Jones 2 B.Williams (c) 3 A.Jones
    4 A.Newman   5 I.Evans
7 S.Tandy   6 J.Bater
         8 J.Thomas
9 J.Spice
         10 S.Connor
         12 G.Henson
              13 S.Parker
11 R.Mustoe   14 S.Terblanche
         15 A.Cashmore

REPLACEMENTS

16	J.Buckland
17	G.Rowntree
18	L.Deacon
19	L.Abraham
20	A.Healey
21	S.Vesty
22	D.Hipkiss

"The players' commitment and ability to play a full 80 minutes was fantastic. It shows the never-say-die attitude which has been a part of this club since long before I joined." Pat Howard

REPLACEMENTS

16	H.Bennett
17	A.Millward
18	L.Bateman
19	L.Beach
20	M.Jones
21	A.Bishop
22	S.Williams

TIGERS MILESTONES

Austin Healey became the third Tigers player to appear in 50 Heineken Cup matches, while the 17-15 victory was Leicester's seventh from their last eight encounters against Welsh sides.

www.leicestertigers.com   119

SEASON REVIEW 2005/06

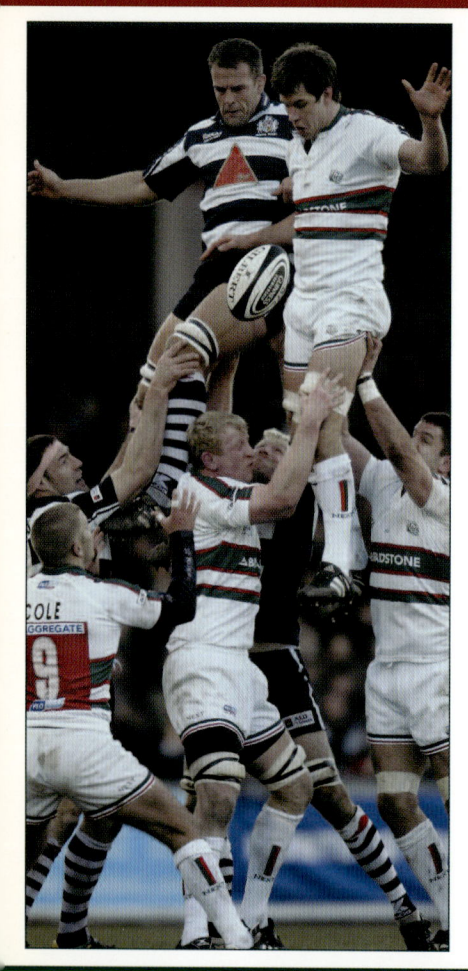

Bristol 15
Leicester Tigers 3

Guinness Premiership
Memorial Stadium
Att: 11,916
Referee: Dean Richards
Tuesday December 27 2005

Tigers slipped from third to fourth place in the Guinness Premiership as they went down 15-3 to a Bristol side determined to extend their stay in the top flight.

The visitors had not tasted victory at the Memorial Ground for over five years and that record looked in little danger of being broken as Tigers rarely troubled their opponents in what was ultimately a disappointing performance.

With 12 changes to the starting line-up, Leicester often looked somewhat disjointed during the early exchanges. Bristol took full advantage, as they refused to allow their opponents time to settle and subsequently dominated for much of the first period. Tigers gave themselves a second-half mountain to climb as they ended the opening 40 minutes with a 15-0 deficit.

Tigers fly-half Ross Broadfoot had the first chance to open the scoring, but Bristol made the away side pay for the youngster's missed kick at goal almost immediately, as Jason Strange slotted a penalty with only three minutes played.

Strange doubled his side's lead after eight minutes, before adding his third successful attempt of the afternoon ten minutes later.

And 9-0 quickly became 12-0, when Tigers were penalised for a fourth time and again Strange was on target. Leicester No 8 Will Johnson was then sent to the sin-bin, allowing the Bristol outside-half to stretch the advantage to 15 points.

Broadfoot's second-half penalty provided scant consolation for Tigers, who lost centre Daryl Gibson to a long-term shoulder injury only minutes into his first-team comeback.

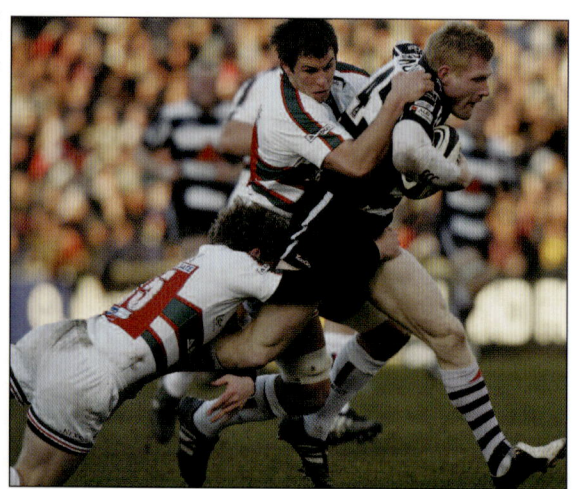

SEASON REVIEW 2005/06

TIGER TIMELINE

			SCORE	MIN
🏉	P	Strange	3-0	7
🏉	P	Strange	6-0	8
🏉	P	Strange	9-0	16
🏉	P	Strange	12-0	18
🏉	P	Strange	15-0	29
	S	Smith Gibson		29
YC		Johnson		29

HALF TIME 15-0

🏉	P	Broadfoot	15-3	49
	S	Holford Morris		56
	S	Humphreys Broadfoot		56
	S	Skinner Abraham		57
	S	Kay Cullen		58
	S	Bemand Cole		66
	S	Taukafa Buckland		68

FULL TIME 15-3

Key
Player coming on
Player going off

LEICESTER TIGERS

- 15 S.Vesty
- 14 D.Hipkiss
- 11 T.Varndell
- 13 S.Rabeni
- 12 D.Gibson
- 10 R.Broadfoot
- 9 N.Cole
- 8 W.Johnson
- 7 L.Abraham
- 6 B.Deacon
- 5 L.Deacon (c)
- 4 L.Cullen
- 3 J.White
- 2 J.Buckland
- 1 D.Morris

REPLACEMENTS

- 16 E.Taukafa
- 17 M.Holford
- 18 B.Kay
- 19 W.Skinner
- 20 S.Bemand
- 21 I.Humphreys
- 22 O.Smith

BRISTOL

- 1 D.Hilton
- 2 M.Regan
- 3 D.Crompton
- 4 R.Winters
- 5 G.Llewellyn
- 7 J.El Abd
- 6 M.Salter (c)
- 8 D.Ward-Smith
- 9 S.Perry
- 10 J.Strange
- 12 S.Cox
- 13 B.Lima
- 11 D.Lemi
- 14 L.Robinson
- 15 B.Stortoni

REPLACEMENTS

- 16 M.Irish
- 17 S.Nelson
- 18 M.Sambucetti
- 19 G.Lewis
- 20 T.Hayes
- 21 R.Higgitt
- 22 J.Rauluni

"It was a poor performance, probably the poorest since I've been head coach. In the end the buck stops with me, and it's my job to put this right."
Pat Howard

TIGERS MILESTONES

The loss against Bristol was Tigers' first defeat in five matches in all competitions, in what was their first match against Bristol since February 2003.

www.leicestertigers.com   121

SEASON REVIEW 2005/06

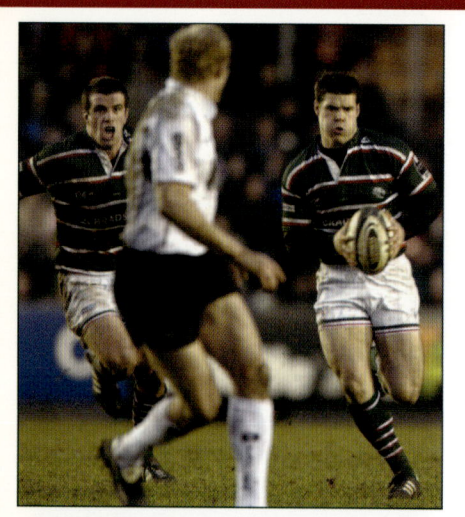

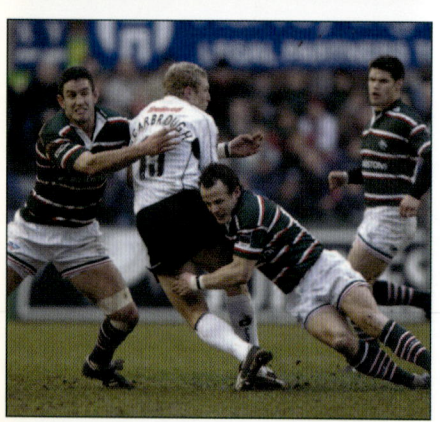

Leicester Tigers 34
Saracens 27

A much-improved performance from Leicester Tigers saw them bounce back from defeat at Bristol to secure a 34-27 victory over Saracens at Welford Road.

Andy Goode kicked 15 points as Pat Howard's side outscored their London opponents by three tries to two to move up a place to third in the Guinness Premiership.

Tigers took the lead through a Goode penalty after just eight minutes, but it was the visitors who scored the first try of the game, as Alan Dickens set up Ben Johnston to touch down in the left-hand corner.

Goode then kicked two penalties in as many minutes, before three points from Saracens outside-half Glen Jackson reduced Tigers' advantage to 9-8 halfway through the first period.

Tigers stretched their lead to 16-8, with referee Roy Maybank awarding a penalty try which Goode converted after Saracens were punished for repeated offences at a series of five-metre scrums.

Darren Morris quickly added a second try for Tigers only two minutes after coming on as a blood replacement, as he powered over to register his first score for the club on 26 minutes.

Goode's fourth penalty made it 24-14 just after half-time, before Tigers were reduced to 13 men in the space of four minutes when both Ben Kay and Graham Rowntree were sent to the sin-bin.

Goode's superb 60-metre penalty took the score to 27-14, but

Guinness Premiership
Welford Road
Att: 16,815
Referee: Roy Maybank
Monday January 2 2006

Jackson added two of his own, before Tom Varndell skipped past two Saracens tacklers to score a classic try from the left wing, with Goode converting to make the score 34-20.

Saracens hit back in injury time with a converted try from Tevita Vaikona, but Tigers held on to secure a vital win.

122 www.leicestertigers.com

SEASON REVIEW 2005/06

TIGER TIMELINE

			SCORE	MIN
	P	Goode	3-0	9
	T	Johnston	3-5	11
	P	Goode	6-5	13
	P	Goode	9-5	18
	P	Jackson	9-8	21
	T+C	Penalty Try/Goode	16-8	23
	S	Morris Rowntree		25
	T	Morris	21-8	27
	S	H.Mitchell Broster		28
	P	Jackson	21-11	30
YC		Vaikona		32
	S	Rowntree Morris		34
	DG	Jackson	21-14	39

HALF TIME 21-14

	P	Goode	24-14	43
	S	Seymour Vyvyan		45
YC		Kay		48
YC		Rowntree		48
	S	Morris Johnson		53
	P	Goode	27-14	55
	S	Cairns Byrne		56
	P	Jackson	27-17	59
	S	Johnson Morris		62
	S	Morris Rowntree		62
	S	Abraham Johnson		62
	S	Varndell Smith		62
	S	Cullen L.Deacon		66
	S	Broster Yates		66
	P	Jackson	27-20	68
	S	Rauluni Dickens		68
	S	Randell Ryder		71
	T+C	Varndell & Goode	34-20	72
	S	Little Powell		74
	T+C	Vaikona & Jackson	34-27	79

FULL TIME 34-27

LEICESTER TIGERS

- 15 S.Vesty
- 14 L.Lloyd
- 11 G.Murphy
- 13 O.Smith
- 12 D.Hipkiss
- 10 A.Goode
- 9 A.Healey
- 8 M.Corry (c)
- 7 S.Jennings
- 6 W.Johnson
- 5 B.Kay
- 4 L.Deacon
- 3 J.White
- 2 G.Chuter
- 1 G.Rowntree

SARACENS

- 1 K.Yates
- 2 S.Byrne
- 3 B.Broster
- 4 K.Chesney
- 5 T.Ryder
- 7 B.Russell
- 6 H.Vyvyan (c)
- 8 B.Skirving
- 9 A.Dickens
- 10 G.Jackson
- 12 A.Powell
- 13 K.Sorrell
- 11 T.Vaikona
- 14 B.Johnston
- 15 D.Scarbrough

REPLACEMENTS

- 16 J.Buckland
- 17 D.Morris
- 18 L.Cullen
- 19 L.Abraham
- 20 N.Cole
- 21 R.Broadfoot
- 22 T.Varndell

"The pack worked very well at the breakdown and I thought again Shane Jennings was pretty special."
Pat Howard

REPLACEMENTS

- 16 M.Cairns
- 17 H.Mitchell
- 18 T.Randell
- 19 D.Seymour
- 20 M.Rauluni
- 21 N.Little
- 22 M.Bartholomeusz

TIGERS MILESTONES

Former Saracens hooker George Chuter has now made 100 appearances for Tigers. His old side have now failed to win at Welford Road in 29 attempts.

www.leicestertigers.com

123

SEASON REVIEW 2005/06

London Irish 25
Leicester Tigers 28

Guinness Premiership
Madejski Stadium
Att: 11,096
Referee: Dave Pearson
Sunday January 8 2006

Leicester Tigers lost Dan Hipkiss, Brett Deacon and Shane Jennings to injury but showed great character to secure a hard-earned 28-25 victory over London Irish at the Madejski Stadium.

The match was dominated by the boots of Andy Goode and Irish fly-half Barry Everitt with both sides only managing a try a piece.

The two number tens exchanged a series of three-pointers and Paul Gustard crashed over for the Exiles before Sam Vesty scored Tigers' only try of the match after half an hour. Geordan Murphy made the initial break from inside his own half, before Austin Healey kicked ahead for Vesty to gather cleanly and touch down under the posts. Goode added the conversion and then another penalty to give Tigers a 16-10 lead.

After 34 minutes, Everitt brought the hosts back to just a three-point deficit with a successful penalty attempt, but Goode replied with a penalty of his own to restore a six-point advantage approaching half-time. A second Everitt drop goal then left Tigers with a slender 19-16 lead at the break.

Three minutes into the second period, Goode stretched that lead with an excellent penalty from well inside his own half to make the score 16-22 to the visitors. The Tigers fly-half continued to make his mark with the boot, but Everitt responded in similar fashion to keep Irish in the game.

In the final minute of the match, Everitt had the chance to level the scores with a penalty from the right-hand side, but fortunately for Pat Howard and his team, the attempt barely left the ground, allowing Tigers to celebrate an important away win.

124 www.leicestertigers.com

SEASON REVIEW 2005/06

TIGER TIMELINE

			SCORE	MIN
🏃	P	Goode	0-3	1
🏃	DG	Everitt	3-3	12
🏃	P	Goode	3-6	15
🟨	YC	Rowntree		19
🏃	S	Varndell Hipkiss		19
🏃	T+C	Gustard + Everitt	10-6	20
🏃	P	Goode	10-9	24
🟨	YC	Horak		24
🏃	T+C	Vesty + Goode	10-16	27
🏃	P	Everitt	13-16	31
🏃	P	Goode	13-19	33
🏃	S	Abraham B.Deacon		39
🏃	DG	Everitt	16-19	40

HALF TIME 16-19

🏃	P	Goode	16-22	43
🏃	P	Everitt	19-22	47
🏃	P	Goode	19-25	49
🏃	S	Murphy Danaher		50
🏃	P	Goode	19-28	61
🏃	S	Ellis Healey		62
🏃	S	Cullen L.Deacon		63
🏃	P	Everitt	22-28	67
🏃	P	Everitt	25-28	73
🏃	S	Buckland Jennings		76

FULL TIME 25-28

Key
Player coming on
Player going off

LEICESTER TIGERS

- 15 S.Vesty
- 14 L.Lloyd
- 11 G.Murphy
- 13 O.Smith
- 12 D.Hipkiss
- 10 A.Goode
- 9 A.Healey
- 8 M.Corry (c)
- 7 S.Jennings
- 6 B.Deacon
- 5 B.Kay
- 4 L.Deacon
- 3 J.White
- 2 G.Chuter
- 1 G.Rowntree

LONDON IRISH

- 1 N.Hatley
- 2 D.Coetzee
- 3 F.Rautenbach
- 4 B.Casey (c)
- 5 K.Roche
- 7 D.Danaher
- 6 P.Gustard
- 8 J.Leguizamon
- 9 P.Hodgson
- 10 B.Everitt
- 12 N.Mordt
- 13 R.Penney
- 11 T.Ojo
- 14 D.Armitage
- 15 M.Horak

REPLACEMENTS

16	J.Buckland
17	D.Morris
18	L.Cullen
19	L.Abraham
20	H.Ellis
21	R.Broadfoot
22	T.Varndell

"Winning is a habit and I think we're getting a bit of confidence now. We've got a big month ahead and we'll have to raise ourselves for Stade next week but there's certainly a good feeling in the squad."
Pat Howard

REPLACEMENTS

16	M.Collins
17	A.Flavin
18	R.Strudwick
19	P.Murphy
20	S.Geraghty
21	J.Storey
22	R.Laidlaw

TIGERS MILESTONES

Andy Goode became only the fifth player to register over 1,000 points in the Premiership. Goode joined an elite list of Jonny Wilkinson, Paul Grayson, Barry Everitt and former Tigers full-back Tim Stimpson.

www.leicestertigers.com

SEASON REVIEW 2005/06

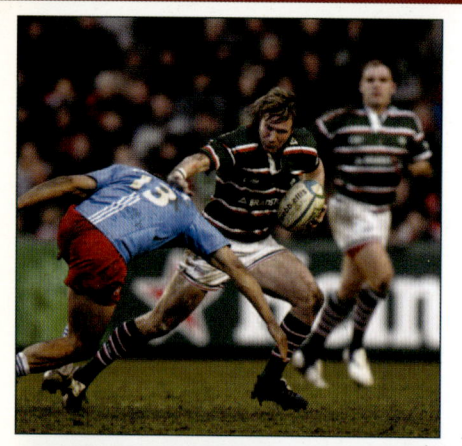

Leicester Tigers 29
Stade Français 22

Heineken Cup
Welford Road
Att: 16,815
Referee: Alan Lewis
Sunday January 15 2006

Leicester Tigers kept their Heineken Cup hopes alive in spectacular fashion as they recorded a last-gasp win over Stade Francais in front of a relieved home crowd.

After arriving at the interval 12-9 behind, Tigers dropped further off the pace as Ignacio Corleto slotted a long-range drop goal to extend his side's lead to 15-9. Although Andy Goode replied with a penalty in the 59th minute, Stade increased their advantage via Mirco Bergamasco's converted interception try.

That left Tigers trailing 22-12 with as little as ten minutes of the match remaining, but Pat Howard's men kept their nerve to eventually run out victors by 29 points to 22. First Andy Goode kicked a 70th-minute penalty to reduce the deficit to a converted score, before the home side drew level following a series of fantastic individual contributions. Goode's imaginative and well-executed chip ahead was expertly collected by Louis Deacon, who charged 25 yards to touch down in the far left-hand corner. Goode then held his nerve under enormous pressure to add the testing touchline conversion.

Tigers pushed on to secure victory and consolidate top spot in one of the most difficult Heineken Cup pools. Dan Hipkiss again proved to be the European hero, as he followed up his final-minute try against the Ospreys with another late score to break Stade hearts. Hipkiss' 79th-minute effort was converted by Goode, whose 19-point contribution proved to be a vital part of another Tigers win.

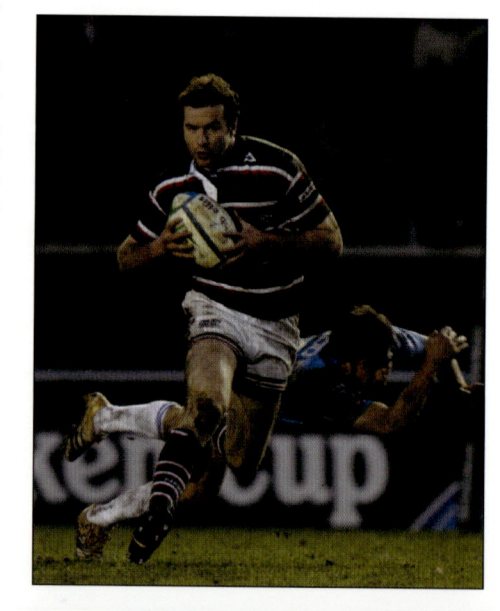

126 www.leicestertigers.com

SEASON REVIEW 2005/06

TIGER TIMELINE

			SCORE	MIN
🏃	P	Goode	3-0	10
🏃	S	Bergamasco Borges		17
🏃	P	Goode	6-0	24
🏃	P	Skrela	6-3	28
🏃	DG	Hernandez	6-6	31
🏃	P	Goode	9-6	32
🏃	P	Skrela	9-9	36
🏃	S	Varndell Lloyd		36
🏃	S	Abraham Jennings		40
🏃	P	Skrela	9-12	40

HALF TIME 9-12

🏃	S	Ellis Healey		54
🏃	DG	Corleto	9-15	56
🏃	T+C	Bergamasco + Skrela	12-22	63
🏃	P	Goode	15-22	71
🏃	T+C	L.Deacon + Goode	22-22	74
🏃	S	Cullen L.Deacon		74
🏃	T+C	Hipkiss + Goode	29-22	79
🏃	S	Marchois James		79
🏃	S	Rabadan Martin		80

FULL TIME 29-22

Key
Player coming on
Player going off

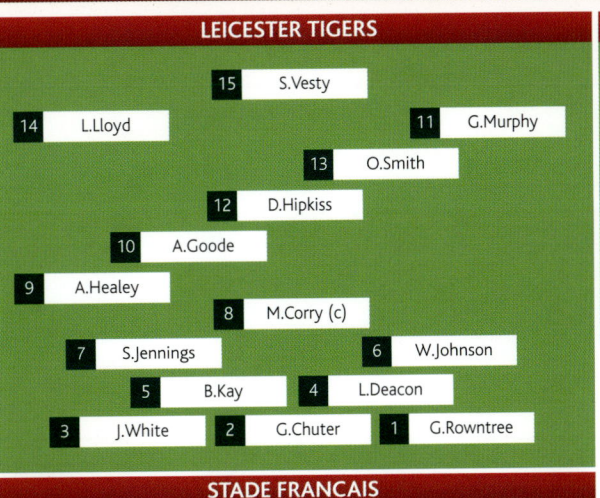

LEICESTER TIGERS

- 15 S.Vesty
- 14 L.Lloyd
- 11 G.Murphy
- 13 O.Smith
- 12 D.Hipkiss
- 10 A.Goode
- 9 A.Healey
- 8 M.Corry (c)
- 7 S.Jennings
- 6 W.Johnson
- 5 B.Kay
- 4 L.Deacon
- 3 J.White
- 2 G.Chuter
- 1 G.Rowntree

STADE FRANCAIS

- 1 S.Marconnet
- 2 D.Szarzewski
- 3 P.De Villiers
- 4 D.Auradou (c)
- 5 M.James
- 7 R.Martin
- 6 S.Parisse
- 8 S.Sowerby
- 9 J.Fillol
- 10 A.Penaud
- 12 D.Skrela
- 13 J.Hernandez
- 11 C.Dominici
- 14 L.Borges
- 15 I.Corleto

REPLACEMENTS

16	J.Buckland
17	M.Holford
18	L.Cullen
19	L.Abraham
20	H.Ellis
21	R.Broadfoot
22	T.Varndell

"In terms of the fight-back, it was just fantastic. The coaches can't take the credit for that - that's all about the players and their belief." **Pat Howard**

REPLACEMENTS

16	B.Kayser
17	Y.Montes
18	A.Marchois
19	P.Rabadan
20	M.Williams
21	G.Messina
22	Mirco Bergamasco

TIGERS MILESTONES

Stade's defeat to Tigers was their first competitive loss against English opposition since Tigers' famous Heineken Cup Final victory in Paris in 2001.

www.leicestertigers.com 127

Clermont Auvergne 27
Leicester Tigers 40

Heineken Cup
Stade Marcel Michelin
Att: 10,000
Referee: Alain Rolland
Friday January 20 2006

Leicester Tigers moved into the last eight of the Heineken Cup with an impressive 40-27 away victory over Clermont Auvergne. Tigers only needed a losing bonus point to secure their passage into the quarter-finals, but they played anything but conservatively as they recorded a five-try demolition of their French opponents.

England Sevens star Tom Varndell scored four of his side's tries as he reminded the national management of his talents ahead of the Six Nations. Dan Hipkiss added the other five-pointer, registering his third try in three successive Heineken Cup games.

The visitors registered the first try of the match with 24 minutes on the clock, as Geordan Murphy put Varndell away in the left-hand corner to give Tigers a slender 8-6 lead.

Tigers made it 15-6 just after the half-hour courtesy of a second Varndell try. Harry Ellis showed great power and strength inside the Clermont 22, allowing his team-mate the space for a try which Goode converted.

Hipkiss then ran in Tigers' third after 38 minutes thanks to a bullocking run by Martin Corry. The Leicester and England captain made valuable yards before off-loading to the young winger, who supplied a confident finish. Goode added the extras before Clermont hit back with a converted try from Anthony Floch, to leave Tigers with a 22-13 advantage at the break.

Just four minutes into the second half, Varndell completed his hat-trick to capture the bonus point, as he proved to be the beneficiary of a sweeping move across the Tigers backline.

Although the 20-year-old's final try of the evening was sandwiched in between two scores for the home team, Tigers left France knowing they had done more than enough to secure a quarter-final berth.

SEASON REVIEW 2005/06

TIGER TIMELINE

			SCORE	MIN
🏃	P	Jones	3-0	5
🏃	P	Jones	6-0	11
🏃	P	Goode	6-3	19
🏃	S	A.Tuilagi Smith		20
🏃	T	Varndell	6-8	25
🏃	T+C	Varndell + Goode	6-15	33
🏃	T+C	Hipkiss + Goode	6-22	38
🏃	T+C	Floch + Jones	13-22	40

HALF TIME 13-22

🏃	S	Barrier Cudmore		41
🏃	T	Varndell	13-27	45
🏃	S	Zerakashvili Scelzo		48
🏃	S	Cullen Kay		49
🏃	P	Goode	13-30	53
🏃	S	Johnson Corry		56
🏃	S	Shvelidze Emmanuelli		58
🏃	S	Miguel Ledesma		59
🏃	S	Audebert Privat		61
🏃	YC	Miguel		62
🏃	S	Ledesma Vermeulen		66
🏃	S	Morris Rowntree		66
🏃	T+C	Audebert + Jones	20-30	67
🏃	S	Healey Ellis		68
🏃	DG	Goode	20-33	69
🏃	T+C	Varndell + Broadfoot	20-40	70
🏃	S	Buckland Chuter		70
🏃	S	Broadfoot Goode		70
🏃	S	Chanal Canale		71
🏃	S	Vermeulen Ledesma		72
🏃	T+C	Paulse + Jones	27-40	74

FULL TIME 27-40

LEICESTER TIGERS

- 15 S.Vesty
- 14 T.Varndell
- 11 G.Murphy
- 13 O.Smith
- 12 D.Hipkiss
- 10 A.Goode
- 9 H.Ellis
- 8 M.Corry (c)
- 7 L.Abraham
- 6 B.Deacon
- 5 B.Kay
- 4 L.Deacon
- 3 J.White
- 2 G.Chuter
- 1 G.Rowntree

CLERMONT AUVERGNE

- 1 L.Emmanuelli
- 2 M.Ledesma
- 3 M.Scelzo
- 4 J.Cudmore
- 5 T.Privat
- 7 M.Dieude
- 6 S.Broomhall
- 8 E.Vermeulen
- 9 P.Mignoni (c)
- 10 S.Jones
- 12 T.Marsh
- 13 G.Canale
- 11 J.Malzieu
- 14 B.Paulse
- 15 A.Floch

REPLACEMENTS

16	J.Buckland
17	D.Morris
18	L.Cullen
19	W.Johnson
20	A.Healey
21	R.Broadfoot
22	A.Tuilagi

"There's a brilliant camaraderie in the squad. To finish as group winners in such a tough pool is a fantastic achievement. It's now time to push on and re-set our goals for the competition."
Pat Howard

REPLACEMENTS

16	B.Miguel
17	G.Shvelidze
18	D.Zirakashvili
19	D.Barrier
20	A.Audebert
21	C.McMullen
22	R.Chanal

TIGERS MILESTONES

Graham Rowntree became the first Englishman to begin 50 Heineken Cup matches, as he made his 350th start for the club.

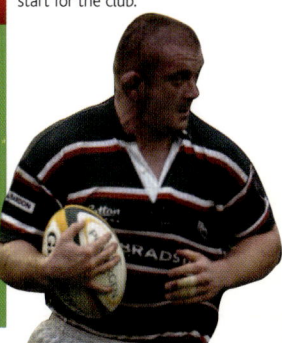

www.leicestertigers.com 129

SEASON REVIEW 2005/06

Leicester Tigers 27
Sale Sharks 27

A superb second-half fightback saw Leicester Tigers secure a 27-27 draw with Sale Sharks at fortress Welford Road. Tigers were in real danger of relinquishing their two-year unbeaten home record as they trailed the league leaders 24-9 at the interval.

Things looked bleak for Tigers after a first half performance which lacked any real quality and saw the returning Lewis Moody given a yellow card. Pat Howard's team had initially started the stronger of the two sides, with Andy Goode kicking a first-minute penalty to give Tigers a 3-0 lead.

However, despite a further penalty and a well-struck drop goal from Goode, it was Sale who dominated the scoring during a disappointing first period. Dean Schofield took advantage of space down the left to run in an easy try before Chris Jones scored Sale's second of the afternoon with 34 minutes played. Goode's England rival, Charlie Hodgson, added four penalties and a conversion to leave the Welford Road faithful in anxious mood ahead of the second 40 minutes.

Thirteen minutes after the re-start, Goode had made significant inroads into the Sale lead, kicking a brace of penalties to reduce the deficit to nine points.

Goode then added further penalties in the 57th and 59th minutes to bring Tigers to within touching distance and raise hopes of a memorable victory.

Tigers played like a different side in comparison to their lack-lustre first-half performance and almost scored their first try of the match when Ollie Smith was grounded just short of the Sale line. Instead, they were forced to settle for a further three points from Goode, who levelled the scores in the 67th minute.

Hodgson then restored Sale's advantage with his first points of the half, before Goode salvaged a hard-earned draw with his eighth successful penalty five minutes from time.

Guinness Premiership
Welford Road
Att: 16,815
Referee: Paul Honiss
Saturday January 28 2006

SEASON REVIEW 2005/06

TIGER TIMELINE

			SCORE	MIN
🏃	P	Goode	3-0	1
🏃	P	Hodgson	3-3	7
🏃	P	Goode	6-3	14
🏃	P	Hodgson	6-6	16
🏃	DG	Goode	9-6	17
✏️	S	Foden Robinson		18
🏉	T+C	Schofield + Hodgson	9-13	21
🏃	P	Hodgson	9-16	26
🏃	T	Jones	9-21	31
🏃	P	Hodgson	9-24	39
🟨	YC	Moody		39
HALF TIME 9-24				
🏃	P	Goode	12-24	43
✏️	S	Abraham Moody		49
✏️	S	A.Tuilagi Rabeni		49
🏃	P	Goode	15-24	53
✏️	S	L.Deacon Kay		53
✏️	S	Sheridan Faure		53
🏃	P	Goode	18-24	57
🏃	P	Goode	21-24	59
✏️	S	Healey Ellis		59
✏️	S	Bruno Titterrell		60
✏️	S	Buckland Chuter		62
✏️	S	Morris Rowntree		64
🏃	P	Goode	24-24	67
✏️	S	Stewart Turner		68
🏃	P	Hodgson	24-27	69
✏️	S	Chuter Buckland		69
✏️	S	Buckland Chuter		72
🏃	P	Goode	27-27	75
✏️	S	Carter Chabal		75
FULL TIME 27-27				

LEICESTER TIGERS

- 15 S.Vesty
- 14 S.Rabeni
- 11 T.Varndell
- 13 L.Lloyd
- 12 O.Smith
- 10 A.Goode
- 9 H.Ellis
- 8 W.Johnson
- 7 L.Moody
- 6 B.Deacon
- 5 B.Kay
- 4 L.Cullen (c)
- 3 J.White
- 2 G.Chuter
- 1 G.Rowntree

REPLACEMENTS

- 16 J.Buckland
- 17 D.Morris
- 18 L.Deacon
- 19 L.Abraham
- 20 A.Healey
- 21 M.Cornwell
- 22 A.Tuilagi

"We know we didn't play very well today and we definitely weren't at our consistent best, but it's been an exceptionally tough month for us and it's now all about making sure we stay on course for the rest of the season."
Pat Howard

SALE SHARKS

- 1 L.Faure
- 2 A.Titterrell
- 3 S.Turner
- 4 C.Jones
- 5 D.Schofield
- 7 M.Lund
- 6 J.White
- 8 S.Chabal
- 9 S.Martens
- 10 C.Hodgson
- 12 R.Todd
- 13 M.Taylor
- 11 C.Mayor
- 14 M.Cueto
- 15 J.Robinson (c)

REPLACEMENTS

- 16 S.Bruno
- 17 A.Sheridan
- 18 B.Stewart
- 19 I.Fernandez Lobbe
- 20 B.Foden
- 21 V.Courrent
- 22 J.Carter

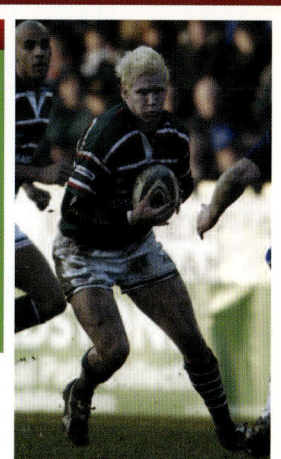

TIGERS MILESTONES

Andy Goode collected a haul of 27 points, as he kicked eight penalties and a drop goal to take his season's tally to 264.

www.leicestertigers.com   131

SEASON REVIEW 2005/06

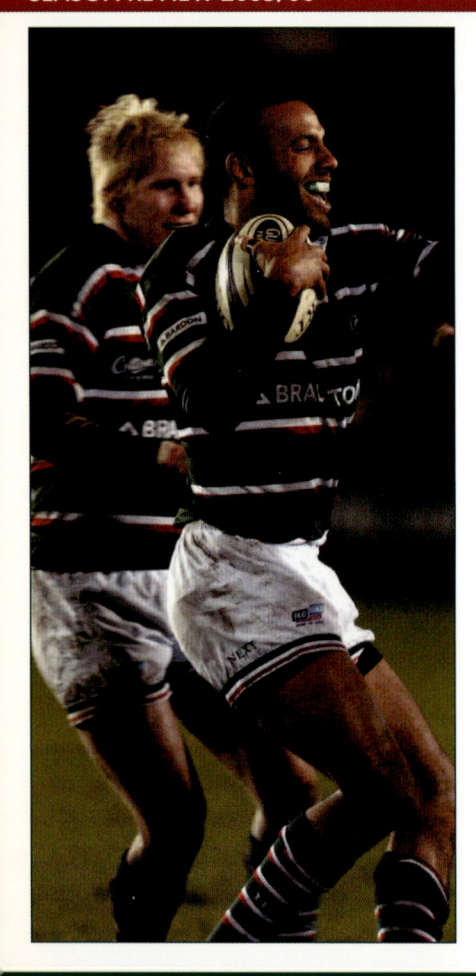

Gloucester 34
Leicester Tigers 16

Leicester Tigers crashed to their first defeat in five matches, as they came unstuck against an impressive Gloucester side at a noisy Kingsholm. Gloucester's victory allowed them to leap-frog Tigers into third place in the Guinness Premiership, leaving Pat Howard and Richard Cockerill's squad clinging to the fourth and final play-off spot.

Guinness Premiership
Kingsholm
Att: 12,500
Referee: Wayne Barnes
Friday February 10 2006

Tigers were punished for failing to take their chances in the first half, as they came apart in the third quarter when Gloucester piled on the pressure and racked up 16 points without reply. Trailing 13-6 at the break, Tigers allowed Gloucester fly-half Ludovic Mercier to kick three penalties in the space of five second-half minutes to leave them 22-6 behind with close to half an hour remaining. With Ollie Smith serving time in the sin-bin, the Cherry and Whites twisted the knife via a controversial penalty try on 63 minutes, with Mercier adding the simple conversion.

Leicester grabbed a consolation try after 75 minutes, when Will Johnson was driven over in the left-hand corner, but it came too late. However, the home side were determined not to be outdone and also finished strongly, as Mark Foster scored Gloucester's third try with two minutes left of normal time.

Tigers did at least have the final word, as replacement hooker Ephraim Taukafa crossed the Gloucester line five minutes into injury time. Unfortunately, that score did little to mask what was ultimately a frustrating evening's work for a Tigers side who had previously been unbeaten in 2006.

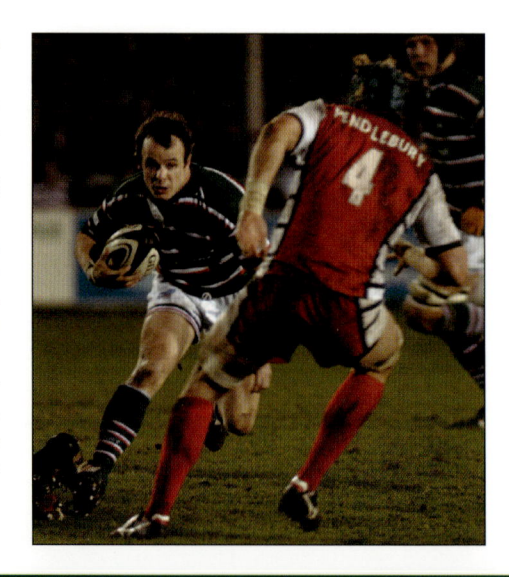

SEASON REVIEW 2005/06

TIGER TIMELINE

			SCORE	MIN
🏃	P	Humphreys	0-3	3
🏃	P	Mercier	3-3	6
✈	T+C	Bailey + Mercier	10-3	14
🏃	P	Humphreys	10-6	24
🏃	P	Mercier	13-6	28
↔	S	Hamilton B.Deacon		33

HALF TIME 13-6

↔	S	Holford Rowntree		41
🏃	P	Mercier	16-6	49
↔	S	Buxton Merriman		50
🏃	P	Mercier	19-6	52
🏃	P	Mercier	22-6	54
🟨	YC	Smith		54
↔	S	Bemand Humphreys		54
↔	S	Wood Powell		57
↔	S	Taukafa Buckland		57
✈	T+C	Penalty Try + Mercier	29-6	60
↔	S	Parkes Elloway		60
↔	S	Eustace Pendlebury		60
↔	S	Skinner Abraham		61
↔	S	Dodge Varndell		61
↔	S	Balding Forrester		65
↔	S	Broadfoot A.Tuilagi		65
🟨	YC	Collazo		67
✈	T	Johnson	29-11	69
✈	T	Foster	34-11	72
✈	T	Taukafa	34-16	78
↔	S	Thirlby Foster		79

FULL TIME 34-16

LEICESTER TIGERS

- 15 S.Vesty
- 14 A.Tuilagi
- 11 T.Varndell
- 13 L.Lloyd
- 12 O.Smith
- 10 I.Humphreys
- 9 A.Healey (c)
- 8 W.Johnson
- 7 L.Abraham
- 6 B.Deacon
- 5 B.Kay
- 4 L.Deacon
- 3 D.Morris
- 2 J.Buckland
- 1 G.Rowntree

GLOUCESTER

- 1 P.Collazo
- 2 R.Elloway
- 3 G.Powell
- 4 J.Pendlebury
- 5 A.Brown
- 7 J.Merriman
- 6 J.Boer (c)
- 8 J.Forrester
- 9 S.Amor
- 10 L.Mercier
- 12 R.Keil
- 13 T.Fanolua
- 11 M.Foster
- 14 J.Bailey
- 15 J.Goodridge

REPLACEMENTS

16	E.Taukafa
17	M.Holford
18	J.Hamilton
19	W.Skinner
20	S.Bemand
21	R.Broadfoot
22	A.Dodge

"We've got to get ourselves in the right frame of mind for the next few games because the players aren't jumping for joy at the moment. It's a real come down to earth for us and we have to bounce back from it." **Pat Howard**

REPLACEMENTS

16	J.Parkes
17	N.Wood
18	A.Eustace
19	A.Balding
20	P.Buxton
21	B.Davies
22	R.Thirlby

TIGERS MILESTONES

The disappointment at Kingsholm was only Tigers' second loss in all competitions since November 18, although it marked their third Guinness Premiership away defeat of the season.

www.leicestertigers.com   133

SEASON REVIEW 2005/06

Leicester Tigers 28
Worcester Warriors 22

Guinness Premiership
Welford Road
Att: 16,815
Referee: David Rose
Friday February 17 2006

Leicester Tigers ran in three tries to maintain their place in the top four of the Guinness Premiership and stretch their unbeaten home record in the competition to 22 games.

However, despite recording a 28-22 victory against Worcester Warriors, Tigers weren't at their fluent best and had to battle hard in the closing minutes to hold on to their six-point lead.

Leo Cullen came to Leicester's rescue twice in injury time, as the former Leinster lock used all his experience to claim a pair of Worcester line-outs five metres from his side's own try line.

The result initially saw Tigers leapfrog Gloucester into third place, although they eventually ended the weekend in the final play-off position after the West Country side won at Newcastle on the Sunday afternoon.

Tigers scored the first try of the match when they launched a crisp attack after winning their own line-out on the Worcester 22. Harry Ellis moved the ball out to Andy Goode, who sent Ollie Smith through unchallenged to touch down between the posts.

Goode added 11 points with the boot in the opening 40 minutes, but Dale Rasmussen crossed for the visitors and Shane Drahm matched the Tigers fly-half point for point to ensure the scores were level at half-time.

With Worcester down to 14 men after the sin-binning of wing Mark Tucker, Tigers regained the lead after 46 minutes as Alesana Tuilagi took Andy Goode's pass, before powering through two tackles to touch down in the right-hand corner.

Two further penalties from Drahm saw Tigers fall a point behind after 58 minutes, but victory was secured when England U21 captain Matt Cornwell was driven over four minutes later.

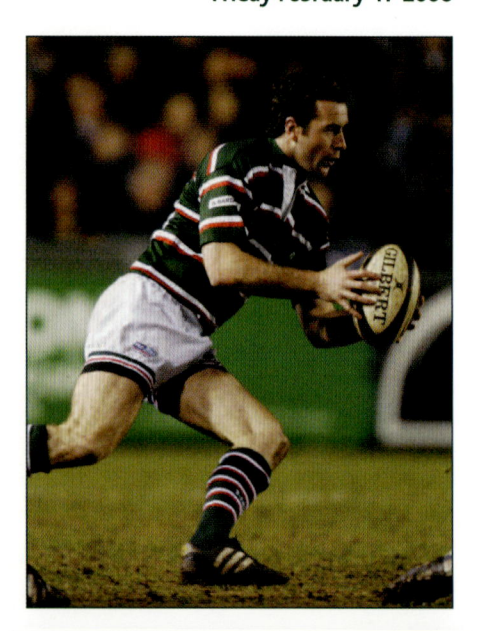

www.leicestertigers.com

SEASON REVIEW 2005/06

TIGER TIMELINE

			SCORE	MIN
🏃	P	Drahm	0-3	6
🏃	T+C	Smith + Goode	7-3	10
🏃	P	Goode	10-3	22
🏃	P	Drahm	10-6	24
🏃	P	Goode	13-6	32
🏃	P	Drahm	13-9	33
🏃	T+C	Rasmussen + Drahm	13-16	36
🏃	P	Goode	16-16	39

HALF TIME 16-16

YC		Tucker		44
🏃	T	A.Tuilagi	21-16	46
🏃	P	Drahm	21-19	50
	S	L Deacon Hamilton		50
	S	Vaili Hickey		50
🏃	P	Drahm	21-22	54
	S	Morris Holford		54
🏃	T+C	Cornwell + Goode	28-22	58
	S	Van Niekerk G Hickie		58
	S	Powell Gomarsall		58
	S	Bemand Ellis		60
	S	Taukafa Chuter		68
	S	Whatling Tucker		68
	S	G.Hickie Van Niekerk		76

FULL TIME 28-22

Key
Player coming on
Player going off

LEICESTER TIGERS

15 G.Murphy
14 A.Tuilagi 11 T.Varndell
13 M.Cornwell
12 O.Smith
10 A.Goode
9 H.Ellis
8 M.Corry (c)
7 S.Jennings 6 L.Moody
5 L.Cullen 4 J.Hamilton
3 J.White 2 G.Chuter 1 M.Holford

WORCESTER WARRIORS

1 T.Windo (c) 2 G.Hickie 3 T.Taumoepeau
4 P.Murphy 5 C.Gillies
7 T.Harding 6 K.Horstmann
8 D.Hickey
9 A.Gomarsall
10 S.Drahm
12 T.Lombard
13 D.Rasmussen
11 M.Tucker 14 G.Trueman
15 N.Le Roux

REPLACEMENTS

16	E.Taukafa
17	D.Morris
18	L.Deacon
19	W.Johnson
20	S.Bemand
21	I.Humphreys
22	A.Dodge

"We're still aiming for the top two in what is a very tight league. We are not where we want to be right now, so every game takes on more importance. We know we have a lot of hard work ahead of us." **Martin Corry**

REPLACEMENTS

16	A.Van Niekerk
17	L.Fortey
18	E.O'Donoghue
19	S.Vaili
20	M.Powell
21	J.Hylton
22	S.Whatling

TIGERS MILESTONES

The win was Tigers' first Premiership victory since the 28-25 defeat of London Irish at the Madejski on January 8.

www.leicestertigers.com   135

SEASON REVIEW 2005/06

Newcastle Falcons 24
Leicester Tigers 16

Guinness Premiership
Kingston Park
Att: 10,200
Referee: Ashley Rowden
Friday February 24 2006

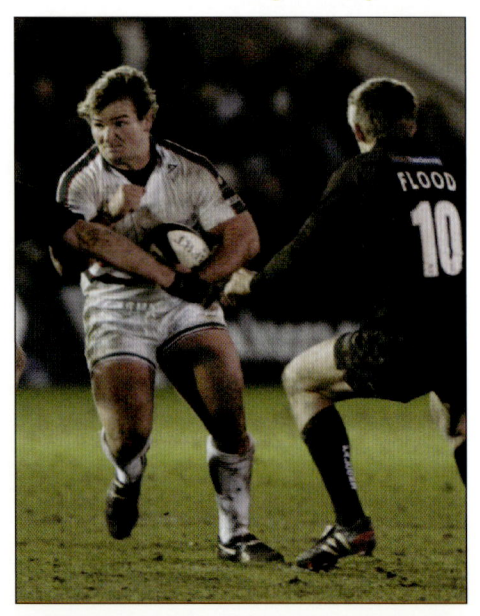

Leicester Tigers crashed to their fifth away defeat of the season, as they lost 24-16 to Newcastle at Kingston Park. Falcons skipper Matt Burke celebrated signing a new two-year contract by kicking a match-winning 21 points, while Tigers flanker Shane Jennings was yellow-carded in the second half to cap a miserable night for Leicester.

Leicester's second defeat in their last three Guinness Premiership games, coupled with London Irish's win over Northampton, meant Tigers dropped out of the play-off places for the only time during the entire 2005/06 season.

The only bright spot for Tigers was a try after 71 minutes for Henry Tuilagi on his first senior appearance of the campaign. The Samoan powerhouse burst on to Austin Healey's pass four minutes after coming off the bench and stormed through from 30 metres out to give his side hope of a comeback.

Sam Vesty's conversion trimmed the deficit to 21-16, but Burke's seventh penalty took the Falcons out of reach with four minutes remaining.

Leicester were never in front against their North-East opponents, although they could have taken the lead with 25 minutes played. Tigers fly-half Ian Humphreys had levelled the scores with two penalties, before Sam Vesty's stunning solo effort was disallowed by referee Ashley Rowden, after a high tackle from Alesana Tuilagi on Newcastle youngster Toby Flood.

Pat Howard's side never recovered from their 15-9 deficit, as two second-half Burke penalties and a Tom May drop goal saw Tigers slip to fifth place in the standings.

www.leicestertigers.com

SEASON REVIEW 2005/06

TIGER TIMELINE

			SCORE	MIN
🏃	P	Burke	3-0	3
🏃	P	Burke	6-0	6
🏃	P	Humphreys	6-3	9
🏃	P	Burke	9-3	11
🏃	P	Humphreys	9-6	14
🏃	P	Humphreys	9-9	25
🏃	P	Burke	12-9	31
🏃	P	Burke	15-9	35

HALF TIME 15-9

🏃	P	Burke	18-9	48
🟨	YC	Jennings		52
	S	Cullen Kay		56
	S	Dodge Smith		57
🏃	S	Taukafa Buckland		59
	S	McCarthy Finegan		63
	S	Charlton Grindal		63
	S	Holford Morris		64
	S	H.Tuilagi Johnson		64
	S	Bemand Humphreys		64
🏃	DG	May	21-9	67
	S	Grimes Parling		68
	T+C	H.Tuilagi + Vesty	21-16	71
	S	Williams Ward		72
	S	Thompson Long		72
	S	Skinner Jennings		72
🏃	P	Burke	24-16	76

FULL TIME 24-16

Key
Player coming on
Player going off

LEICESTER TIGERS

- 15 S.Vesty
- 14 A.Tuilagi
- 11 T.Varndell
- 13 L.Lloyd
- 12 O.Smith
- 10 I.Humphreys
- 9 A.Healey (c)
- 8 W.Johnson
- 7 S.Jennings
- 6 L.Abraham
- 5 B.Kay
- 4 L.Deacon
- 3 D.Morris
- 2 J.Buckland
- 1 G.Rowntree

NEWCASTLE FALCONS

- 1 M.Ward
- 2 A.Long
- 3 R.Morris
- 4 A.Perry
- 5 G.Parling
- 7 B.Woods
- 6 O.Finegan
- 8 A.Buist
- 9 J.Grindal
- 10 T.Flood
- 12 M.Mayerhofler
- 13 M.Tait
- 14 T.May
- 11 A.Elliott
- 15 M.Burke (c)

REPLACEMENTS

16	E.Taukafa
17	M.Holford
18	H.Tuilagi
19	L.Cullen
20	S.Bemand
21	A.Dodge
22	W.Skinner

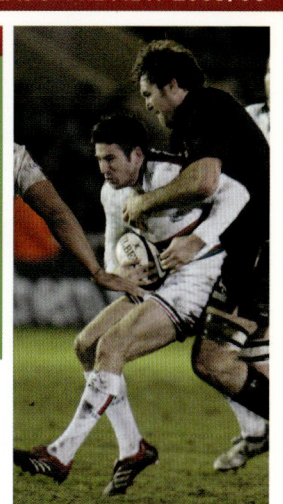

"As usual, we scored more tries than the opposition, but we conceded too many penalties and will have to deal with our ball control, defensive issues and kicking."
Pat Howard

REPLACEMENTS

16	J.Williams
17	M.Thompson
18	M.McCarthy
19	S.Grimes
20	O.Phillips
21	H.Charlton
22	D.Walder

TIGERS MILESTONES

This was Tigers' 35th meeting with Newcastle and was only their eighth loss, with 24 wins. The defeat saw Tigers slip out of the Guinness Premiership play-off places for the only time during the season.

www.leicestertigers.com 137

SEASON REVIEW 2005/06

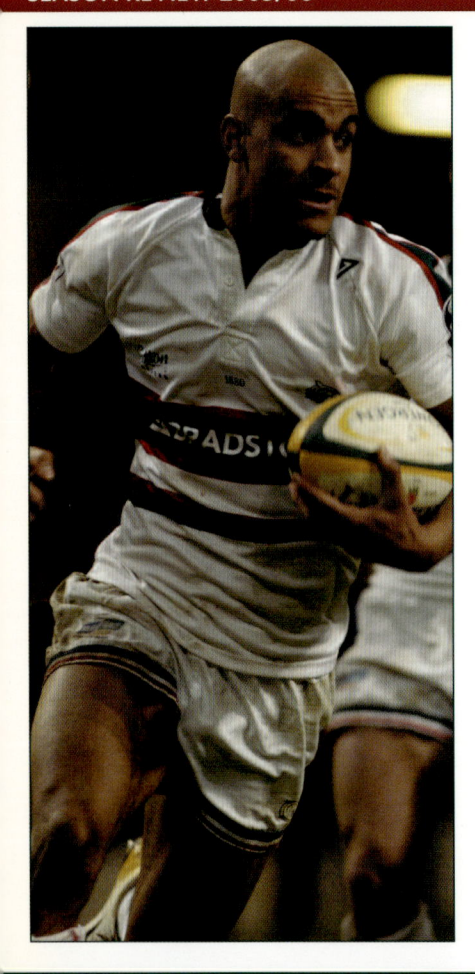

Leicester Tigers 17
London Wasps 22

Powergen Cup semi-final
Millennium Stadium
Att: 50,811
Referee: Nigel Owens
Saturday March 4 2006

Tigers were knocked out at the semi-final stage of the Powergen Cup, as they lost 22-17 to London Wasps at Cardiff's Millennium Stadium. Leicester outscored their opponents by three tries to one, but 17 points from the boot of Jeremy Staunton dashed Tigers' hopes of a place in the Twickenham final.

Scrum-half Austin Healey returned to the scene of his 2002 Heineken Cup Final magic, creating scores for Tom Varndell and Leon Lloyd either side of the break. Dan Hipkiss also crossed for an injury-time consolation, but Tigers were left to rue their indiscipline, as Staunton slotted four first-half penalties. Ayoola Erinle's break-away try with six minutes left to play eventually capped a miserable day for Pat Howard and his side.

Tigers fell behind after six minutes, as Staunton kicked his first penalty. Leicester were then penalised for slowing the ball down, with Staunton's 40-metre penalty making it 6-0.

Tigers' frustration deepened when Staunton's penalty made it 9-0 to Wasps with 30 minutes played.

However, Leicester hit back with an unconverted try three minutes later. Lloyd challenged Josh Lewsey, following Healey's clever chip kick, allowing Varndell to pick up the loose ball and sweep past his marker to touch down in the left-hand corner.

Healey's break then enabled Geordan Murphy to send Lloyd over on the right-hand side seven minutes after the break. Lloyd's score recuced the deficit to two points, but Staunton's fifth penalty and Enrinle's converted try took the game out of Tigers' reach.

SEASON REVIEW 2005/06

TIGER TIMELINE

			SCORE	MIN
	P	Staunton	0-3	9
	P	Staunton	0-6	11
	P	Staunton	0-9	30
	S	Jennings H.Tuilagi		32
	T	Varndell	5-9	33
	P	Staunton	5-12	39

HALF TIME 5-12

	T	Lloyd	10-12	47
	S	J.Dawson McKenzie		50
	P	Staunton	10-15	59
	S	Haskell O'Connor		64
	S	Ellis Healey		64
	S	M.Dawson Reddan		65
	S	Brooks Abbott		65
	T+C	Erinle + Staunton	10-22	74
	S	Cullen Kay		75
	S	Holford Rowntree		78
	S	McKenzie Payne		79
	T+C	Hipkiss + Goode	17-22	81

FULL TIME 17-22

Key
Player coming on
Player going off

LEICESTER TIGERS

- 15 S.Vesty
- 14 G.Murphy
- 11 T.Varndell
- 13 L.Lloyd
- 12 D.Hipkiss
- 10 A.Goode
- 9 A.Healey
- 8 H.Tuilagi
- 7 L.Moody
- 6 M.Corry (c)
- 5 B.Kay
- 4 L.Deacon
- 3 J.White
- 2 G.Chuter
- 1 G.Rowntree

LONDON WASPS

- 1 A.McKenzie
- 2 R.Ibanez
- 3 T.Payne
- 4 S.Shaw
- 5 R.Birkett
- 7 J.O'Connor
- 6 J.Worsley
- 8 L.Dallaglio (c)
- 9 E.Reddan
- 10 J.Staunton
- 12 S.Abbott
- 13 F.Waters
- 11 T.Voyce
- 14 J.Lewsey
- 15 A.Erinle

REPLACEMENTS

16	J.Buckland
17	M.Holford
18	L.Cullen
19	S.Jennings
20	H.Ellis
21	M.Cornwell
22	A.Tuilagi

"We have to learn how the referees want us to play the game. It's vital that we put things right and cut out the penalties that have cost us so dearly."
Ben Kay

REPLACEMENTS

16	J.Barrett
17	J.Dawson
18	G.Skivington
19	J.Haskell
20	M.Dawson
21	J.Brooks
22	M.Van Gisbergen

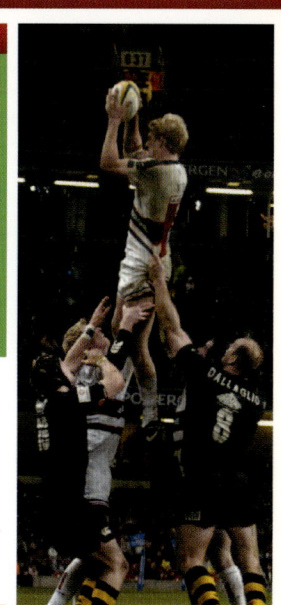

TIGERS MILESTONES

Tigers were appearing in their 18th domestic cup semi-final and hoping to reach the final for the first time since a 9-3 win over Sale at Twickenham in 1997.

www.leicestertigers.com 139

SEASON REVIEW 2005/06

Leicester Tigers 26
Leeds Tykes 23

Leicester Tigers moved back into the top four of the Guinness Premiership after a heart-stopping win over Leeds Tykes at a muddy Welford Road. Will Skinner's try in the fifth minute of injury time snatched a dramatic victory that saw them finish the weekend in fourth position.

Tigers had slipped out of the play-off places after just one win in their previous four Premiership games, but they reignited their title chances in a dramatic clash through first-half tries from James Buckland, Sam Vesty and Ollie Smith.

Pat Howard's team seemed to be in control as they led 19-6 at half-time, but converted scores from Tom Biggs and Justin Marshall, together with a third penalty from Italian outside-half Roland De Marigny, threatened to turn the result in Leeds' favour.

Tigers appeared to be heading for defeat when Biggs crossed for the visitors with only four minutes left to play. De Marigny added the conversion to give Leeds a 23-19 lead that looked set to end Leicester's 26-month unbeaten home record.

However, Tigers showed great character to eventually secure an invaluable five points, as Austin Healey's penalty earned a line-out 10 metres from the Tykes line, setting the platform for Skinner's winning try.

After a powerful catch and drive, the 22-year-old flanker was adjudged to have grounded the ball following Chris White's consultation with the video referee. Sam Vesty's conversion put the seal on a stunning fightback against a passionate and committed Leeds outfit.

Guinness Premiership
Welford Road
Att: 16,815
Referee: Chris White
Friday March 10 2006

140 www.leicestertigers.com

SEASON REVIEW 2005/06

TIGER TIMELINE

			SCORE	MIN
🏃	P	De Marigny	0-3	3
🏃	T+C	Buckland + Vesty	7-3	8
🏃	T	Vesty	12-3	16
🏃	P	De Marigny	12-6	21
🏃	T+C	Smith + Vesty	19-6	23
	S	Gerber Shelley		33
	S	H.Tuilagi Abraham		39

HALF TIME 19-6

	S	Abraham H.Tuilagi		41
🏃	P	De Marigny	19-9	47
	S	Morris Rowntree		51
	S	Rawlinson Bulloch		54
	S	H.Tuilagi Abraham		56
	S	Murphy Hooper		60
	S	Balshaw Blackett		60
	S	Reid Dunbar		60
	S	Hamilton Cullen		66
	T+C	Marshall +De Marigny	19-16	67
	S	Skinner Jennings		72
🏃	T+C	Biggs + De Marigny	19-23	75
🏃	T+C	Skinner + Vesty	26-23	80

FULL TIME 26-23

Key
Player coming on
Player going off

LEICESTER TIGERS

- 15 S.Vesty
- 14 L.Lloyd
- 11 A.Tuilagi
- 13 O.Smith
- 12 D.Hipkiss
- 10 A.Healey (c)
- 9 S.Bemand
- 8 L.Deacon
- 7 S.Jennings
- 6 L.Abraham
- 5 B.Kay
- 4 L.Cullen
- 3 M.Holford
- 2 J.Buckland
- 1 G.Rowntree

LEEDS TYKES

- 1 K.Lensing
- 2 G.Bulloch
- 3 M.Shelley
- 4 S.Hooper (c)
- 5 T.Palmer
- 7 R.Parks
- 6 J.Dunbar
- 8 N.Thomas
- 9 J.Marshall
- 10 R.De Marigny
- 12 L.Blackett
- 13 C.Jones
- 11 C.Bell
- 14 A.Snyman
- 15 T.Biggs

REPLACEMENTS

16	E.Taukafa
17	D.Morris
18	J.Hamilton
19	W.Skinner
20	H.Tuilagi
21	R.Broadfoot
22	A.Dodge

"There were plenty of positives to take out off the match, especially our never-say-die attitude. We showed a lot of determination and patience in order to get ourselves into a scoring position in injury time and finish with the winning try."

Pat Howard

REPLACEMENTS

16	R.Gerber
17	R.Rawlinson
18	C.Murphy
19	R.Reid
20	M.McMillan
21	I.Balshaw
22	A.Craig

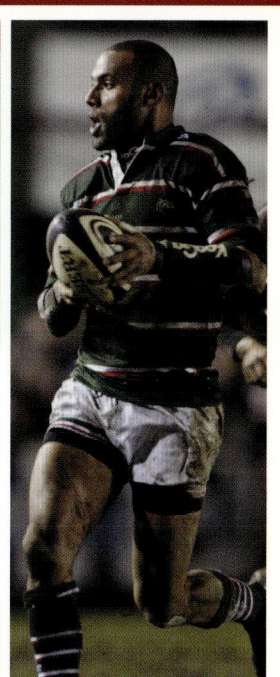

TIGERS MILESTONES

This was Leeds Tykes' sixth loss in six visits to Welford Road, with Will Skinner's late score ensuring Tigers remained unbeaten in their last 23 Premiership matches at the stadium.

www.leicestertigers.com   141

SEASON REVIEW 2005/06

Leicester Tigers 42
Barbarians 52

Friendly
Welford Road
Att: 8,304
Referee: Andrew Small
Friday March 17 2006

Leicester Tigers and the Barbarians treated a crowd of 8,304 to a feast of red-hot rugby at freezing Welford Road. The annual challenge match produced 14 tries, some breath-taking moves and an evening of great entertainment.

The Ba-Baas outscored the home side by eight tries to six, with two scores in the last eight minutes wrapping up a ten-point victory.

Leicester head coach Pat Howard made a well-received comeback, as he partnered Matt Smith in the centres.

Tigers' Brent Wilson and Barbarians winger Simon Danielli scored the pick of the tries in the space of seven second-half minutes.

New Zealander Wilson touched down for his second try of the night with 25 minutes remaining, after breaking through three tackles in midfield and holding off a succession of challenges to wriggle over in the left-hand corner.

Border Reivers star and Scottish international Danielli then sprinted half the length of the pitch to score another sensational solo effort moments later.

The Ba-Baas followed tradition by attacking from all areas of the field and selecting a side packed with stars from across the globe. The starting XV included players from Australia, South Africa, Samoa, Tonga, England, Ireland, Scotland, Wales and the United States of America, with the appearance of Wallaby World Cup winner Joe Roff delighting the Welford Road crowd.

A young Tigers side followed the Ba-Baas example by moving the ball wide whenever the opportunity presented itself. They were rewarded with three tries in each half, as they came close to recording a memorable win.

SEASON REVIEW 2005/06

TIGER TIMELINE

			SCORE	MIN
T		Hanley	0-5	9
T+C		A.Tuilagi + Humphreys	7-5	11
S		Pienaar B.Deacon		15
T+C		Bemand + Humphreys	14-5	22
T+C		Afeaki + Hercus	14-12	27
T+C		Wilson + Humphreys	21-12	32
T+C		Danielli + Hercus	21-19	36

HALF TIME 21-19

				MIN
T+C		Webber + Hercus	21-26	41
S		Webber Byrne		41
S		R.Thomas Evans		41
S		MacDonald Yates		41
S		Budgett Afeaki		41
S		Chamberlain Sititi		41
S		Edwards Powell		41
S		Stcherbina Erinle		41
S		Breeze Danielli		41
T+C		A.Tuilagi + Humphreys	28-26	49
S		Owen Howard		49
TC		Hercus	28-33	51
T		Mustchin	28-38	62
T+C		Wilson + Humphreys	35-38	65
T+C		F.Tuilagi + Humphreys	42-38	67
S		Boulton Morris		70
T+C		Danielli + Hercus	42-45	72
S		Kay Montagu		73
S		Wright Bemand		73
S		Whitehead Taukafa		78
T+C		Powell + Hercus	42-52	79

FULL TIME 42-52

LEICESTER TIGERS

- 15 R.Broadfoot
- 14 A.Tuilagi
- 11 A.Dodge
- 13 M.Smith
- 12 P.Howard
- 10 I.Humphreys
- 9 S.Bemand (c)
- 8 B.Deacon
- 7 W.Skinner
- 6 B.Wilson
- 5 D.Montagu
- 4 J.Hamilton
- 3 D.Morris
- 2 E.Taukafa
- 1 J.Rawson

BARBARIANS

- 1 K.Yates
- 2 S.Byrne (c)
- 3 B.Evans
- 4 I.Afeaki
- 5 H.Louw
- 7 S.Sititi
- 6 M.Mustchin
- 8 G.Lewis
- 9 M.Powell
- 10 M.Hercus
- 12 A.Erinle
- 13 F.Waters
- 14 S.Danielli
- 11 S.Hanley
- 15 J.Roff

REPLACEMENTS

16	P.Boulton
17	R.Cockerill
18	C.Whitehead
19	A.Wright
20	F.Tuilagi
21	R.Owen
22	B.Pienaar

"Playing in the side lets you get to know the players a bit better as it gives you a different insight. I wanted to see if the guys would rise to the challenge against top-class opposition, and some of the lads really stepped up."
Pat Howard

REPLACEMENTS

16	R.Webber
17	N.Budgett
18	G.Chamberlain
19	D.Edwards
20	M.Stcherbina
21	B.Breeze
22	M.MacDonald

TIGERS MILESTONES

This was the Barbarians 50th victory at Welford Road, where the invitational side have also played sides such as an Eric Thornloe XV and the Midlands. Of the 85 matches between Tigers and the Ba-Baas, Leicester have won 36, the Barbarians 45 and five further games drawn.

SEASON REVIEW 2005/06

Bath Rugby 12
Leicester Tigers 19

Guinness Premiership
Recreation Ground
Att: 10,600
Referee: Chris White
Saturday March 25 2006

Leicester Tigers clinched their third Guinness Premiership away win of the season at a rain-lashed Rec to tighten their grip on an all-important play-off place. Andy Goode's confident kicking display guided Leicester to their first away win in the competition since January 8, as the England No. 10 contributed 14 points with the boot.

Leon Lloyd's try and Goode's 11 points in the first half proved decisive as Tigers struck a blow against their Heineken Cup quarter-final opponents.

Goode and Bath outside-half Chris Malone exchanged two penalties apiece, before Lloyd scored the only try of the match as the game approached the half-hour mark. Tigers attacked the heart of Bath's defence through a series of powerful drives, creating the space for Goode's long pass to find Lloyd, who dived over in the right-hand corner.

Tigers led 16-9 at the interval but restarted without Lewis Moody, after the England and Lions flanker was yellow-carded for coming in at the side of a ruck two minutes before the break.

Both sides struggled to combat the wet conditions and the crowd had to wait until the 71st minute to see the try-line threatened again. This time, Bath were denied a score when Duncan Bell spilled Joe Maddock's pass only five metres short of the Leicester line.

Goode's penalty in the 78th minute put Tigers further clear, before Malone struck back a minute later to hand the home side a glimmer of hope.

Bath pushed to level the scores with the final play of the game as Malone aimed a kick towards the corner in the dying seconds, but Lloyd won the battle for the ball with Bath winger David Bory, leaving Tigers to come away with a valuable four points.

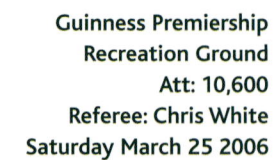

SEASON REVIEW 2005/06

TIGER TIMELINE

			SCORE	MIN
🏃	P	Goode	0-3	7
🏃	P	Goode	0-6	15
🏃	P	Malone	3-6	22
🏃	P	Malone	6-6	27
	T+C	Lloyd + Goode	6-13	29
🏃	P	Malone	9-13	37
🟨	YC	Moody		37
🏃	P	Goode	9-16	39

HALF TIME 9-16

				MIN
	S	Cornwell	Hipkiss	48
	S	Filise	Flatman	60
	S	Short	Grewcock	60
	S	Dixon	Mears	70
	S	Williams	Walshe	70
	S	Abendanon	Stephenson	70
	S	Feau'nati	Lipman	71
🏃	P	Goode	9-19	74
	S	Healey	Ellis	74
🏃	P	Malone	12-19	77
	S	Skinner	Jennings	77

FULL TIME 12-19

Key
Player coming on
Player going off

LEICESTER TIGERS

- 15 S.Vesty
- 14 G.Murphy
- 11 L.Lloyd
- 13 O.Smith
- 12 D.Hipkiss
- 10 A.Goode
- 9 H.Ellis
- 8 M.Corry (c)
- 7 L.Moody
- 6 S.Jennings
- 5 L.Deacon
- 4 B.Kay
- 3 J.White
- 2 J.Buckland
- 1 G.Rowntree

BATH RUGBY

- 1 D.Flatman
- 2 L.Mears
- 3 D.Bell
- 4 S.Borthwick (c)
- 5 D.Grewcock
- 7 M.Lipman
- 6 A.Beattie
- 8 G.Delve
- 9 N.Walshe
- 10 C.Malone
- 12 J.Maddock
- 13 A.Higgins
- 11 D.Bory
- 14 S.Finau
- 15 M.Stephenson

REPLACEMENTS

- 16 E.Taukafa
- 17 M.Holford
- 18 L.Cullen
- 19 W.Skinner
- 20 A.Healey
- 21 M.Cornwell
- 22 A.Tuilagi

"There were two sets of forwards out there that were very competitive and that meant it was always likely to be a dogged affair. I thought the conditions made it tough, but our pack were very controlled and aggressive."
Pat Howard

REPLACEMENTS

- 16 P.Dixon
- 17 T.Filise
- 18 P.Short
- 19 Z.Feau'nati
- 20 A.Williams
- 21 A.Dunne
- 22 N.Abendanon

TIGERS MILESTONES

This was Tigers' 30th win at The Rec and their 95th victory over their West Country rivals in 158 meetings.

www.leicestertigers.com 145

SEASON REVIEW 2005/06

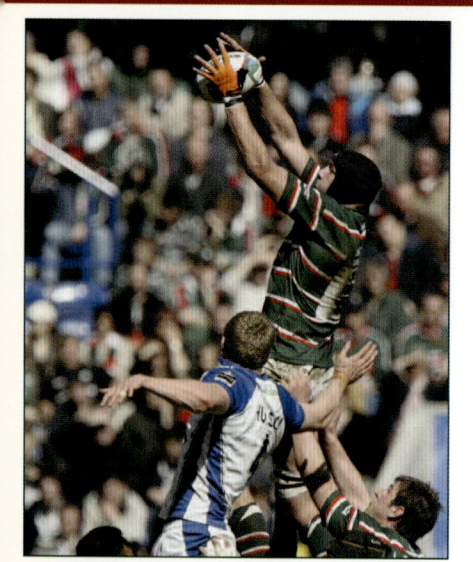

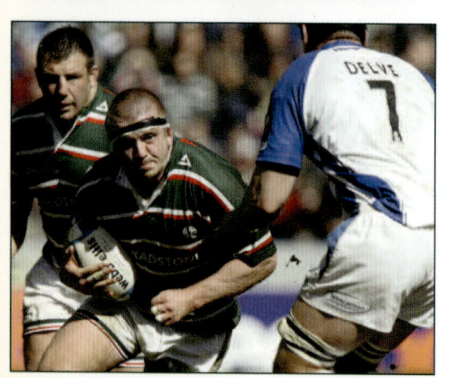

Leicester Tigers 12
Bath Rugby 15

Leicester Tigers suffered Heineken Cup heartbreak as they lost 15-12 to Bath at the Walkers Stadium. The narrow defeat saw Tigers bow out at the quarter-final stage of the competition they won so gloriously in 2001 and 2002. Pat Howard's side were unable to produce the superb form which had seen them record earlier victories over Stade Francais, the Ospreys (twice) and Clermont Auvergne (twice), as they slipped to one of their most disappointing defeats of the season.

Tigers got off to a bright start as Andy Goode effortlessly slotted a 50-metre penalty to give them a second-minute lead. Chris Malone's equalising three-pointer four minutes later set the tone for the match however, as the pendulum swung back and forth between the two sides.

The two No. 10s exchanged another penalty apiece before Malone was again on target after 28 minutes to put Bath in front at 9-6. In keeping with the nature of the match, the lead only lasted a minute before Goode kicked his third successful penalty.

The second half was another tight affair, with Goode re-establishing a three-point advantage after 43 minutes, before Bath again drew level via Malone's fourth penalty of the afternoon. The decisive score arrived with 61 minutes on the clock, as Bath's Australian-born outside-half gave the West Country side a lead they never relinquished.

The match ended in controversy, as referee Joel Jutge reduced the game to passive scrums after Bath pair David Flatman and Taufaao Filise were both sin-binned. Tigers piled on the pressure in the closing stages and looked certain to score as they created a number of chances in the final few minutes. However, despite spending long spells camped on the visitors' line, Leicester were unable to find a way through.

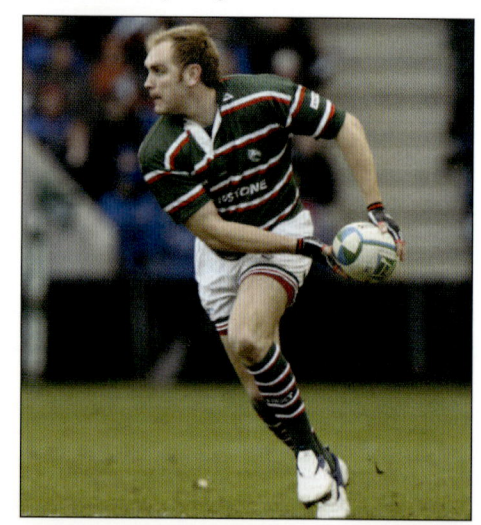

Heineken Cup quarter-final
Walkers Stadium
Att: 32,500
Referee: Joel Jutge
Saturday April 1 2006

www.leicestertigers.com

SEASON REVIEW 2005/06

TIGER TIMELINE

		SCORE	MIN
P	Goode	3-0	2
P	Malone	3-3	6
P	Goode	6-3	19
P	Malone	6-6	28
P	Malone	6-9	32
P	Goode	9-9	34
S	Short Hudson		37

HALF TIME 9-9

S	Buckland Chuter		41
P	Goode	12-9	45
S	Flatman Bell		50
P	Malone	12-12	52
S	Healey Ellis		59
P	Malone	12-15	62
S	A.Tuilagi Lloyd		63
S	Lipman Delve		63
S	Cheeseman Crockett		66
S	Abraham Jennings		67
YC	Flatman		69
S	Bell Lipman		70
YC	Filise		71

FULL TIME 12-15

Key
Player coming on
Player going off

LEICESTER TIGERS

- 15 S.Vesty
- 14 L.Lloyd
- 11 G.Murphy
- 13 O.Smith
- 12 D.Hipkiss
- 10 A.Goode
- 9 H.Ellis
- 8 M.Corry (c)
- 7 S.Jennings
- 6 L.Moody
- 5 B.Kay
- 4 L.Deacon
- 3 J.White
- 2 G.Chuter
- 1 G.Rowntree

BATH RUGBY

- 1 T.Filise
- 2 L.Mears
- 3 D.Bell
- 4 J.Hudson
- 5 D.Grewcock
- 7 G.Delve
- 6 A.Beattie
- 8 Z.Feau'nati (c)
- 9 N.Walshe
- 10 C.Malone
- 12 O.Barkley
- 13 A.Crockett
- 11 D.Bory
- 14 A.Higgins
- 15 M.Stephenson

REPLACEMENTS

- 16 J.Buckland
- 17 M.Holford
- 18 L.Cullen
- 19 L.Abraham
- 20 A.Healey
- 21 M.Cornwell
- 22 A.Tuilagi

"We were our own worst enemies. We had opportunities to score all over the place in the last 10 minutes and didn't take them, so we have no complaints." **Pat Howard**

REPLACEMENTS

- 16 P.Dixon
- 17 D.Flatman
- 18 P.Short
- 19 M.Lipman
- 20 A.Williams
- 21 T.Cheeseman
- 22 L.Best

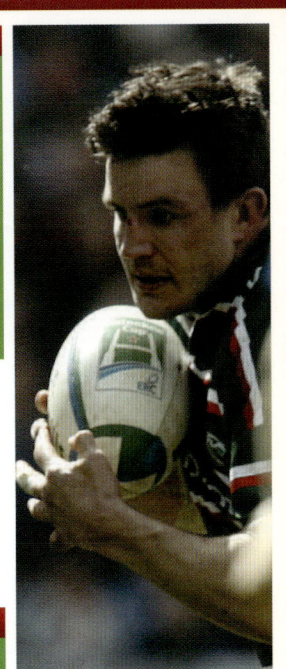

TIGERS MILESTONES

The match against Bath was Leicester's seventh Heineken Cup quarter-final and their fifth in the last six years.

www.leicestertigers.com

SEASON REVIEW 2005/06

Northampton Saints 19
Leicester Tigers 24

Tom Varndell's try double fired Leicester Tigers to a thrilling 24-19 win over Northampton Saints in the Guinness Premiership at a packed Franklin's Gardens.

Varndell was restored to the starting line-up after missing the last four matches through his commitments with England Sevens and the 20-year-old winger grabbed a try in each half to keep Leicester in the play-off places.

Varndell took his try tally this season to 16 in 24 games, with Alesana Tuilagi also crossing for Tigers, who led 14-13 at the break.

Pat Howard's side responded magnificently after receiving criticism for the manner of their Heineken Cup exit at the hands of Bath. Tigers showed a willingness to attack from deep, with the back three of Tuilagi, Varndell and Geordan Murphy looking particularly dangerous.

The visitors took the lead as early as the third minute when Varndell finished off a sweeping move that began with Tuilagi racing half the length of the field. They scored their second try five minutes before the break, as the Samoan winger set off on another 50-metre run to outpace the Northampton cover and touchdown in the left-hand corner.

Northampton fought back through the boot of Bruce Reihana, however, to leave Tigers trailing 19-14 with 54 minutes played. Leicester showed great character to eventually see off their East Midlands rivals, with Varndell's second try, a Sam Vesty penalty and an Andy Goode conversion earning Tigers local bragging rights and a vital victory.

Guinness Premiership
Franklin's Gardens
Att: 13,493
Referee: Tony Spreadbury
Friday April 14 2006

www.leicestertigers.com

SEASON REVIEW 2005/06

TIGER TIMELINE

			SCORE	MIN
T		Varndell	0-5	3
C		Vesty	0-7	3
YC		Spencer		7
YC		Rowntree		7
S		Holford L.Deacon		10
P		Reihana	3-7	12
P		Reihana	6-7	17
S		L.Deacon Holford		18
T+C		Dan Browne + Reihana	13-7	29
T+C		A.Tuilagi + Vesty	13-14	35

HALF TIME 13-14

S	Buckland Chuter	41
S	Holford Rowntree	41
S	Smith Murphy	41
P	Reihana	16-14	46
P	Reihana	19-14	51
S	Gibson Hipkiss	51
P	Vesty	19-17	54
S	Goode Healey	55
S	Lewitt Tupai	58
S	Harding Fox	58
S	Budgen Barnard	62
S	Jennings Moody	62
T+C	Varndell + Goode	19-24	63
S	Hamilton Kay	66
S	Gerard Lord	68
YC	Holford		78

FULL TIME 19-24

LEICESTER TIGERS

- 15 G.Murphy
- 14 A.Tuilagi
- 11 T.Varndell
- 13 D.Hipkiss
- 12 S.Vesty
- 10 A.Healey
- 9 S.Bemand
- 8 M.Corry (c)
- 7 L.Moody
- 6 L.Deacon
- 5 B.Kay
- 4 L.Cullen
- 3 J.White
- 2 G.Chuter
- 1 G.Rowntree

NORTHAMPTON SAINTS

- 1 T.Smith
- 2 S.Thompson (c/c)
- 3 P.Barnard
- 4 Damien Browne
- 5 M.Lord
- 7 D.Fox
- 6 P.Tupai
- 8 Daniel Browne
- 9 M.Robinson
- 10 C.Spencer
- 12 D.Quinlan
- 13 J.Clarke
- 11 B.Cohen
- 14 S.Lamont
- 15 B.Reihana (c/c)

REPLACEMENTS

- 16 J.Buckland
- 17 M.Holford
- 18 J.Hamilton
- 19 S.Jennings
- 20 O.Smith
- 21 D.Gibson
- 22 A.Goode

"We had to come out and answer some of our critics and prove to ourselves that we are capable of playing a different type of rugby. Today we decided to try to match a team who try to run the ball. We showed we were ready for that challenge." **Pat Howard**

REPLACEMENTS

- 16 D.Richmond
- 17 C.Budgen
- 18 D.Gerard
- 19 B.Lewitt
- 20 S.Harding
- 21 J.Howard
- 22 R.Kydd

TIGERS MILESTONES

Tigers' victory was their third over Northampton this season and their first at Franklin's Gardens since a 16-3 triumph on November 9. 2002.

www.leicestertigers.com 149

SEASON REVIEW 2005/06

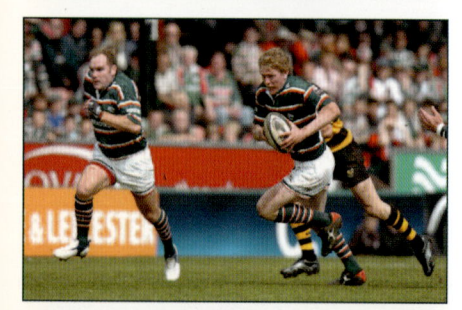

Leicester Tigers 20
London Wasps 19

Tom Varndell scored a sensational first-half hat-trick to help Leicester Tigers move into second place in the Guinness Premiership. The young winger's efforts secured a nail-biting 20-19 win over defending champions London Wasps as Tigers rejoined the top two for the first time since January.

Tigers got off to the perfect start, as Varndell touched down with only 63 seconds on the clock. Andy Goode's long pass found the 20-year-old with a yard of space wide on the left wing, with Varndell then making his 60-metre sprint finish look far easier than it should have been. The England international outpaced his opposite number, Thom Evans, before sublimely side-stepping Mark van Gisbergen's challenge to leave the Welford Road crowd in jubilant mood.

Jeremy Staunton's fifth-minute drop goal kept the visitors in touch early on and van Gisbergen's penalty following a high tackle on Paul Sackey closed the gap to a single point after 14 minutes.

Goode's penalty opened up a four-point lead, before Varndell's second try took Tigers further ahead. The Premiership's leading scorer took Scott Bemand's pass on halfway, before squeezing past two challenges in less than five yards of space to score one of the tries of the season.

Van Gisbergen reduced the arrears with a well-taken penalty after 32 minutes, but Leicester hit back immediately as Varndell bagged his third try of the match with 33 minutes played. Goode's restart bounced invitingly for Shane Jennings in the Wasps 22 and his pass released Varndell who raced clear.

Van Gisbergen then kicked another penalty to leave Tigers leading 20-12 at half-time, before Paul Sackey's 54th-minute converted try left Tigers clinging to a one-point advantage for the remaining 26 minutes of the match.

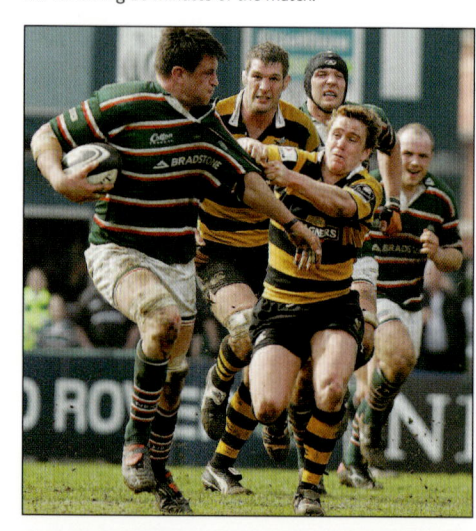

Guinness Premiership
Welford Road
Att: 16,815
Referee: Dave Pearson
Saturday April 22 2006

150   www.leicestertigers.com

SEASON REVIEW 2005/06

TIGER TIMELINE

			SCORE	MIN
🏃	T+C	Varndell + Goode	7-0	2
🏃	DG	Staunton	7-3	6
🏃	P	Van Gisbergen	7-6	15
🏃	P	Goode	10-6	22
🏃	T	Varndell	15-6	25
🏃	P	Van Gisbergen	15-9	32
🏃	T	Varndell	20-9	33
🏃	P	Van Gisbergen	20-12	40

HALF TIME 20-12

🏃	S	Chuter Buckland	49
🏃	S	Lloyd A.Tuilagi	49
🏃	S	Gibson Healey	52
🏃	T+C	Sackey+Van Gisbergen 20-19	53
🏃	S	Abbott Evans	54
🏃	S	J.Ward Ibanez	55
🏃	S	Vaa Bracken	59
🏃	S	Hamilton Cullen	64
🏃	S	Cornwell Smith	64
🏃	S	Bracken Payne	69
🏃	S	Skinner Jennings	72

FULL TIME 20-19

Key
Player coming on
Player going off

LEICESTER TIGERS

- 15 A.Goode
- 14 A.Tuilagi
- 11 T.Varndell
- 13 O.Smith
- 12 S.Vesty
- 10 A.Healey
- 9 S.Bemand
- 8 M.Corry (c)
- 7 S.Jennings
- 6 L.Deacon
- 5 B.Kay
- 4 L.Cullen
- 3 J.White
- 2 J.Buckland
- 1 M.Holford

REPLACEMENTS

16	G.Chuter
17	D.Young
18	J.Hamilton
19	W.Skinner
20	L.Lloyd
21	M.Cornwell
22	D.Gibson

LONDON WASPS

- 1 T.Payne
- 2 R.Ibanez
- 3 P.Bracken
- 4 S.Shaw
- 5 R.Birkett
- 7 M.Lock
- 6 D.Leo
- 8 L.Dallaglio (c)
- 9 E.Reddan
- 10 J.Staunton
- 12 R.Hoadley
- 13 A.Erinle
- 11 T.Evans
- 14 P.Sackey
- 15 M.Van Gisbergen

REPLACEMENTS

16	J.Ward
17	J.Va'a
18	J.Haskell
19	J.Barrett
20	J.Honeyben
21	A.King
22	S.Abbott

> "We know we are a good side. We have the ability to score tries and our defence has been pretty impressive, but we just aren't killing teams off."
> **Pat Howard**

TIGERS MILESTONES

This was Wasps' 16th defeat in 16 visits to Welford Road. It was Tigers' first win over the Londoners this season, having drawn 29-29 at the Causeway Stadium in September and been edged out in the Powergen Cup semi-final in March.

www.leicestertigers.com 151

SEASON REVIEW 2005/06

Leicester Tigers survived a late onslaught from Saracens at Vicarage Road to clinch a fifth straight win and guarantee a place in the top four of the Guinness Premiership.

Saracens threw everything at the visitors in the dying moments, but Tigers hung on to their slender lead to keep their title ambitions alive as they secured an all-important play-off spot.

Tom Varndell scored his 13th try in the competition this season and his sixth in the last three games, but Tigers failed to capitalise on a number of other scoring opportunities and were left clinging to a one-point advantage. Andy Goode was the architect of Varndell's score with a cross-field kick towards the right-hand corner. The bounce wrong-footed Dan Scarbrough and Varndell pounced to touch down, with Goode adding the most difficult of conversions.

In the end, Tigers relied on eight points from the boot of returning No. 10 Andy Goode, who partnered England colleague, Harry Ellis, at half back.

Sarries led 12-7 after 48 minutes, but Tigers trimmed the deficit to two points three minutes later through a Goode penalty. The Leicester fly-half then belted a 40-metre penalty between the posts after 56 minutes to put Tigers ahead for the first time in the match.

New Zealander, Glen Jackson, was off target with a penalty attempt three minutes later that would have put Saracens back in front, before Tigers wasted a chance to go further clear with nine minutes left when they were penalised for crossing just five metres short of the line. In the end, Pat Howard and his side were happy to leave Watford with a victory that kept them in the hunt for silverware.

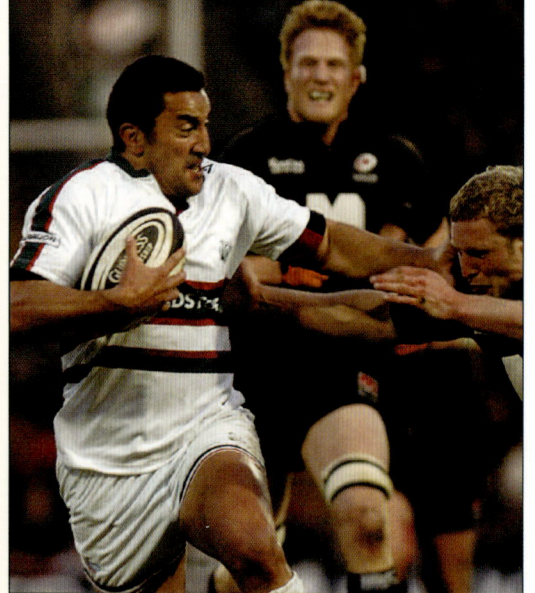

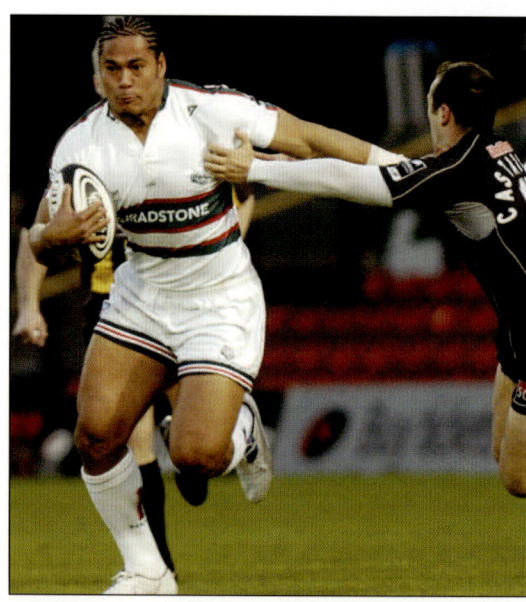

Saracens 12
Leicester Tigers 13

Guinness Premiership
Vicarage Road
Att: 9,828
Referee: Chris White
Friday April 28 2006

152 www.leicestertigers.com

SEASON REVIEW 2005/06

TIGER TIMELINE

			SCORE	MIN
🏃	P	Jackson	3-0	13
🏃	P	Jackson	6-0	25
🏃	P	Jackson	9-0	27
🏃	T+C	Varndell + Goode	9-7	31

HALF TIME 9-7

🏃	S	Healey Ellis		41
🏃	P	Jackson	12-7	47
🏃	P	Goode	12-10	51
🏃	S	Ellis Healey		51
🏃	P	Goode	12-13	56
🏃	S	Rauluni Bracken		56
🏃	S	Jennings L.Deacon		58
🏃	S	Cairns Byrne		59
🏃	S	Lloyd Smith		59
🏃	S	Hamilton Cullen		60
🏃	S	Healey Ellis		60
🏃	S	Vesty Murphy		68
🏃	S	Lloyd Yates		70
🏃	S	Holford Morris		70
🏃	S	Seymour Ben T.Russell		72
🏃	S	Buckland Chuter		73
🏃	S	Haughton Castaignede		76

FULL TIME 12-13

Key
Player coming on
Player going off

LEICESTER TIGERS

- 15 G.Murphy
- 14 A.Tuilagi
- 11 T.Varndell
- 13 O.Smith
- 12 D.Gibson
- 10 A.Goode
- 9 H.Ellis
- 8 M.Corry (c)
- 7 L.Moody
- 6 L.Deacon
- 5 B.Kay
- 4 L.Cullen
- 3 J.White
- 2 G.Chuter
- 1 D.Morris

SARACENS

- 1 K.Yates
- 2 S.Byrne
- 3 C.Visagie
- 4 S.Raiwalui
- 5 T.Ryder
- 7 B.Russell
- 6 K.Chesney
- 8 H.Vyvyan (c)
- 9 K.Bracken
- 10 G.Jackson
- 12 K.Sorrell
- 13 B.Johnston
- 11 T.Vaikona
- 14 D.Scarbrough
- 15 T.Castaignede

REPLACEMENTS

16	J.Buckland
17	M.Holford
18	J.Hamilton
19	S.Jennings
20	A.Healey
21	L.Lloyd
22	S.Vesty

"This is the point of the season where we've got to really concentrate and switch on. We've got to ensure we make every training session, every recovery session and every match count."
Lewis Moody

REPLACEMENTS

16	M.Cairns
17	N.Lloyd
18	B.Broster
19	D.Seymour
20	M.Rauluni
21	D.Harris
22	R.Haughton

TIGERS MILESTONES

Tom Varndell's first-half try set a new Premiership record of six consecutive tries, following his hat-trick against London Wasps and his brace at Northampton Saints.

www.leicestertigers.com 153

SEASON REVIEW 2005/06

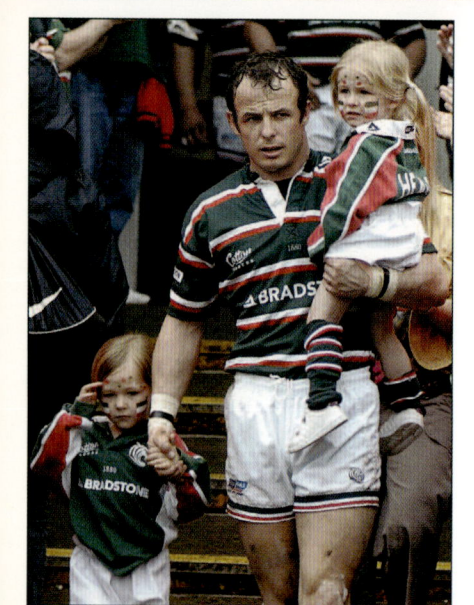

Leicester Tigers 32
Bristol 3

Leicester Tigers secured a home Guinness Premiership semi-final after a 32-3 victory over battling Bristol. A capacity crowd saw Tigers outscore their opponents by five tries to nil as their search for Premiership glory continued.

Despite the wet conditions, Tigers repeated their recent desire to spread the ball wide and counter-attack from deep. After Geordan Murphy and Jason Strange had exchanged penalties, Leicester scored their first try of the match through hooker George Chuter. Pat Howard's side ignored a comfortable chance of three points, as captain Austin Healey chose to kick for the corner from a close-range penalty. Leo Cullen's line-out catch saw the Tigers pack power over from ten metres, with Chuter emerging with ball in hand to give Tigers an 8-3 lead after 31 minutes.

Leicester soon picked up their second try of the afternoon when Healey took a late switch off Alesana Tuilagi. The fly-half hit the line at pace before feeding Tom Varndell, who raced in from 20-metres.

Tigers led 13-3 at the break and started the second half in impressive fashion, as they scored their third try on 46 minutes. Tuilagi made 35 metres before off-loading superbly to Scott Bemand just inside the Bristol 22. The ball was then recycled left, where Darren Morris gave the scoring pass to Chuter, who claimed his second try of the day.

Four minutes later, Tigers secured a bonus point after Sam Vesty's clever grubber was taken expertly by Tuilagi who went over in the left-hand corner. Another classic catch and drive then paved the way for Michael Holford to score his fourth try for the club. Fellow replacement Andy Goode added a difficult conversion to give Tigers an unassailable 32-3 lead.

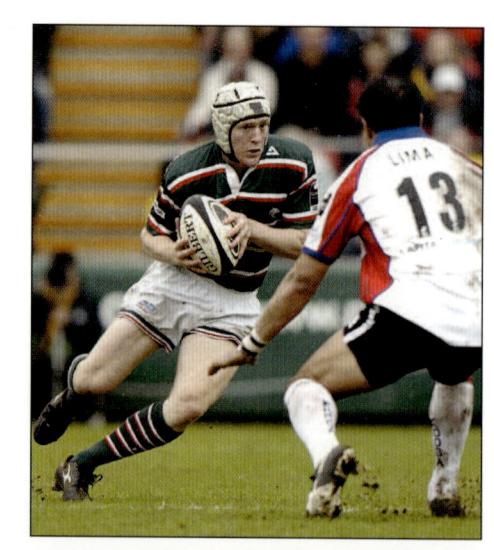

Guinness Premiership
Welford Road
Att: 16,815
Referee: Ashley Rowden
Saturday May 6 2006

SEASON REVIEW 2005/06

TIGER TIMELINE

			SCORE	MIN
	P	Murphy	3-0	3
	S	Johnson Cullen		14
	S	Vesty Murphy		16
	S	Cullen Johnson		19
	P	Strange	3-3	23
	S	Murphy Vesty		23
	T	Chuter	8-3	28
	T	Varndell	13-3	33
	S	Vesty Murphy		35

HALF TIME 13-3

	S	Holford Rowntree		44
	T	Chuter	18-3	46
	T+C	A.Tuilagi + Vesty	25-3	51
	S	Buckland Chuter		54
	S	Johnson Jennings		54
	S	Goode Lloyd		54
	YC	Lewis		58
	T+C	Holford+Goode	32-3	59
	S	Ellis Varndell		59
	S	Rauluni Nicholls		60
	S	Gray Strange		62
	S	N.Clark Nelson		63
	S	Corry A.Tuilagi		68
	S	Morgan Lewis		69
	S	Hayes Stortoni		69

FULL TIME 32-3

Key
Player coming on
Player going off

LEICESTER TIGERS

- 15 G.Murphy
- 14 A.Tuilagi
- 11 T.Varndell
- 13 L.Lloyd
- 12 D.Gibson
- 10 A.Healey (c)
- 9 S.Bemand
- 8 L.Deacon
- 7 L.Moody
- 6 S.Jennings
- 5 L.Cullen
- 4 J.Hamilton
- 3 D.Morris
- 2 G.Chuter
- 1 G.Rowntree

BRISTOL

- 1 M.Irish
- 2 S.Nelson
- 3 D.Crompton (c)
- 4 R.Winters
- 5 M.Sambucetti
- 7 C.Short
- 6 G.Lewis
- 8 D.Ward-Smith
- 9 G.Nicholls
- 10 J.Strange
- 12 S.Cox
- 13 B.Lima
- 11 M.Stanojevic
- 14 L.Robinson
- 15 B.Stortoni

REPLACEMENTS

16	J.Buckland
17	M.Holford
18	M.Corry
19	W.Johnson
20	H.Ellis
21	S.Vesty
22	A.Goode

"This was a game we had to win. We made a few mistakes but we were trying to play. The mid-season malaise has disappeared and we are now appreciating that to win these games you have to start playing a bit of rugby." **Austin Healey**

REPLACEMENTS

16	D.Hilton
17	N.Clark
18	C.Morgan
19	I.Grieve
20	J.Rauluni
21	D.Gray
22	T.Hayes

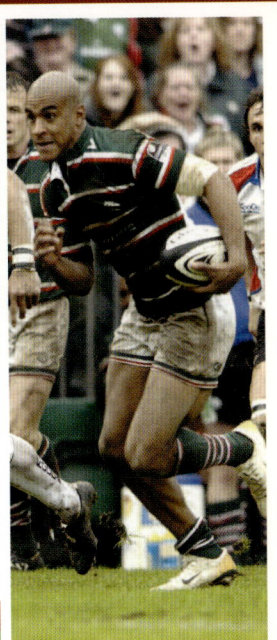

TIGERS MILESTONES

The victory over Bristol ensured Tigers went through the entire league season undefeated at Welford Road for the sixth time in the nine-season history of the Premiership.

www.leicestertigers.com 155

SEASON REVIEW 2005/06

Leicester Tigers 40
London Irish 8

Leicester Tigers booked a place in the Guinness Premiership Final with a 40-8 thrashing of London Irish at Welford Road. Tigers outscored their semi-final opponents by five tries to one in an unexpectedly one-sided affair.

Guinness Premiership semi-final
Welford Road
Att: 14,069
Referee: Dave Pearson
Sunday May 14 2006

Tigers continued where they left off against Bristol as they showed the confidence to move the ball the width of the field. Tigers' front five set the platform for some now customary entertainment from the home side's backline, with Alesana Tuilagi, Harry Ellis, Geordan Murphy and replacement Leon Lloyd the major beneficiaries.

Tuilagi scored the first try of the match with just over a quarter of an hour played, before Olivier Magne replied for the Exiles.

The highlight of the game came on 33 minutes, when a superb break from man-of-the-match Ellis resulted in Tigers' second try of the afternoon. The scrum-half justified his Tigers recall when he raced 30 metres, breaking through Hodgson's tackle and outpacing the cover to claim a superb individual score. Fly-half Andy Goode added a well-struck conversion, before landing a magnificent 53-metre penalty on the stroke of half-time. Goode's effort brought a huge roar from the Welford Road faithful and saw Tigers enter the break 20-5 in front.

Replacement Leon Lloyd then raced fully 65 metres to score a superb interception try with his very first touch of the match.

Ellis then chipped through himself, with Murphy beating Hodgson to the bounce before tapping the ball up into his hands in what must rank as one of the most skilful pieces of play seen this season. The Irishman touched down to rapturous applause to put Leicester 33-8 in front with only 11 minutes remaining.

Tigers then capped a great team display when Lloyd latched on to Ollie Smith's bouncing pass after the outside centre had made a telling break. Lloyd again outpaced the cover to sprint home and leave the final score-line 40-8 in Tigers' favour.

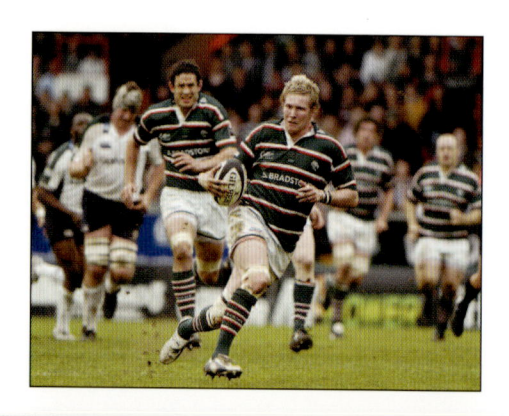

156 www.leicestertigers.com

SEASON REVIEW 2005/06

TIGER TIMELINE

		SCORE	MIN
P	Goode	3-0	7
YC	Hodgson		13
T+C	A.Tuilagi + Goode	10-0	15
YC	Kay		24
T	Magne	10-5	25
T+C	Ellis + Goode	17-5	32
P	Goode	20-5	40

HALF TIME 20-5

S	Healey Ellis		41
S	Johnson Corry		42
S	Paice Russell		46
P	Catt	20-8	51
S	Ellis Healey		52
S	Corry Johnson		55
S	Kennedy Magne		55
P	Goode	23-8	56
S	Lloyd Varndell		58
T	Lloyd	28-8	60
S	Buckland Chuter		62
S	Murphy Leguizamon		63
S	Tiesi Feau'nati		63
S	Hamilton Cullen		66
T+C	Murphy & Goode	35-8	67
S	Holford Rowntree		68
S	Johnson Corry		68
S	Vesty A.Tuilagi		68
S	Healey Ellis		70
S	Warren Hatley		73
T	Lloyd	40-8	73
S	Everitt Tagicakibau		75
S	Willis Hodgson		75

FULL TIME 40-8

LEICESTER TIGERS

- 15 G.Murphy
- 14 A.Tuilagi
- 11 T.Varndell
- 13 O.Smith
- 12 D.Gibson
- 10 A.Goode
- 9 H.Ellis
- 8 M.Corry (c)
- 7 L.Moody
- 6 S.Jennings
- 5 B.Kay
- 4 L.Cullen
- 3 J.White
- 2 G.Chuter
- 1 G.Rowntree

REPLACEMENTS

- 16 J.Buckland
- 17 M.Holford
- 18 J.Hamilton
- 19 W.Johnson
- 20 A.Healey
- 21 L.Lloyd
- 22 S.Vesty

LONDON IRISH

- 1 N.Hatley
- 2 R.Russell
- 3 R.Skuse
- 4 B.Casey
- 5 K.Roche
- 7 O.Magne
- 6 D.Danaher
- 8 J.Leguizamon
- 9 P.Hodgson
- 10 R.Flutey
- 12 D.Feau'nati
- 13 M.Catt (c)
- 11 S.Tagicakibau
- 14 T.Ojo
- 15 D.Armitage

REPLACEMENTS

- 16 T.Warren
- 17 D.Paice
- 18 N.Kennedy
- 19 P.Murphy
- 20 G.Tiesi
- 21 B.Willis
- 22 B.Everitt

"We wanted to hold on to the ball and make an impression because we felt that was the right way to deal with London Irish."
Pat Howard

TIGERS MILESTONES

Tigers have now won their last seven matches against London Irish and are undefeated against the Exiles since May 3 2003.

www.leicestertigers.com 157

SEASON REVIEW 2005/06

Leicester Tigers fell at the final hurdle, as they missed out on the Guinness Premiership crown, losing 45-20 to Sale Sharks at a rain-soaked Twickenham. The appalling weather conditions dictated the match throughout, with both sides unable to impose their favoured expansive, attacking style.

Tigers conceded three first-half tries as their dreams of Premiership glory ended at RFU headquarters for the second successive year.

Sale made the brighter start in their first Premiership Final, as they opened the scoring after Charlie's Hodgson's clever cross-kick found England wing Mark Cueto, who touched down in the right-hand corner. Hodgson then kicked the first of his six penalties to give Sale an 8-0 lead with eight minutes played.

Tigers replied almost immediately, as Shane Jennings showed great courage to charge down Hodgson's clearance, allowing Ollie Smith to beat the Sale defence to the ball and hack through. Lewis Moody gathered, before sliding over from three metres out. Andy Goode added a superb conversion, 10 metres in from the right touchline.

With continuity a difficulty due to the increasingly wet weather, the remainder of the first half proved to be a stop-start affair, but it was Sale who added a further two tries to lead 23-10 at the break.

Despite James Hamilton's late try, Tigers were unable to prevent Sale from maintaining a comfortable lead via the boot of England fly-half Hodgson.

Substitute Chris Mayor then sealed the Guinness Premiership title for the Cheshire side with an interception try following some last-gasp attacking from Tigers. Valentin Courrent's simple conversion was the final play of the game, leaving Sale to celebrate a 45-20 victory and the Guinness Premiership title.

Sale Sharks 45
Leicester Tigers 20

Guinness Premiership Final
Twickenham
Att: 58,000
Referee: Dave Pearson
Saturday May 27 2006

158 www.leicestertigers.com

SEASON REVIEW 2005/06

TIGER TIMELINE

		SCORE	MIN
P	Hodgson	3-0	3
T	Cueto	8-0	8
T+C	Moody + Goode	8-7	9
T	Lund	13-7	17
P	Hodgson	16-7	31
P	Goode	16-10	36
T+C	Ripol + Hodgson	23-10	40

HALF TIME 23-20

S	Schofield Fernandez Lobbe		41
P	Goode	23-13	43
P	Hodgson	26-13	45
S	Vesty A.Tuilagi		46
P	Hodgson	29-13	48
S	Bruno Titterrell		51
S	Stewart Turner		51
S	L.Deacon Jennings		51
S	Healey Ellis		51
S	Hamilton Cullen		54
S	Holford Rowntree		59
S	Buckland Chuter		62
P	Hodgson	32-13	63
S	Lloyd Smith		64
S	Day Chabal		66
S	Mayor Taylor		67
DG	Hodgson	35-13	70
T+C	Hamilton + Goode	35-20	74
S	Foden Wigglesworth		74
S	Chabal Jones		76
P	Hodgson	38-20	78
S	Courrent Seveali'i		79
T+C	Mayor + Courrent	45-20	80

FULL TIME 45-20

LEICESTER TIGERS

- 15 G.Murphy
- 14 A.Tuilagi
- 11 T.Varndell
- 13 O.Smith
- 12 D.Gibson
- 10 A.Goode
- 9 H.Ellis
- 8 M.Corry (c)
- 7 L.Moody
- 6 S.Jennings
- 5 B.Kay
- 4 L.Cullen
- 3 J.White
- 2 G.Chuter
- 1 G.Rowntree

SALE SHARKS

- 1 L.Faure
- 2 A.Titterrell
- 3 S.Turner
- 4 C.Jones
- 5 I.Fernandez Lobbe
- 7 M.Lund
- 6 J.White
- 8 S.Chabal
- 9 R.Wigglesworth
- 10 C.Hodgson
- 12 E.Seveali'i
- 13 M.Taylor
- 11 O.Ripol Fortuny
- 14 M.Cueto
- 15 J.Robinson (c)

REPLACEMENTS

- 16 J.Buckland
- 17 M.Holford
- 18 J.Hamilton
- 19 L.Deacon
- 20 A.Healey
- 21 L.Lloyd
- 22 S.Vesty

"It wasn't a 40-8 margin in the semi-final against London Irish, and I don't think the distance between the two teams in the final necessarily reflected the game, but they were the better team, no question."
Pat Howard

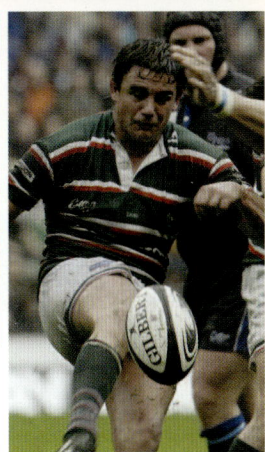

REPLACEMENTS

- 16 S.Bruno
- 17 B.Stewart
- 18 D.Schofield
- 19 C.Day
- 20 B.Foden
- 21 V.Courrent
- 22 C.Mayor

TIGERS MILESTONES

Tigers' defeat at Twickenham meant they finished as Guinness Premiership runners-up for the second consecutive season.

www.leicestertigers.com 159

DEVELOPMENT TEAM

DEVELOPMENT TEAM

GUINNESS A LEAGUE REVIEW

We start the new campaign with a great deal of optimism. I know I speak for all the lads when I say we're looking forward to it. The players have worked incredibly hard over the summer and now they can't wait to get back into the swing of things.

Everyone knows of the much-talked-about 'Welford Road factor' when it comes to the senior team's fantastic home record, but your support can have an equally important impact on the success of our development system. We've had some massive crowds for A League games in the past, including a European record of 12,769 for last May's Guinness Final against Harlequins. We really hope that level of support continues as it's a big part of getting our younger players ready to play in the Guinness Premiership. To run out in front of a passionate and enthusiastic crowd gives the lads a taste of what it will be like if they do make the step up. From a coaching perspective, it also allows us to assess how they deal with the added pressures of a playing in front of a large number of fans. In short, big crowds are a good thing for all of us here at Tigers.

Winning the Guinness A League for the second successive year last season was a great achievement, and one which everyone at the club was rightly proud of. However, it's not something we'll be dwelling on or living off. Development rugby is all about securing the future of Leicester Tigers, so focusing on the past isn't the way forward.

Instead, we'll be concentrating on preparing a new set of players for the challenges of first-team rugby. The development squad has nurtured a great deal of talent over recent years, and we'll be doing everything we can to ensure that continues this season. A number of youngsters have already demonstrated their ability to perform at A League level through their efforts during the summer. Greig Tonks has looked good in training and scored a try in the pre-season match with Nottingham, while Mitchell Culpin took his chance on the senior tour to France. The performances of Jack Cobden and Chris Munday have also suggested that they'll have a big part to play in the development side this year.

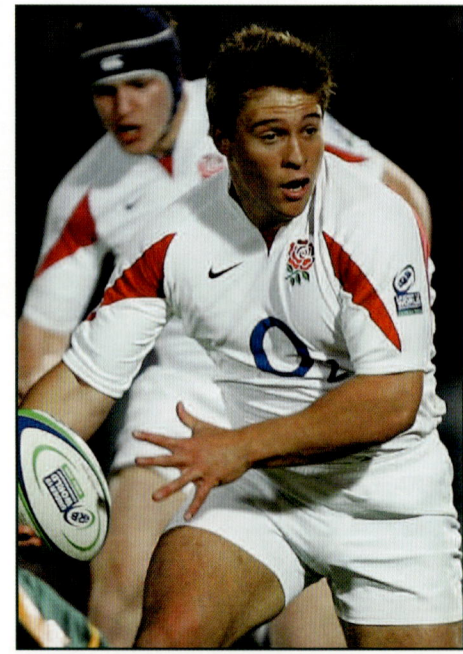

162 www.leicestertigers.com

GUINNESS A LEAGUE REVIEW

When we look at the next tier of players – those guys who've been a part of last year's development squad and are now looking to become central figures within the set-up – I think we have further grounds to be optimistic. Tom Youngs, Dan Cole, Ollie Dodge and Alex Shaw all showed great potential last season. The same can be said of Matt Smith, who is now a full-time member of the first-team squad, and Ben Pienaar, who will now be training with the senior side on a regular basis.

As well as allowing young players the opportunity to progress, the A League also provides a competitive and testing arena for those first-team players coming back from injury. Last season, the likes of Seru Rabeni and Scott Bemand benefited greatly from exposure to match conditions in the development system and I'm sure this coming year other returning Tigers will experience the same advantages.

If we can continue to provide that vital stepping-stone between first-team rugby and the rest of the club, then I'm certain we can produce plenty more individual and collective success stories. I hope you'll all be with us to help us achieve those goals.

Here's to the new season.

Andy Key
Head of Rugby Development

GUINNESS A LEAGUE FINAL

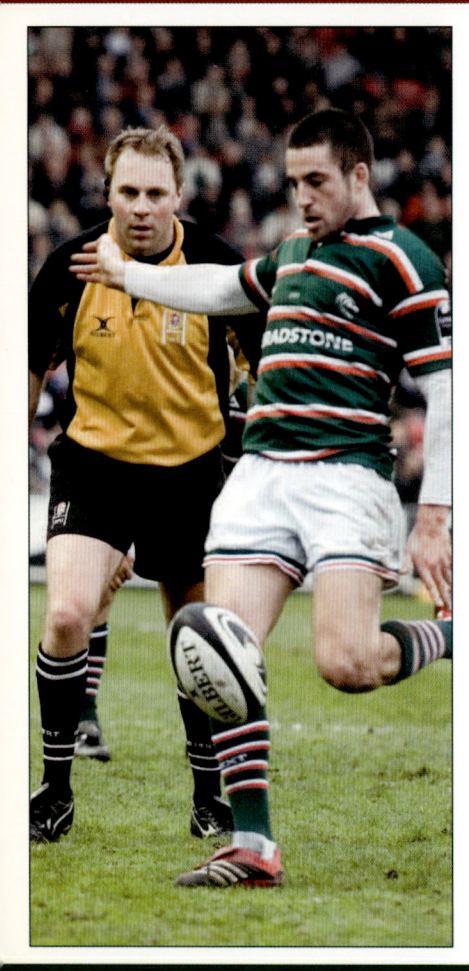

Leicester Tigers Development XV 26
NEC Harlequins Development XV 17

Leicester Tigers Development XV retained the Guinness A League championship with an enthralling victory in front of a record-breaking crowd at Welford Road. Tigers clinched a thrilling 26-17 win over NEC Harlequins to secure their second successive A League crown, after late tries from Scott Bemand and Tom Croft saw them overturn a 34-32 first-leg deficit.

Guinness A League
Welford Road
Att: 12,769
Monday April 24 2006

12,769 supporters (the highest for any second team game in Europe) watched Tigers claw their way to glory after they trailed 17-14 at the beginning of the third quarter. Andy Key's side started brightly, wiping out Quins first-leg lead within the opening five minutes. Full back Matt Smith orchestrated the evening's first try via a decisive midfield break which allowed scrum half Rob Springall to cross. Ian Humphreys added the extras before Will Skinner's stunning 65-metre solo effort took Tigers ten points clear on aggregate. Skinner turned over opposition ball inside his own half, before evading the covering defenders to register what would be his last try in a Leicester shirt. Humphreys slotted an excellent touchline conversion, before Adrian Jarvis pulled back three points for the visitors to leave Tigers leading 14-3 at the break.

Quins grabbed the first try of the second half after 48 minutes when Pablo Bouza crossed, with Jarvis converting to close the gap to 14-10 on the night and to just two points on aggregate. Simon Keogh then put the away side ahead after 53 minutes with an impressive individual score to give Dean Richards' outfit a 17-14 lead and a five-point advantage over the two legs.

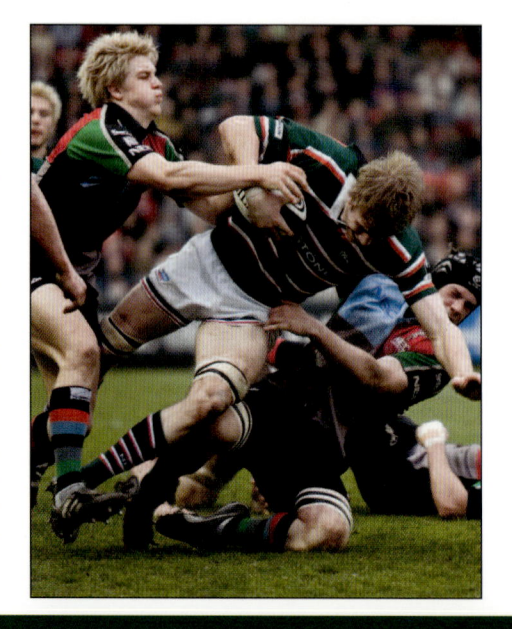

GUINNESS A LEAGUE FINAL

LEICESTER TIGERS DEVELOPMENT XV

15	M.Smith
14	S.Rabeni
13	D.Hipkiss
12	M.Cornwell (c)
11	A.Dodge
10	I.Humphreys
9	R.Springall
8	W.Johnson
7	W.Skinner
6	T.Croft
5	D.Montagu
4	J.Hamilton
3	D.Young
2	J.Buckland
1	D. Cole

REPLACEMENTS

16	C.Whitehead
17	J.Rawson
18	B.Pienaar
19	B.Wilson
20	S.Bemand
21	T.Youngs
22	O.Dodge

"The Guinness A League is absolutely vital. We've always felt that the most important thing for any player's development is to have meaningful competition at the right level." **Andy Key**

NEC HARLEQUINS DEVELOPMENT XV

1	A.Rogers
2	A C Repetto
3	L.Ward
4	J. Inglis
5	G.Robson
7	T.Guest
6	P.Bouza
8	T.Diprose (c)
9	I.Vass
10	A.Jarvis
12	M.Deane
13	T.Masson
11	C.Amesbury
14	H.Barratt
15	M.Brown

REPLACEMENTS

16	A.Croall
17	M.Lambert
18	L.Sherriff
19	D.Clayton
20	A.Thompstone
21	J.Turner-Hall
22	S.Keogh (41)

Tigers refused to panic however, and a brace of tries in the closing ten minutes ensured the A League title remained at Welford Road. A fantastic break from Humphreys set the platform for Bemand to cross after 70 minutes, with the replacement number nine turning provider minutes later, as his clever reverse pass created the space for Croft to crash over. Humphreys successfully added the first of the two conversion attempts to leave the players celebrating a hard-fought victory and the fans celebrating a memorable evening's entertainment.

www.leicestertigers.com

MATT HAMPSON CHALLENGE

England U-21 and Leicester Tigers Development XV put on a fantastic display of free-flowing rugby in May's Matt Hampson Challenge Match. Both sides showed tremendous ambition throughout the evening and gave the 6,256 crowd a great deal of entertainment.

The event raised a substantial amount of money for Matt's trust and, unsurprisingly, the match was played in a fitting spirit.

With both teams moving the ball at every opportunity, it was the home side who registered the opening score when turn-over ball saw Matt Smith float a long pass to Matt Cornwell who off-loaded to Alex Dodge, before Will Skinner beat the last man for pace to touch down in the left hand corner.

England hit back a minute later via an easy penalty to reduce the arrears to two points, before Sale's Michael Hills scored their first try on 27 minutes, following a superb run and off-load from debutant fly half Sam Robinson.

England full back Mike Brown then drew two men, before off-loading behind the tacklers to give left wing Paul Diggin a simple run-in. Hills then claimed his second try after breaking off unseen from a strong rolling maul, with Brown adding the difficult extras to give Jim Mallinder's side a 22-5 lead at half-time.

It was Tigers who registered the first points of the second half when replacement Vavae Tuilagi sprinted through to score a sensational team try after 52 minutes. Smith's miss pass found Cornwell ten metres from his own line, before the Tigers captain passed to centre-partner Youngs whose strength took him up to half way. Youngs then showed good ball skills to feed Tuilagi, whose delight in scoring was clear for all to see.

Tigers continued to build momentum when Scott Bemand's charge down resulted in Cornwell throwing a sharp cut out pass to England U-19 winger Ollie Dodge, who scored in the left hand corner.

The impressive Brown, who was England's star performer, then scored a fantastic individual try after 68 minutes to give his side a 27-17 lead. England added a further score before the close, with Wasps back row James Haskell racing in after Gloucester's Will Matthews had made the initial break. Replacement Jamie Lennard's assured conversion was the final play of the match and left England U-21 as 36-17 winners.

MATT HAMPSON CHALLENGE

ACADEMY STRUCTURE

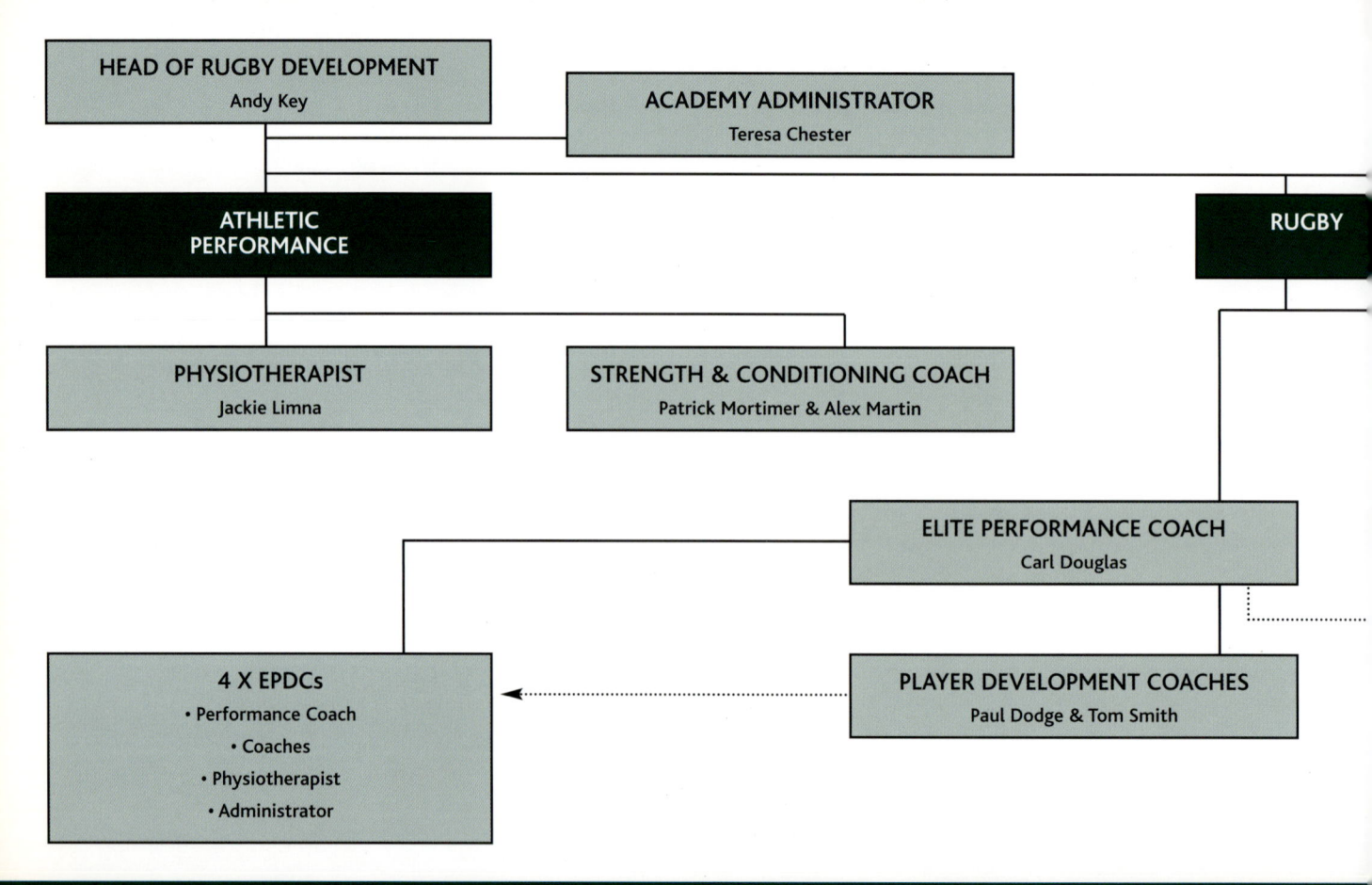

HEAD OF RUGBY DEVELOPMENT
Andy Key

ACADEMY ADMINISTRATOR
Teresa Chester

ATHLETIC PERFORMANCE

RUGBY

PHYSIOTHERAPIST
Jackie Limna

STRENGTH & CONDITIONING COACH
Patrick Mortimer & Alex Martin

ELITE PERFORMANCE COACH
Carl Douglas

PLAYER DEVELOPMENT COACHES
Paul Dodge & Tom Smith

4 X EPDCs
- Performance Coach
- Coaches
- Physiotherapist
- Administrator

ACADEMY STRUCTURE

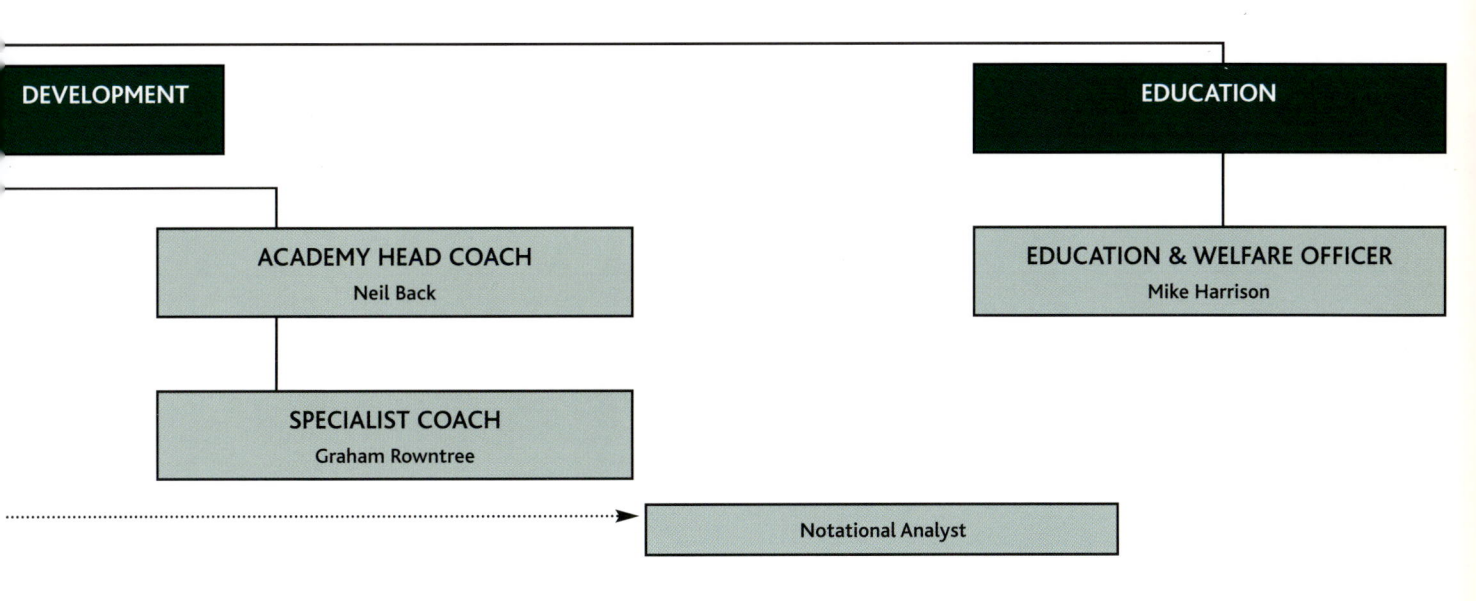

- **DEVELOPMENT**
  - **ACADEMY HEAD COACH** — Neil Back
    - **SPECIALIST COACH** — Graham Rowntree
  - Notational Analyst

- **EDUCATION**
  - **EDUCATION & WELFARE OFFICER** — Mike Harrison

ACADEMY COACHES

Teresa Chester

RUGBY ADMINISTRATOR

Teresa joined Leicester Tigers in September 1999, initially assisting Jo Hollis and working within the club's community department. She now holds the role of rugby administrator and is responsible for a wide variety of issues, ranging from looking after all aspects of academy administration, to ordering every piece of kit worn by the entire Tigers set-up.

Teresa was born and raised in Leicestershire, having been educated at Lutterworth Grammar School. Prior to starting a family, Teresa continued her county links as she worked for another popular local firm in Everards Brewery.

Jackie Limna

ACADEMY PHYSIOTHERAPIST

Jackie obtained her degree in physiotherapy in Bristol, before going on to get a Masters degree in Sports Medicine from Trinity College in Dublin.

She was employed by the NHS for six years, as well as working for National League club Western-Super Mare and the Somerset Rugby Union. Jackie has also helped out with the RFUW in their Elite Regional Programme.

Jackie joined Leicester Tigers in 2004/05 and her main role is within Tigers' Academy, although she also helps out with the first team and Tigers' development team.

Ray Needham

ACADEMY KIT-MAN

Ray joined Tigers in 1973 after successfully studying for a degree at Exeter University. He made 129 first team appearances up until 1982, before spending a season coaching the Leicester Tigers Extras.

From 1984 he was a fully qualified RFU coach, working with Leicester youth until 1989. Ray continued to teach at Allderman Newtons throughout the majority of his coaching career between 1973-2000. He has since taken up his current role as academy kitman.

Patrick Mortimer

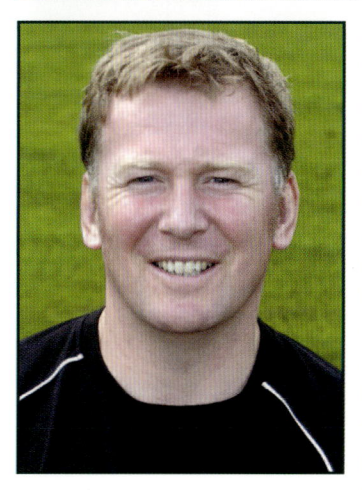

ACADEMY CONDITIONING COACH

Paddy has had extensive experience in the rugby world, having played and coached for many years. Forced out of rugby at the tender age of 23, he obtained a degree in Physical Education from the Manchester Metropolitan University and is currently completing his accreditation as a sports psychologist. He is also an experienced strength and conditioning coach.

Paddy, who was born in the Lake District, played college rugby as well as representing Sale's second team. His coaching experiences saw him take on the posts of assistant coach for Fylde, Sale Heriots Rugby and a head coach's role at Liverpool St Helens.

Paddy also taught physical education and lectured Sport Psychology at Manchester Metropolitan University and Edinburgh University. He was assistant manager of Gloucester's Rugby Academy, Sports Psychologist for British International Rowing, has had private clients of varying sport disciplines as well as serving the RFU as its Sports Science Co-ordinator for Referees. Paddy is currently a representative on UK Athletics' Senior Sports Science Performance Group and is one of a pair of Senior Sports Psychologists for UKathletics.

ACADEMY SEASON REVIEW 2005/06

ACADEMY REVIEW WITH ANDY KEY

2005/06 proved to be another fantastic year for all of us involved with Tigers Academy. We had a great season on the pitch, culminating with the Development side retaining their Guinness A League trophy with victory over NEC Harlequins at the end of April. The lads showed a great deal of character throughout a demanding season, and more importantly a number of youngsters put their hands up for inclusion in the club's first team.

A large number of academy players played a major role in the A League success, which is particularly pleasing for us all. The tournament has been very clearly used as a tool for helping their personal development, so to achieve such success with so many young players, is obviously a massive bonus.

We also had an impressive year at U-20 level, where so many of our players have shown the potential to progress even further. From a development point of view, our trips into France as part of the 1880 celebrations were another huge step forward, whilst our EPDC elite development centres continue to offer a great deal of optimism for the future. We have four of these centres, based at Swaffam, Oval Park, Newark and then an alternating home at Stafford and Burton. These institutions provide the breeding ground for our future stars, so we thank the coaches and staff at all four centres for the wonderful job they do in developing these youngsters.

We are also very proud that a large number of our academy players received international honours during the 2005/06 season.

Greig Tonks Jack Cobden, Spencer Eke and Chris Mundy have all represented England at U-18 group, while Ollie Dodge, Tom Youngs, Dan Cole, Alex Shaw, and Rob Springall gained England caps at U-19 level.

The academy also produced two of England's U-21 Grand Slam winning side. Tigers Development captain Matt Cornwell led his country to the shadow Six Nations, alongside 2004/05's Academy Player of the Year Tom Croft.

They were joined at that level by lock Ian Nimmo and prop David Young, who both won caps for Scotland U-21. All these players have pushed themselves hard throughout the year and their selection is a reward for all their effort and commitment.

Congratulations also go to Matt Smith and Tom Croft, who leave Tigers Academy having been given first team contracts. Tom and Matt have been outstanding this year and will no doubt improve even further as they gain more first team opportunities. We will be watching their progress closely.

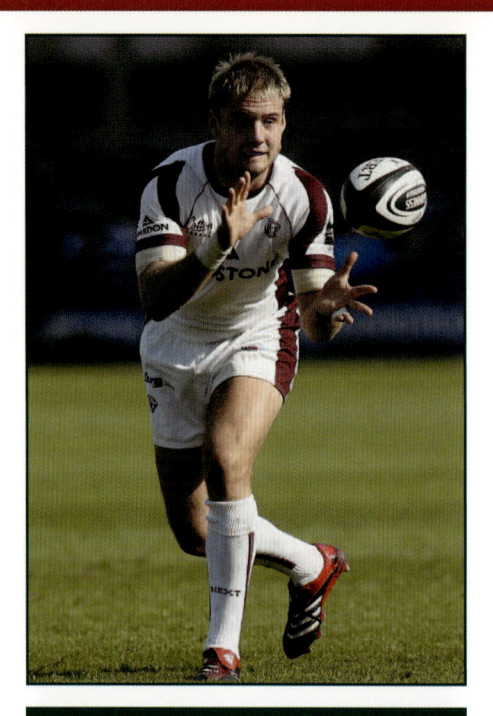

"The older players rubbing shoulders with the young lads may give them some of the experience and game understanding that's invaluable. That's the breeding ground for development - playing alongside and against better players who can improve your game."

– Tigers technical director, Neil Back.

ACADEMY SEASON REVIEW 2005/06

> "The prominence of the A League means lads get regular rugby in a worthwhile competition, and as a mindset and an attitude, that is vital to their overall development."
> – *Tigers forwards coach, Richard Cockerill.*

ACADEMY PROFILES

RICKIE ALEY
Full back
5'8"
65 kg
16/8/90

PHIL BOULTON
Prop
6'3"
127 kg
14/12/86

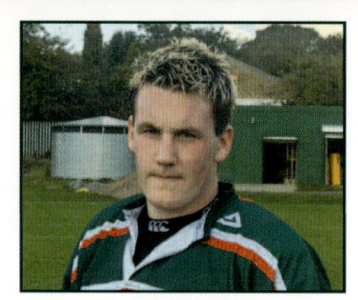

ANDY BROWN
Prop
6'
101 kg
1/10/89

DAN COLE
Prop
6'3"
120 kg
9/5/87

BEN AVENT
Back row
5'10"
88 kg
20/12/89

ADAM BRAY
Hooker
6'1"
110 kg
5/1/87

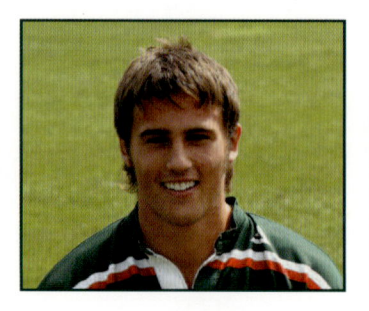

JACK COBDEN
Centre
6'2"
92 kg
26/3/89

TOM COLLETT
Hooker
5'10"
90 kg
5/1/89

ACADEMY PROFILES

MITCHELL CULPIN
Centre
5'9"
78 kg
14/3/89

SPENCER EKE
Scrum half
5'9"
75 kg
3/3/88

GREGOR GILLANDERS
Second row
6'4"
108 kg
12/4/88

SAM HERRINGTON
Second row
6'5"
117 kg
2/10/86

OLLIE DODGE
Wing/centre
6'2"
95 kg
27/8/87

CHRIS FLETCHER
Centre
5'10"
88 kg
28/10/87

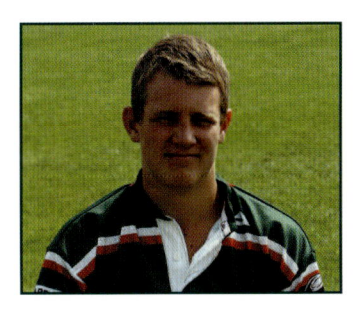

SAM HARRISON
Scrum half
5'9"
75 kg
7/4/90

WILL HURRELL
Wing
6'1"
94 kg
15/1/90

ACADEMY PROFILES

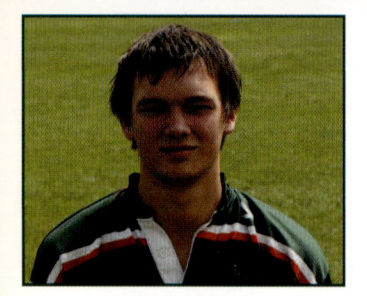

DAN HURST
Second row
6'4"
92 kg
11/09/88

WILL LAWSON
Centre
5'9"
78 kg
19/1/90

TOM McGREGOR
Second row
6'5"
105 kg
26/2/90

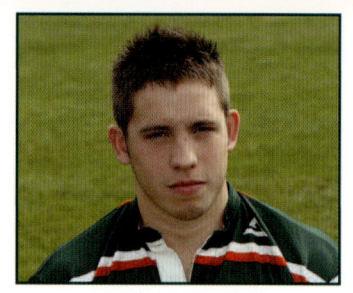

CHRIS MUNDY
Back row
6'
92 kg
10/9/87

MAURI KEISERIE
Second row
6'4"
105 kg
22/11/88

NATHANIEL LOWERS
Wing
6'5"
96 kg
26/02/90

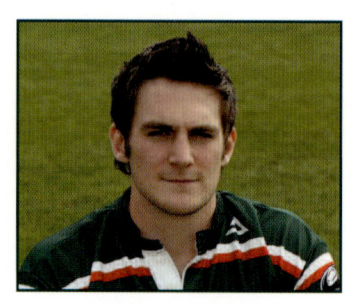

AIDEN McNULTY
Fly half
6'
90 kg
21/10/87

RYAN OWEN
Wing
6'2"
94 kg
4/10/86

ACADEMY PROFILES

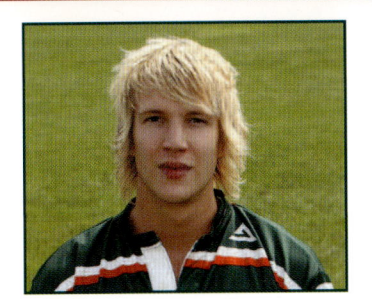

KARL PALLAS
Centre
6'1"
78 kg
24/1/90

BEN PIENAAR
Back row
5'10"
100 kg
10/9/86

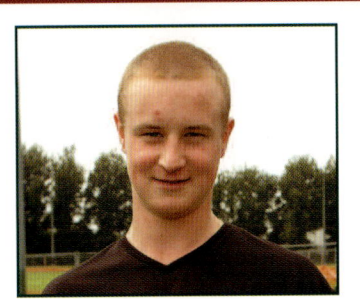

IAN SAXELBY
No. 8
6'3"
97 kg
22/5/89

ROB SPRINGALL
Scrum half
5'10"
89 kg
23/1/87

ADAM PARKINS
Prop
6'5"
137 kg
26/12/89

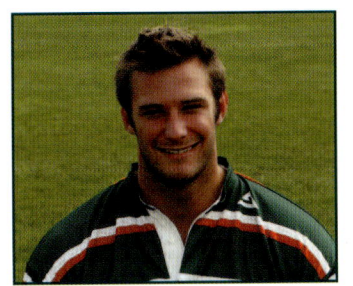

GREG SAMMONS
Hooker
5'11"
102 kg
31/12/87

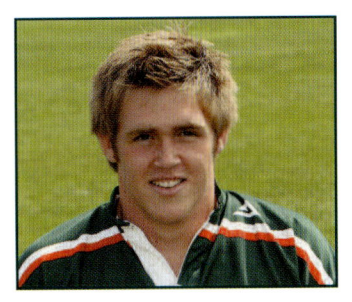

ALEX SHAW
Second row/Back row
6'3"
107 kg
31/3/87

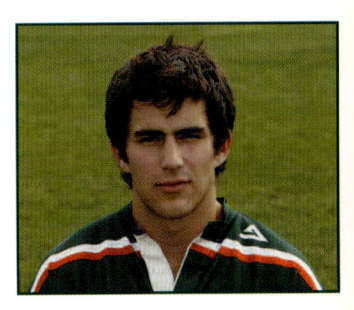

TOM STRICKLAND
Fly half
6'
80 kg
11/10/88

ACADEMY PROFILES

JOE TATE
Prop
5'9"
104 kg
12/1/89

VAVAE TUILAGI
Wing
6'3"
94 kg
15/06/88

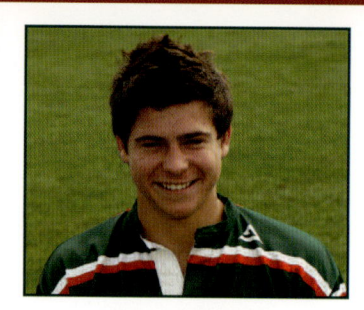

BEN YOUNGS
Fly half
5'10"
76 kg
5/9/89

GREIG TONKS
Full back/centre
6'1"
88 kg
20/5/89

ADAM VARLEY
Back row
6'2"
94 kg
3/10/87

TOM YOUNGS
Centre
5'8"
102 kg
28/01/87

ACADEMY PROFILES

www.leicestertigers.com

GUINNESS PREMIERSHIP GUIDE 2006-07

www.leicestertigers.com

GUINNESS PREMIERSHIP GUIDE 2006-07

www.leicestertigers.com 181

CLUB DETAILS

THE SQUAD	Pos	Born	Age	Ht	Wt	Debut	2005-6 All Games App	Try	Pts	Premiership App	Try	Pts	Tigers Career All Games App	Try	Pts	League Games App	Try	Pts	Since Last Try	Caps
Luke Abraham	BR	26 Sep 83	22	6'2"	16st 2	21 Dec 02	6+11	-	-	5+6	-	-	7+19	1	5	5+11	1	5	18	-
Scott Bemand	SH	21 Sep 78	27	5'11"	13st 9	11 Sep 04	5+4	1	5	4+4	-	-	18+14	3	15	15+10	2	10	4	-
Paul Boulton	P					17 Mar 06	0+1	-	-	-	-	-	0+1	-	-	-	-	-	-	-
Ross Broadfoot	FH	8 Mar 85	21	5'11"	14st 2	11 Sep 04	5+6	-	30	4+4	-	28	9+10	-	59	7+8	-	52	-	-
James Buckland	H	21 Sep 81	24	5'11"	17st 2	11 Sep 04	6+15	1	5	6+9	1	5	11+32	1	5	10+22	1	5	9	-
George Chuter	H	9 Jul 76	29	5'10"	15st 7	31 Mar 01	28+2	6	30	17+2	3	15	81+32	15	75	55+21	7	35	3	EN 2
Neil Cole	SH	30 Oct 79	26	5'11"	12st 8	12 Nov 05	1+3	-	-	1+2	-	-	1+3	-	-	1+2	-	-	-	-
Matt Cornwell	C	16 Jan 85	21	6'0"	14st 8	2 Oct 04	7+4	3	15	3+4	3	15	9+13	3	15	5+10	3	15	3	-
Martin Corry	BR	12 Oct 73	32	6'5"	18st 1	30 Aug 97	23+1	-	-	13+1	-	-	210+12	20	100	133+8	12	60	34	EN 45/L 6
Tom Croft	L/BR	7 Nov 85	20	6'5"	16st 2	12 Nov 05	2	-	-	2	-	-	2	-	-	2	-	-	-	-
Leo Cullen	L	9 Jan 78	28	6'6"	17st 5	3 Sep 05	18+10	-	-	14+6	-	-	18+10	-	-	14+6	-	-	-	IR 18
Brett Deacon	FL	7 Mar 82	24	6' 4"	17st 0	13 Sep 03	16+1	1	5	10	-	-	33+9	2	10	24+7	1	5	8	-
Louis Deacon	L	7 Oct 80	25	6'6"	18st 1	12 Aug 00	21+6	2	10	14+4	1	5	117+19	4	20	78+14	2	10	15	EN 3
Alex Dodge	C	17 Nov 84	21	6'2"	15st 6	18 Mar 05	1+2	-	-	0+2	-	-	1+3	-	-	0+2	-	-	-	-
Harry Ellis	SH	17 May 82	24	5'10"	13st 5	25 Aug 01	18+5	5	25	10+2	2	10	91+30	26	130	59+18	12	60	2	EN 13
Daryl Gibson	C	2 Mar 75	31	5'11"	15st 6	13 Sep 03	11+2	-	-	8+2	-	-	64+3	11	55	45+3	9	45	15	NZ 19
Andy Goode	FH	3 Apr 80	26	5'11"	15st 7	2 Oct 98	25+5	1	347	15+4	-	225	128+21	22	1193	75+14	15	784	24	EN 7
James Hamilton	L	17 Nov 82	23	6'8"	19st 3	13 Sep 03	11+11	3	15	7+10	3	15	19+16	4	20	12+14	4	20	1	-
Austin Healey	UB	26 Oct 73	32	5'10"	13st 7	26 Aug 96	17+15	3	15	14+8	1	5	212+36	61	332	143+23	40	216	19	EN 51/L 2
Dan Hipkiss	C	4 Jun 82	23	5'10"	14st 4	24 Aug 02	17+5	5	25	12+1	1	5	24+12	8	40	17+7	3	15	5	-
Michael Holford	P	11 Aug 82	23	5'11"	16st 8	19 Oct 03	9+15	4	20	8+11	4	20	18+20	4	20	14+15	4	20	3	-
Pat Howard	C/FH	14 Nov 73	32	5'10"	13st 9	5 Sep 98	1	-	-	-	-	-	91+5	11	57	62+3	7	37	2	AU 20
Ian Humphreys	FH	24 Apr 82	24	5'11"	12st 7	30 Sep 05	4+2	-	37	2+1	-	15	4+2	-	37	2+1	-	15	-	-
Shane Jennings	FL	8 Jul 81	24	6'0"	16st 2	3 Sep 05	25+4	3	15	16+3	1	5	25+4	3	15	16+3	1	5	18	-
Will Johnson	BR	18 Mar 74	32	6'4"	16st 6	16 Apr 94	12+7	1	5	10+4	1	5	157+53	10	50	93+35	3	15	4	-
Ben Kay	L	14 Dec 75	30	6'4"	19st 0	11 Sep 99	26+5	2	10	18+2	1	5	148+31	9	45	91+19	6	30	21	EN 41/L 1
Leon Lloyd	W/C	22 Sep 77	28	6'4"	15st 1	16 Oct 96	24+6	11	55	16+5	4	20	222+22	82	410	139+14	36	180	2	EN 5
Daniel Montagu	L	10 Sep 83	22	6'4"	17st 2	3 Mar 04	1	-	-	-	-	-	2+2	-	-	0+1	-	-	-	-
Lewis Moody	FL	12 Jun 78	27	6'3"	16st 2	25 Aug 96	12	1	5	8	1	5	119+42	23	115	75+26	11	55	1	EN 40/L 2
Alejandro Moreno	P	26 Apr 73	33	6'1"	17st 6	3 Sep 05	11+1	-	-	6+1	-	-	11+1	-	-	6+1	-	-	-	AR 3/IT 4
Darren Morris	P	24 Sep 74	31	6'1"	19st 9	13 Sep 03	13+7	1	5	8+6	1	5	56+20	1	5	38+15	1	5	10	WA 18/L 1
Geordan Murphy	FB/W	19 Apr 78	28	6'1"	13st 5	14 Nov 97	23	3	18	13	2	13	170+15	73	571	100+10	46	353	2	IR 42/L 1
Ryan Owen	W					17 Mar 06	0+1	-	-	-	-	-	0+1	-	-	-	-	-	-	-

www.leicestertigers.com

CLUB DETAILS

| | | | | | | | 2005-6 Season for Tigers ||| ||| Tigers Career ||| ||| Since Last ||
| | | | | | | | All Games ||| Premiership ||| All Games ||| League Games ||| ||
THE SQUAD	Pos	Born	Age	Ht	Wt	Debut	App	Try	Pts	App	Try	Pts	App	Try	Pts	App	Try	Pts	Try	Caps
Ben Pienaar	BR	10 Sep 86	19	5'10"	15st 10	17 Mar 06	0+1	-	-	-	-	-	0+1	-	-	-	-	-	-	-
Seru Rabeni	C	27 Dec 78	27	6'2"	16st 6	5 Sep 04	2+2	-	-	2+1	-	-	14+4	8	40	12+3	6	30	9	FJ 21/PI 3
John Rawson	P	6 Apr 75	31	5'7"	17st 3	5 Feb 05	1	-	-	-	-	-	2+4	-	-	0+4	-	-	-	-
Graham Rowntree	P	18 Apr 71	35	6'0"	17st 3	23 Oct 90	19+1	-	-	13	-	-	361+36	18	87	211+23	5	25	54	EN 54/L 2
Will Skinner	FL	8 Feb 84	22	5'11"	14st 9	26 Apr 03	5+7	2	10	3+6	2	10	12+24	5	25	10+16	4	20	4	-
Matt Smith	FB/C	15 Nov 85	20	6'3"	15st 17	Mar 06	1	-	-	-	-	-	1	-	-	-	-	-	-	-
Ollie Smith	C/W	14 Aug 82	23	6'1"	15st 4	16 Aug 00	26+4	2	10	17+4	2	10	122+20	31	155	80+13	17	85	8	EN 5
Ephraim Taukafa	H	26 Jun 76	29	5'11"	16st 5	21 Nov 04	2+7	1	5	1+6	1	5	3+9	1	5	1+7	1	5	4	TG 15
Alesana Tuilagi	W	24 Feb 81	25	6'1"	17st 7	11 Sep 04	18+6	7	35	14+3	5	25	24+19	17	85	17+12	9	45	2	WS 10
Anitelea Tuilagi	UB	5 Jun 86	19	6'1"	15st 2	12 Nov 05	0+1	-	-	0+1	-	-	0+1	-	-	0+1	-	-	-	WS 8
Freddie Tuilagi	W/C	9 Jun 71	34	5'11"	15st 28	Oct 00	0+1	1	5	-	-	-	72+10	16	80	45+4	8	40	1	WS 16
Henry Tuilagi	BR	12 Aug 76	29	6'1"	19st 8	13 Sep 03	1+2	1	5	0+2	1	5	24+23	8	40	17+18	6	30	3	WS 4
Tom Varndell	W	16 Sep 85	20	6'3"	15st 4	6 Nov 04	24+5	21	105	18+3	14	70	31+7	29	145	24+4	20	100	3	EN 3
Sam Vesty	FH	26 Nov 81	24	6'0"	14st 4	24 Aug 02	22+7	2	27	15+5	2	27	67+25	7	111	46+16	4	54	9	-
Julian White	P	14 May 73	33	6'1"	18st 8	29 Nov 03	19+2	-	-	13+2	-	-	49+6	2	10	32+4	-	-	28	EN 35/L 3
Chris Whitehead	H	9 May 86	20	6'3"	16st 3	17 Mar 06	0+1	-	-	-	-	-	0+1	-	-	-	-	-	-	-
Brent Wilson	FL	9 Sep 81	24	6'5"	17st	17 Mar 06	1	2	10	-	-	-	1	2	10	-	-	-	1	-
Alex Wright	SH	23 Jun 86	19	5'8"	11st 7	3 Mar 04	0+1	-	-	-	-	-	0+3	1	5	-	-	-	3	-
David Young	P	18 Feb 85	21	6'1"	17st 7	3 Dec 05	0+1	-	-	-	-	-	0+1	-	-	-	-	-	-	-
Penalty Tries								1	5											
TIGERS TOTALS FOR							540+206	97	914	360+137	58	578	All games: Played 36, Won 22, Drawn 3, Lost 11								
TOTALS AGAINST								53	724		29	468	Premiership: Played 24, Won 15, Drawn 3, Lost 6								

THE KICKERS	Misses	Succ%	C	PG	DG	C	PG	DG	C	PG	DG	C	PG	DG	Att	Career%
Ross Broadfoot	10	52.38%	3	8	-	2	8	-	10	13	-	8	12	-	41	56.10%
Andy Goode	52	71.27%	51	78	2	30	54	1	195	204	27	128	136	15	567	70.37%
Austin Healey	1	-	-	-	-	-	-	-	3	1	6	2	-	4	11	36.36%
Ian Humphreys	5	75.00%	8	7	-	-	5	-	8	7	-	-	5	-	20	75.00%
Geordan Murphy	2	33.33%	-	1	-	-	1	-	49	33	3	24	23	2	130	63.08%
Sam Vesty	3	72.73%	7	1	-	7	1	-	17	14	-	8	6	-	56	55.36%
TIGERS TOTALS	73	69.20%			69	95	2	39	69	1						
OPPONENTS	57	73.11%			39	116	11	22	85	8						

CLUB PROFILES

NAME OF CLUB	Bath Rugby
FOUNDED	1865
STADIUM ADDRESS	Recreation Ground, Spring Gardens, Bath BA2 6PW
STADIUM CAPACITY	10,500
CLUB SWITCHBOARD	01225 325 200
CLUB OFFICIALS	Chairman: Andrew Brownsword
	Chief Executive: Bob Calleja
	Acting Head Coach: Steve Meehan
	Forwards Coach: Mark Bakewell
	Captain: Steve Borthwick
WEBSITE	www.bathrugby.com

CLUB PROFILES

PLAYING SQUAD

Always a tough prospect up front, where England locks Steve Borthwick and Danny Grewcock are among the best around, especially in the line-out. A big pack is backed up by some quick backs, with young full-back Nick Abendanon and returning centre Shaun Berne among the most eye-catching. Olly Barkley and Chris Malone are assured goal-kickers anywhere inside 55 metres. Great things are expected of rugby league recruit Chev Walker in the centre.

ONE TO WATCH

David Flatman

The England international prop has endured a couple of frustrating years with persistent Achilles problems. But after returning from an ankle sprain in the second half of last season, he has enjoyed a pre-season free from injury. His size and power in the scrum, lifting ability in the line-out and work around the park, together with his experience from seven years in professional rugby and eight England caps, make him a vital member of the squad.

INS & OUTS

IN

Shaun Berne *(fly-half, NSW Waratahs)*, Chev Walker *(centre, Leeds Rhinos RL)*, Matt Banahan *(lock, London Irish)*, Pietro Travagli *(scrum-half, Viadana)*, Jonny Faamatuainu *(lock, Otahuhu)*, Eliota Fuimaono-Sapolu *(centre, Auckland University)*.

OUT

Taufa'ao Felise *(prop, Cardiff)*, Lee Best *(full-back, Worcester Warriors)*, James Hudson *(lock, London Irish)*, Andy Dunne *(fly-half, Ireland)*, Frikkie Welsh *(wing, Blue Bulls)*, Mike Baxter *(scrum-half, Pertemps Bees)*.

www.leicestertigers.com

CLUB PROFILES

BATH RUGBY SQUAD LIST

Surname	Christian name	Position	Height (Metric)	Height (Imp)	Weight (Metric)	Weight (Imp)	DOB	Honours
Abendanon	Nick	Full back/Wing	1.79m	5ft 10in	82kg	13st 0lb	27/08/86	
Banahan	Matt	Lock	2.00m	6ft 7in	109kg	17st 3lb	30/12/86	
Barkley	Olly	Fly half/Centre	1.78m	5ft 10in	92kg	14st 6lb	28/11/81	England
Barnes	David	Prop	1.83m	6ft 0in	112kg	17st 10lb	29/07/76	
Beattie	Andy	Back row	1.96m	6ft 5in	118kg	18st 8lb	06/09/78	
Bell	Duncan	Prop	1.88m	6ft 2in	126kg	19st 8lb	01/10/74	England
Berne	Shaun	Centre	1.81m	5ft 11in	87kg	13st 10lb	08/01/79	
Borthwick	Steve	Lock	1.98m	6ft 6in	110kg	17st 5lb	12/10/79	England
Bory	David	Wing	1.80m	5ft 11in	93kg	14st 9lb	08/03/76	France
Brooker	Chris	Hooker	1.78m	5ft 10in	108kg	17st 0lb	31/05/86	
Cheeseman	Tom	Centre	1.83m	6ft 0in	90kg	14st 2lb	22/03/86	
Crockett	Alex	Centre	1.80m	5ft 11in	93kg	14st 9lb	20/11/81	
Davey	Spencer	Centre	1.85m	6ft 1in	96kg	15st 2lb	03/02/83	
Davis	Ryan	Full back/Fly half/Centre	1.68m	5ft 6in	88kg	13st 12lb	11/11/85	
Delve	Gareth	Back row	1.91m	6ft 3in	114kg	18st 0lb	30/12/82	Wales
Dixon	Pieter	Hooker	1.80m	5ft 11in	105kg	16st 7lb	17/10/77	
Faamatuainu	Jonny	Lock	1.95m	6ft 5in	106kg	16st 5lb	29/12/83	Samoa
Feaunati	Zak	Number 8	1.88m	6ft 2in	118kg	18st 8lb	23/07/73	Samoa
Fidler	Rob	Lock	1.96m	6ft 5in	116kg	18st 4lb	21/09/74	England
Flatman	David	Prop	1.85m	6ft 1in	120kg	18st 12lb	21/01/80	England
Fuiamaono-Sapolu	Eliota	Centre	1.83m	6ft 0in	107kg	16st 8lb		Samoa
Goodman	Chris	Back row	1.88m	6ft 2in	106kg	16st 5lb	06/07/85	
Grewcock	Danny	Lock	1.98m	6ft 6in	120kg	18st 10lb	07/11/72	England/Lions
Hawkins	Rob	Hooker	1.83m	6ft 0in	104kg	16st 4lb	14/04/83	
Higgins	Andrew	Centre	1.81m	5ft 11in	85kg	13st 6lb	13/07/81	

www.leicestertigers.com

BATH RUGBY SQUAD LIST

Surname	Christian name	Position	Height (Metric)	Height (Imp)	Weight (Metric)	Weight (Imp)	DOB	Honours
Hughes	George	Centre	1.81m	5ft 11in	92kg	14st 6lb	24/03/87	
Jarvis	Aaron	Prop	1.83m	6ft 0in	114kg	18st 0lb	20/05/86	
Lipman	Michael	Back row	1.85m	6ft 1in	99kg	15st 7lb	16/01/80	England
Loader	Christian	Prop	1.78m	5ft 10in	117kg	18st 6lb	26/10/73	Wales
Maddock	Joe	Full back/Wing	1.73m	5ft 8in	84kg	13st 5lb	20/12/78	
Malone	Chris	Fly half	1.83m	6ft 0in	93kg	14st 9lb	08/01/78	
Mangeolles	Michael	Centre	1.80m	5ft 11in	93kg	14st 9lb	13/10/86	
Mears	Lee	Hooker	1.75m	5ft 9in	100kg	15st 8lb	05/03/79	England
Miller	James	Back row	1.91m	6ft 3in	98kg	15st 6lb	09/02/87	
Myerscough	Mike	Lock	1.96m	6ft 5in	98kg	15st 6lb	28/05/86	
Ovens	Laurence	Prop	1.85m	6ft 1in	112kg	17st 10lb	06/09/85	
Perry	Matt	Full back	1.85m	6ft 1in	88kg	13st 12lb	27/01/77	England/Lions
Scaysbrook	James	Back row	1.91m	6ft 3in	98kg	15st 6lb	01/01/82	
Short	Peter	Back row/Lock	1.95m	6ft 5in	112kg	17st 10lb	10/06/79	
Stephenson	Michael	Wing	1.82m	6ft 0in	82kg	13st 0lb	28/09/80	England
Smith	Dan	Back row/Lock	1.96m	6ft 5in	112kg	17st 10lb	23/10/84	
Stevens	Matt	Prop	1.83m	6ft 0in	121kg	19st 0lb	01/10/82	England/Lions
Travalgi	Pietro	Scrum half	1.82m	6ft 0in	88kg	13st 11lb	28/04/81	Italy
Walker	Chev	Centre	1.91m	6ft 3in	101kg	15st 9lb	10/09/82	
Walshe	Nick	Scrum half	1.78m	5ft 10in	85kg	13st 6lb	01/11/74	England
Ward	Dave	Hooker	1.83m	6ft 0in	100kg	15st 8lb	21/05/85	
Williams	Andy	Scrum half	1.81m	5ft 11in	88kg	13st 12lb	07/02/81	Wales
Wood	Martyn	Scrum half	1.78m	5ft 10in	94kg	14st 11lb	25/04/77	England

CLUB PROFILES

CLUB PROFILES

DIRECTIONS & MAP

Leave M4 at Junction 18 and use Bath's Park & Ride facilities wherever possible. For Lambridge Park & Ride, follow the A46 to Bath, then follow the signs for the town centre on the A4. After the first set of traffic lights the Lambridge Park & Ride (Bath Rugby's training ground) is immediately on your left. There are also council-run Park & Ride schemes signposted within the city.

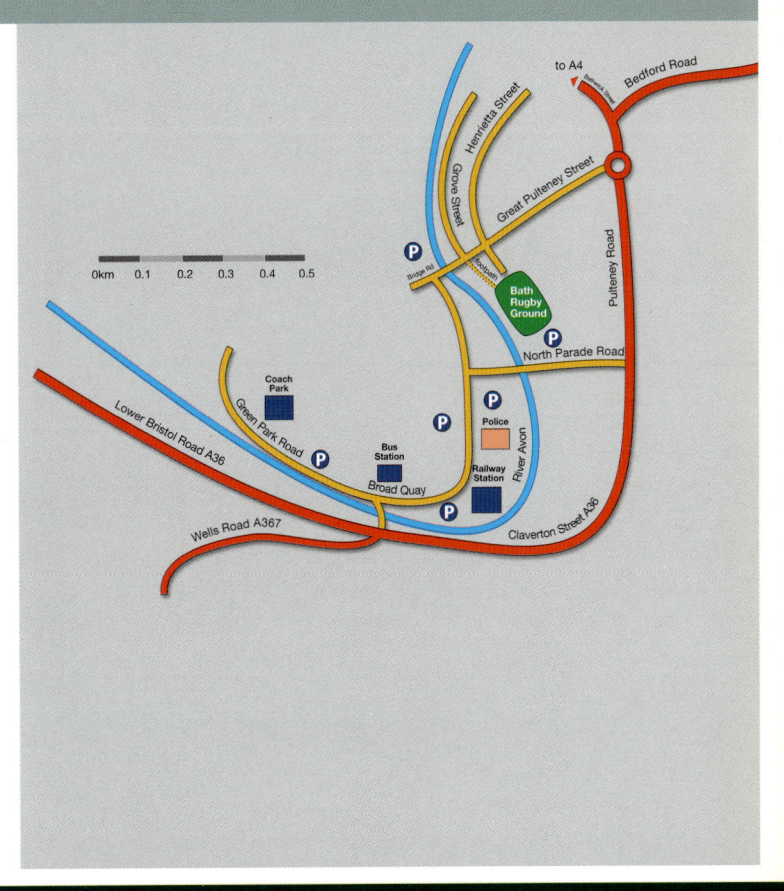

www.leicestertigers.com 189

CLUB PROFILES

BRISTOL RUGBY

NAME OF CLUB	Bristol Rugby
FOUNDED	1888
STADIUM ADDRESS	The Memorial Stadium, Filton Avenue, Horfield, Bristol BS7 0AQ
STADIUM CAPACITY	11,796
CLUB SWITCHBOARD	0117 952 0500
CLUB OFFICIALS	Chief Executive: **David White** Head Coach: **Richard Hill** Assistant Coaches: **Martin Haag, Paul Hull** Captain: **Matt Salter**
WEBSITE	www.bristolrugby.co.uk

CLUB PROFILES

PLAYING SQUAD

A busy summer on the recruitment front, Bristol were particularly pleased with the capture of Dave Hill from New Zealand, though he has club commitments Down Under until part of the way through the season. Scrum-half Shaun Perry made a massive impression last season and is targeting an England call-up. They are a cosmopolitan lot down in the West Country now with internationals from Hong Kong and the Cook Islands as well as Italy and Argentina.

ONE TO WATCH

Shaun Perry
The former Coventry scrum-half set the Guinness Premiership alight last season in his first term in the top flight of professional rugby. He rose from being a National One player to leading out England A as captain and missed out on a senior England tour only after a wrist injury. Now the challenge is to follow that season with another impressive one, though in Richard Hill he has the best tutor possible.

INS & OUTS

IN

Justin Wring *(prop, Otley)*, Alfie Too'ala *(back row, Plymouth Albion)*, Craig Morgan *(wing, Cardiff)*, Brian O'Riordan *(scrum-half, Leinster)*, Luke Arscott *(full-back, Plymouth Albion)*, Sean Hohneck *(lock, Waikato Chiefs)*, Walter Pozzebon *(centre, Treviso)*, Dave Hill *(fly-half, Waikato Chiefs)*, Ulia Ulia *(back row)*.

OUT

Sean Marsden *(wing, Glasgow)*, Olly Kohn *(lock, Harlequins)*, Ollie Hodge *(lock, released)*, Jon Pritchard *(centre, released)*, Chris Morgan *(back row, released)*, Martin Rospide *(released)*, Ross Blake *(scrum-half, released)*, Mark Denney *(centre, released)*, Jake Rauluni *(scrum-half, Leeds Tykes)*.

www.leicestertigers.com   191

CLUB PROFILES

BRISTOL RUGBY SQUAD LIST

Surname	Christian name	Position	Height (Metric)	Height (Imp)	Weight (Metric)	Weight (Imp)	DOB	Honours
Arscott	Luke	Full back	1.85m	5ft 11in	99kg	15st 8lb	07/07/84	
Budgett	Nathan	Lock	2.01m	6ft 6in	108kg	17st 0lb	02/11/75	Wales
Clark	Neil	Hooker	1.80m	5ft 11in	102kg	16st 0lb	08/10/84	
Clarke	Alex	Prop	1.80m	5ft 11in	108kg	17st 0lb	09/01/81	
Cox	Sam	Centre	1.83m	6ft 0in	87kg	13st 10lb	12/11/80	
Crompton	Darren	Prop	1.88m	6ft 2in	114kg	18st 0lb	12/09/72	
El Abd	Joe	Flanker	1.90m	6ft 2in	102kg	16st 0lb	23/02/80	
Going	Vaughan	Full back	1.79m	5ft 11in	90kg	14st 2lb	26/08/72	Hong Kong
Gray	Danny	Fly half	1.78m	5ft 10in	83kg	13st 0lb	21/05/83	
Grieve	Iain	Back row	1.95m	6ft 4in	104kg	16st 5lb	19/02/87	
Hallam	Chris	Scrum half	1.79m	5ft 8in	83kg	13st 1lb	28/02/84	
Hayes	Tommy	Fly half	1.83m	6ft 0in	91kg	14st 4lb	13/12/73	Cook Islands
Higgitt	Rob	Centre	1.88m	6ft 2in	92kg	14st 7lb	12/08/81	
Hill	David	Fly half/centre	1.88m	6ft 1in	100kg	15st 10lb	31/07/78	New Zealand
Hilton	Dave	Prop	1.80m	5ft 11in	106kg	16st 10lb	03/04/70	Scotland
Hobson	Jason	Prop	1.80m	5ft 11in	108kg	17st 0lb	10/02/83	
Hohneck	Sean	Lock	2.03m	6ft 8in	116kg	18st 0lb	08/01/79	
Irish	Mark	Prop	1.86m	6ft 1in	108kg	17st 0lb	25/08/81	
Lemi	David	Wing	1.74m	5ft 9in	75kg	11st 12lb	10/02/82	Samoa
Lewis	Geraint	Back row	1.91m	6ft 3in	102kg	15st 8lb	12/01/74	Wales
Lima	Brian	Wing	1.82m	6ft 0in	97kg	15st 4lb	25/01/72	Samoa
Llewellyn	Gareth	Second row	1.99m	6ft 6in	114kg	17st 7lb	27/02/69	Wales
Maggs	Ashley	Centre	1.93m	6ft 3in	96kg	15st 2lb	15/05/86	
Martin-Redman	Richard	Number 8/Flanker	1.91m	6ft 3in	108kg	17st 0lb	18/01/82	
Morgan	Craig	Full back/Wing	1.85m	6ft 0in	92kg	14st 4lb		Wales
Nelson	Saul	Hooker	1.78m	5ft 10in	93kg	14st 9lb	11/04/80	
Nicholls	Greg	Scrum half	1.73m	5ft 8in	76kg	12st 0lb	10/12/83	

BRISTOL RUGBY SQUAD LIST

Surname	Christian name	Position	Height (Metric)	Height (Imp)	Weight (Metric)	Weight (Imp)	DOB	Honours
O'Riordan	Brian	Scrum half	1.84m	5ft 11in	86kg	13st 7lb	04/02/81	
Perry	Shaun	Scrum half	1.78m	5ft 10in	95kg	15st 0lb	04/05/78	
Pozzebon	Walter	Centre	1.84m	6ft 0in	92kg	14st 4lb	12/06/79	Italy
Reay	Andy	Centre	1.83m	6ft 0in	94kg	14st 12lb	01/04/83	
Regan	Mark	Hooker	1.78m	5ft 10in	96kg	15st 2lb	28/01/72	England
Robinson	Lee	Wing	1.88m	6ft 2in	109kg	17st 1lb	30/12/80	
Salter	Matt	Back row	1.93m	6ft 4in	103 kg	16st 4lb	12/02/76	
Sambucetti	Mariano	Second row	1.96m	6ft 5in	109kg	17st 1lb	23/10/79	Argentina
Short	Craig	Back row	1.87m	6ft 2in	101 kg	16st 0lb	06/26/75	
Stanojevic	Marko	Wing	1.80m	5ft 11in	80kg	12st 7lb	01/10/79	
Stortoni	Bernardo	Full back	1.85m	6ft 1in	91kg	14st 4lb	17/12/76	Argentina
Strange	Jason	Fly half	1.77m	5ft 10in	84kg	13st 3lb	08/10/73	
Thompson	Wayne	Prop	1.83m	6ft 0in	102kg	16st 3lb	19/03/84	
Taumalolo	Josh	Full back	1.83m	5ft 10in	93kg	14st 9lb	08/07/76	Tonga
Tooala	Alfie	Back row	1.84m	5ft 11in	115kg	18st 1lb	30/01/80	Samoa
Ward-Smith	Dan	Number 8	1.93m	6ft 4in	115kg	17st 8lb	02/01/78	
Winters	Roy	Second row	1.93m	6ft 4in	112kg	17st 10lb	13/12/75	
Wring	Justin	Prop	1.93m	6ft 3in	123kg	18st 8lb	04/01/72	

CLUB PROFILES

194　www.leicestertigers.com

CLUB PROFILES

DIRECTIONS & MAP

From the North, West and East: Exit the M4 at junction 19 and join the M32. Travel along the M32 for 3.1 miles until you reach junction 2. Take the third exit signposted Horfield and Southmead and follow the road through a division and a roundabout both of which have clear signs reading Memorial Stadium. Once through this area, you join Muller Road and should continue to drive along it for 1.4 miles until you come to a signal-controlled crossroads. Turn left into Filton Avenue, where the ground is located on the left.

From the South: Exit the M5 at junction 16 signposted A38 Thornbury and Filton. At the roundabout, head right signposted A38 Filton. Travel along the A38 (Gloucester Road) for 4.3 miles as you enter the outer suburbs of Bristol. Pass Filton Airport on your right, the Royal Mail sorting office, an American Golf retail outlet on your left and the Royal George and Wellington pubs. At a set of traffic lights immediately past a small shop called Satellite Warehouse and before Polypipe Timber, take an unsignposted left turn into Filton Avenue where you'll see the ground on your right.

PARKING

All of the areas around the ground are residential and you'll have to battle for spaces. But finding a space within a five to ten minute walk is relatively easy - parking on Muller Road is a popular choice, as is Gloucester Road although this is often more difficult. There are many other roads across the other side of Gloucester Road - travel past the Wellington pub along Kellaway Avenue and you'll find another area of roads often used for matchday parking.

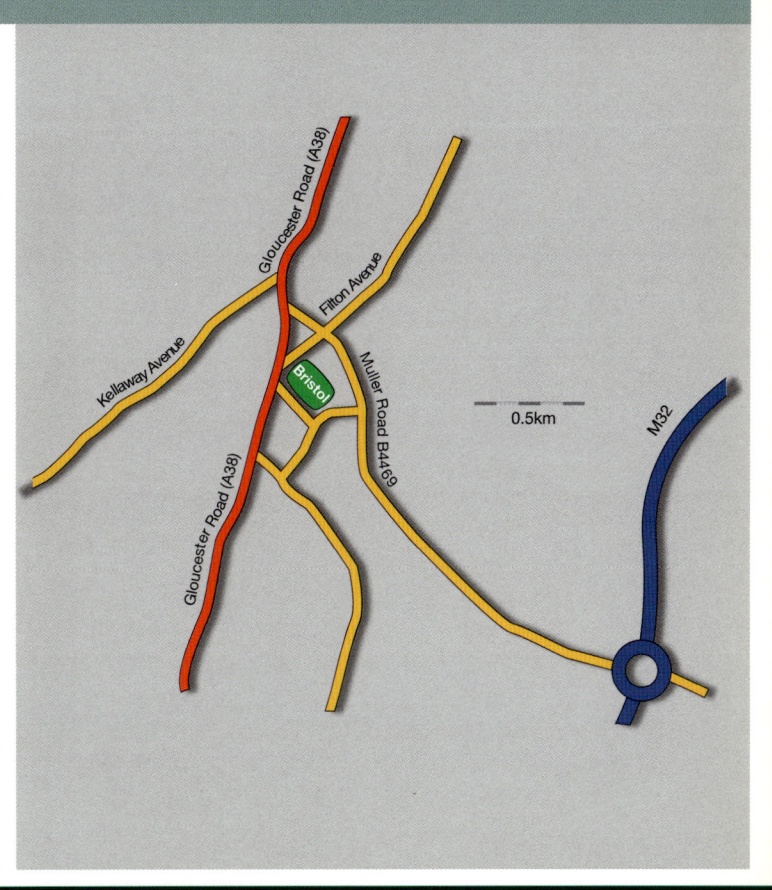

www.leicestertigers.com 195

CLUB PROFILES

NAME OF CLUB	Gloucester Rugby
FOUNDED	1873
STADIUM ADDRESS	Kingsholm Stadium, Kingsholm Road, Kingsholm, Gloucester GL1 3AX
STADIUM CAPACITY	12,500
CLUB SWITCHBOARD	01452 300951
CLUB OFFICIALS	Chairman: **Tom Walkinshaw**
	Managing Director: **Ken Nottage**
	Head Coach: **Dean Ryan**
	Coach: **Bryan Redpath**
	Captain: **Peter Buxton**
WEBSITE	www.gloucesterrugby.co.uk

CLUB PROFILES

PLAYING SQUAD

Christian Califano is an experienced, battle-hardened prop who will make a big impression on the Guinness Premiership. The arrival of Iain Balshaw is an eye-catching one as he returns to the West Country following a short spell at Leeds Tykes which ended with relegation last season. Terry Fanolua will be a big miss and it was a surprise to see Phil Vickery leave the club, but Dean Ryan will be happy with the make-up of the squad, while neutrals are looking forward to seeing exciting young backs Ryan Lamb and Anthony Allen.

ONE TO WATCH

Ryan Lamb
Fly-half Lamb burst on to the scene during Gloucester's march towards the European Challenge Cup Final last season. A play-making No.10 with flair and vision, Lamb expects to be a marked man this season, though Gloucester believe he has the ability to thrive.

INS & OUTS

IN

Christian Califano *(prop, Agen)*, Iain Balshaw *(full-back, Leeds Tykes)*, Ross McMillan *(hooker, Nottingham)*, Carlos Nieto *(prop, Viadana)*, Rory Lawson *(scrum-half, Edinburgh)*, Will James *(lock, Cornish Pirates)*.

OUT

Terry Fanolua *(centre, Brive)*, Marcel Garvey *(wing, Worcester Warriors)*, Quinton Davids *(lock, Cheetahs)*, Duncan McRae *(fly-half, retired)*, Henry Paul *(centre, Harlequins RL)*, James Parkes *(hooker, Leeds)*, Gary Powell *(prop, Cardiff Blues)*, Phil Vickery *(prop, Wasps)*

www.leicestertigers.com

CLUB PROFILES

GLOUCESTER RUGBY SQUAD LIST

Surname	Christian name	Position	Height (Metric)	Height (Imp)	Weight (Metric)	Weight (Imp)	DOB	Honours
Adams	Jack	Centre	1.82m	6ft 0in	95kg	16st 5lb	17/09/86	
Allen	Anthony	Centre	1.80m	5ft 10in	90kg	14st 3lb	01/09/86	
Azam	Olivier	Hooker	1.85m	6ft 0in	115kg	18st 2lb	21/10/74	France
Bailey	James	Wing	1.80m	5ft 10in	83kg	13st 2lb	05/08/83	
Balding	Adam	Number 8	1.88m	6ft 2in	111kg	17st 7lb	07/12/79	
Balshaw	Iain	Full back/Wing	1.83m	5ft 10in	95kg	14st 7lb	14/04/79	England/Lions
Boer	Jake	Flanker	1.87m	6ft 1in	105kg	16st 8lb	01/11/75	
Bortolami	Marco	Lock	1.95m	6ft 6in	110kg	17st 2lb	12/06/80	Italy
Brown	Alex	Lock	2.00m	6ft 7in	113kg	17st 5lb	17/05/79	England
Buxton	Peter	Back row	1.92m	6ft 3in	112kg	17st 9lb	21/08/78	
Califano	Christian	Prop	1.80m	5ft 10in	113kg	17st 5lb	16/05/72	France
Collazo	Patrice	Prop	1.85m	6ft 1in	110kg	17st 3lb	27/04/74	France
Davies	Brad	Outside half	1.77m	5ft 9in	89kg	14st 1lb	13/02/83	
Davies	Mefin	Hooker	1.78m	5ft 10in	95kg	16st 5lb	02/09/72	Wales
Elloway	Rob	Hooker	1.83m	6ft 0in	98kg	15st 4lb	09/11/83	
Eustace	Adam	Lock	1.95m	6ft 4in	108kg	17st 0lb	09/01/79	
Forrester	James	Number 8	1.95m	6ft 5in	99kg	15st 9lb	09/02/81	England
Forster	Jack	Prop	1.82m	6ft 0in	119kg	18st 6lb	19/03/87	
Foster	Mark	Wing/Centre	1.83m	6ft 0in	91kg	14st 3lb	02/09/83	
Goodridge	Jon	Full back	1.86m	6ft 1in	87kg	13st 8lb	26/02/81	
Hazell	Andy	Flanker	1.83m	6ft 0in	94kg	14st 9lb	25/04/78	England
James	Will	Lock	1.95m	6ft 6in	122kg	19st 8lb	22/12/76	
Keil	Rudi	Centre	1.85m	6ft 1in	93kg	14st 1lb	08/12/77	
Lamb	Ryan	Fly half	1.76m	5ft 9in	81kg	12st 10lb	18/05/86	
Lawson	Rory	Scrum half	1.76m	5ft 9in	82kg	12st 8lb	12/03/81	

198 www.leicestertigers.com

CLUB PROFILES

GLOUCESTER RUGBY SQUAD LIST

Surname	Christian name	Position	Height (Metric)	Height (Imp)	Weight (Metric)	Weight (Imp)	DOB	Honours
McMillan	Ross	Hooker	1.88m	6ft 2in	110kg	17st 2lb	02/06/87	
Mercier	Ludovic	Fly half	1.80m	5ft 10in	90kg	14st 0lb	01/11/76	
Merriman	James	Flanker	1.83m	6ft 0in	95kg	14st 7lb	17/01/84	
Morgan	Olly	Full back	1.89m	6ft 3in	89kg	14st 1lb	03/11/85	
Miller	Dean	Flanker	1.89m	6ft 3in	103kg	15st 3lb	13/09/87	
Narraway	Luke	Back row	1.90m	6ft 3in	100kg	15st 8lb	07/09/83	
Nieto	Carlos	Prop	1.85m	6ft 1in	110kg	17st 2lb	28/04/76	Italy
Pendlebury	Jonathan	Lock	1.94m	6ft 5in	104kg	16st 5lb	15/01/83	
Richards	Peter	Scrum half	1.75m	5ft 9in	94kg	14st 12lb	10/03/78	England
Sigley	Terry	Prop	1.88m	6ft 2in	123kg	19st 2lbs	12/10/78	
Simpson-Daniel	James	Wing/Centre	1.82m	6ft 0in	79kg	12st 7lb	30/05/82	England
Thirlby	Rob	Wing	1.86m	6ft 2in	89kg	14st 0lb	02/03/79	
Thomas	Haydn	Scrum half	1.73m	5ft 8in	78kg	12st 4lb	17/09/82	
Tindall	Mike	Centre	1.88m	6ft 2in	100kg	15st 8lb	18/10/78	England/Lions
Tuohy	Dan	Lock	1.99m	6ft 6in	108kg	17st 0lb	18/06/85	
Walker	Willie	Fly half	1.80m	5ft 10in	90kg	14st 0lb	19/05/78	
Wood	Nick	Prop	1.86m	6ft 2in	108kg	17st 0lb	09/01/83	

www.leicestertigers.com

CLUB PROFILES

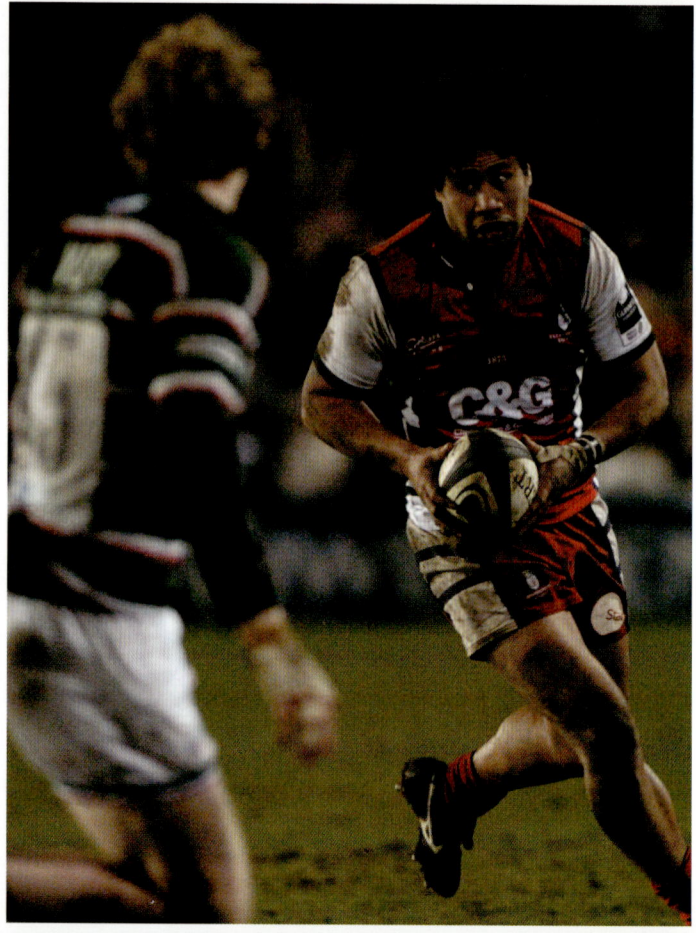

200 www.leicestertigers.com

CLUB PROFILES

DIRECTIONS & MAP

Gloucester Rugby Park and Ride: The club's Park and Ride facility runs every 20 minutes for two hours before and after each home Guinness Premiership fixture. Supporters' vehicles can be securely parked at the British Energy overspill car park at Barnwood which is signposted around the city with yellow AA road signs. Swanbrook Bus Company provide the shuttle service at £1 for adults and 50p for all concessions. More than 600 cars can use this facility into Kingsholm and it is easy for all supporters with excellent access from junction 11A of M5.

Directions: From the North, South or East - Leave the M5 at junction 11 and follow signs for Gloucester A40. Follow the dual carriageway to roundabout, turn right following A40 signs to Gloucester/Ross on Wye. Follow the dual carriageway to the next roundabout (Longford Roundabout), and turn left, following A38 signs to City Centre. Go straight across another roundabout (Tewkesbury Road Roundabout), following signs to City Centre; you are now on the Kingsholm Road. Kingsholm Stadium is approximately 800 yards on the right. There is a Park & Ride scheme at the British Energy overspill car park at Barnwood which is signposted around the city with yellow AA road signs. More than 600 cars can use this facility into Kingsholm and it is easy for all supporters with excellent access from junction 11A of M5. The service runs every 20 minutes for two hours before and after each home league fixture.

By Rail – the station is just a few minutes' walk from Gloucester Rugby Club. Come out of the station, turn right and follow the road towards Kingholm.

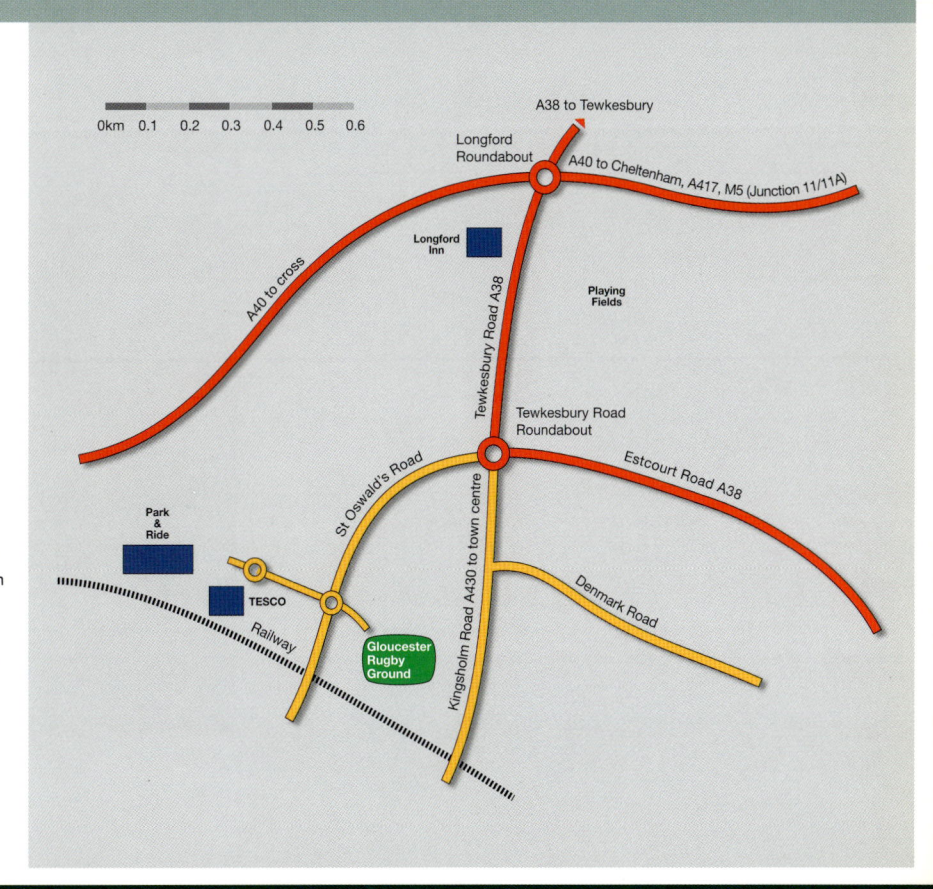

www.leicestertigers.com 201

CLUB PROFILES

NEC HARLEQUINS OF LONDON

NAME OF CLUB	NEC Harlequins
FOUNDED	1866
STADIUM ADDRESS	Twickenham Stoop Stadium, Langhorn Drive, Twickenham, Middlesex TW2 7SX
STADIUM CAPACITY	12,700
CLUB SWITCHBOARD	0208 410 6000
CLUB OFFICIALS	Chief Executive: Mark Evans
	Managing Director: Tony Copsey
	Director of Rugby: Dean Richards
	Captain: Paul Volley
OFFICIAL WEBSITE	www.quins.co.uk

CLUB PROFILES

PLAYING SQUAD

After promotion at the first attempt from National One, Dean Richards knew he would need more strength in depth in his squad. Will Greenwood and Tony Diprose were denied a swan-song season in the top flight as they retired in the summer, but Quins have signed genuine quality in Hal Luscombe and Stuart Abbott, rich potential in Dave Strettle and Danny Care, and a ready-made captain in flanker Paul Volley who returns after a spell in France. Richards is big on a "club" feel at Quins as they look to re-establish themselves among the elite.

ONE TO WATCH

Nick Easter
Having originally joined Quins on a three-month trial in August 2004, the back-row forward went on to be named the club's Player of the Season at the end of the 2004/05 and 2005/06 seasons. He played at blindside throughout his first year at The Stoop, before switching to No.8 last season, where he started in the team ahead of former England international Tony Diprose. A powerful runner with ball in hand, Easter was a regular try-scorer in the promotion-winning season in 2005/06.

INS & OUTS

IN
Dave Strettle *(wing, Rotherham)*, Hal Luscombe *(centre, Newport Gwent Dragons)*, Danny Care *(scrum-half, Leeds Tykes)*, Will Skinner *(flanker, Leicester Tigers)*, Stuart Abbott *(centre, London Wasps)*, Paul Volley *(flanker, Castres)*, Chris Hala'uifa *(back row, Rotherham)*, Peter Cook *(prop, Nottingham)*, Nicolas Spanghero *(lock, Castres)*, Mike Ross *(prop, Cork)*.

OUT
Kevin Burke *(lock, London Welsh)*, Will Greenwood *(centre, retired)*, Ian Vass *(scrum-half, Northampton Saints)*, Henry Barratt *(centre, Cornish Pirates)*, Pablo Bouza *(lock, Leeds)*, Darren Clayton *(back row, Coventry)*, Tony Diprose *(No.8, retired)*, Duncan James *(scrum-half, released)*, Agustin Costa Repetto *(hooker, released)*, Kiba Richards *(wing, released)*, Mike Worsley *(prop, released)*.

CLUB PROFILES

HARLEQUINS SQUAD LIST

Surname	Christian name	Position	Height (Metric)	Height (Imp)	Weight (Metric)	Weight (Imp)	DOB	Honours
Abbott	Stuart	Centre	1.83m	6ft 0in	90kg	14st 3lb	03/06/78	England
Arnesbury	Charlie	Wing	1.83m	6ft 0in	88kg	13st 12lb	08/04/86	
Brown	Mike	Full back/Wing	1.83m	6ft 0in	90kg	14st 3lb	04/09/85	
Care	Danny	Scrum half	1.75m	5ft 9in	76kg	12st 2lb	02/01/87	
Cook	Peter	Prop	1.78m	5ft 10in	102kg	16st 0lb	25/12/82	
Croall	Aston	Prop	1.83m	6ft 0in	112kg	17st 9lb	10/07/84	
Deane	Mel	Centre	1.78m	5ft 10in	90kg	14st 3lb	16/01/75	
Duffy	Gavin	Full back/Centre	1.85m	6ft 1in	92kg	14st 7lb	18/09/84	Ireland
Easter	Nick	Back row	1.93m	6ft 4in	115kg	18st 2lb	15/08/75	
Evans	Jim	Lock	2.01m	6ft 7in	107kg	16st 12lb	02/08/80	
Fuga	Tani	Hooker	1.80m	5ft 11in	103kg	16st 3lb	14/07/73	Samoa
Gues	Tom	Back row	1.93m	6ft 4in	107kg	8st 7lb	05/07/84	
Hala'Ufia	Chris	Back row	1.96m	6ft 5in	105kg	16st 5lb	24/10/78	Tonga
Harder	George	Wing	1.85m	6ft 1in	103kg	16st 3lb	22/06/74	Samoa
Hayter	James	Hooker	1.88m	6ft 2in	105kg	16st 8lb	14/08/78	
Inglis	James	Lock	1.96m	6ft 5in	105kg	16st 7lb	26/08/86	
Jarvis	Adrian	Fly half	1.88m	6ft 2in	88kg	13st 12lb	12/12/83	
Jones	Ceri	Prop	1.83m	6ft 0in	118kg	18st 8lb	19/06/77	
Keogh	Simon	Wing/Scrum half	1.75m	5ft 9in	88kg	13st 12lb	05/09/79	
Kohn	Olly	Lock	2.01m	6ft 7in	124kg	19st 6lb	19/05/81	
Lambert	Mark	Prop	1.90m	6ft 3in	121kg	19st 1lb	19/02/85	
Luscombe	Hal	Centre	1.90m	6ft 3in	93kg	14st 9lb	23/01/81	Wales
Masson	Tosh	Centre	1.81m	5ft 11in	94kg	14st 12lb	27/02/85	

www.leicestertigers.com

CLUB PROFILES

HARLEQUINS SQUAD LIST

Surname	Christian name	Position	Height (Metric)	Height (Imp)	Weight (Metric)	Weight (Imp)	DOB	Honours
Mehrtens	Andrew	Fly half	1.78m	5ft 10in	89kg	14st 0lb	28/04/73	New Zealand
Mial	Simon	Lock	1.93m	6ft 4in	109kg	17st 3lb	13/03/76	
Monye	Ugo	Wing	1.85m	6ft 1in	92kg	14st 6lb	13/04/83	
Nebbett	Ricky	Prop	1.81m	5ft 11in	113kg	17st 12lb	16/08/77	
Richards	Jimmy	Hooker	1.75m	5ft 9in	100kg	15st 11lb	11/12/75	
Robshaw	Chris	Back row	1.88m	6ft 2in	102kg	16st 0lb	04/06/86	
Robson	George	Lock	1.96m	6ft 5in	109kg	17st 2lb	04/11/85	
Rogers	Alex	Prop	1.91m	6ft 3in	111kg	17st 7lb	16/12/86	
Ross	Mike	Prop	1.88m	6ft 2in	124kg	19st 6lb	21/12/79	
Sherriff	Luke	Back row	1.93m	6ft 4in	103kg	16st 3lb	15/02/79	
So'olato	Steve	Scrum half	1.78m	5ft 10in	88kg	13st 12lb	11/05/77	Samoa
Skinner	Will	Flanker	1.80m	5ft 11in	90kg	14st 3lb	08/02/84	
Spanghero	Nicolas	Lock	2.00m	6ft 7in	120kg	18st 0lb	21/10/76	
Strettle	David	Wing	1.83m	6ft 0in	78kg	12st 4lb	23/07/83	
Turner-Hall	Jordan	Centre	1.83m	6ft 0in	102kg	16st 0lb	05/01/88	
Volley	Paul	Back row	1.85m	6ft 1in	106kg	16st 8lb	02/11/71	
Vos	Andre	Back row	1.96m	6ft 5in	105kg	16st 8lb	09/01/75	South Africa
Ward	Lorne	Prop	1.85m	6ft 1in	118kg	18st 9lb	16/02/77	
Williams	Tom	Full back	1.80m	5ft 11in	90kg	14st 2lb	12/01/83	

www.leicestertigers.com

CLUB PROFILES

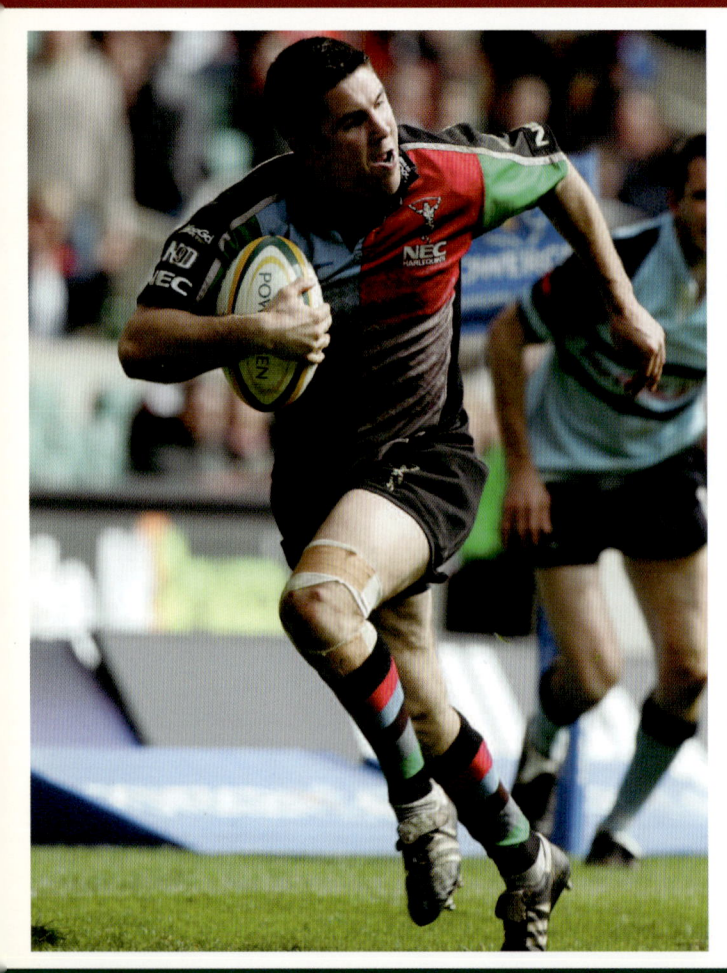

CLUB PROFILES

DIRECTIONS & MAP

By Road:
From the M3: Follow the M3 until it ends at the Sunbury roundabout. Continue up the A316 Chertsey Road, over three roundabouts. Continue for two miles. With Twickenham stadium on your left, Quins' ground is on the right. U-turn at the RFU roundabout. Enter the Stoop via Langhorn Drive, 450 yards on your left.

From the M4: Leave the M4 at Junction 3. Take the third exit of the roundabout for the A312, towards Feltham (A3006). Continue along the A312 for 4.5 miles. At the A305/A316 roundabout, turn left on to the A316. Follow the A316 Chertsey Road, over three roundabouts. Continue for two miles. With Twickenham stadium on your left, Quins' ground is on the right. U-turn at the RFU roundabout. Enter the Stoop via Langhorn Drive, 450 yards on your left.

By train: Twickenham station is served by trains from London Waterloo and Reading, with more services and routes accessible via Clapham Junction. Upon leaving the station, turn right towards Twickenham stadium and left at the mini-roundabout. Take the first left into Court Way and then left into Craneford Way and continue on until you reach the stadium. The Twickenham Stoop is at the end of the road on the right.

www.leicestertigers.com

CLUB PROFILES

NAME OF CLUB	Leicester Tigers
FOUNDED	1880
STADIUM ADDRESS	Leicester Tigers, Aylestone Road, Leicester LE2 7TR
STADIUM CAPACITY	16,000
CLUB SWITCHBOARD	08701 28 34 30
CLUB OFFICIALS	Chairman: Peter Tom CBE
	Chief Executive: Peter Wheeler
	Managing Director: David Clayton
	Head Coach: Pat Howard
	Forwards Coach: Richard Cockerill
	Captain: Martin Corry
WEBSITE	www.leicestertigers.com

CLUB PROFILES

PLAYING SQUAD

Austin Healey retired, Will Johnson departed and Graham Rowntree moved into coaching at the end of last season, while head coach Pat Howard strengthened an already impressive squad with six summer signings. Martin Castrogiovanni, an Italy international prop signed from Calvisano, could prove to be a real find, while Paul Burke adds experienced competition for Andy Goode at fly-half. The international periods hit the selection process with so many players in England's Elite Player Squad, while there are also likely call-ups for players from Ireland and the Pacific Island nations. There is still a good mix of youth and experience, and home-grown talent with imported signings, and Tigers now include eight Irishmen in the first-team squad, led by the mercurial Geordan Murphy.

ONE TO WATCH

Johne Murphy
Name-sake Geordan has made a massive impression since joining Tigers nine years ago, and the club have high hopes that Johne will make his mark in similar fashion. The 22-year-old signed for Tigers from Irish club Lansdowne in October 2005 after impressing during a one-month trial at the club. He attended the same school as Ireland and Lions star Geordan but they are not related.

A full-back or wing, he steps up to the first-team squad this season following a series of eye-catching early performances in the Development XV and full recovery from a serious knee injury.

INS & OUTS

IN
Jordan Crane (*back row, Leeds Tykes*), Paul Burke (*fly half, Munster*), Gavin Hickie (*hooker, Worcester*), Frank Murphy (*scrum half, Munster*), Martin Castrogiovanni (*prop, Calvisano*), Marcos Ayerza (*prop, Cardenal Newman*).

OUT
Darren Morris (*prop, Worcester*), Ross Broadfoot (*fly half, Bedford*), Alex Dodge (*wing/centre, Nottingham*), Dan Montagu (*lock, Nottingham*), Will Skinner (*flanker, NEC Harlequins*), Brent Wilson (*back row, Newcastle*), Will Johnson (*back row, Coventry*), Alex Wright (*scrum half, released*), Ephraim Taukafa (*hooker, released*), John Rawson (*prop, released*), Austin Healey (*retired*).

www.leicestertigers.com 209

CLUB PROFILES

LEICESTER TIGERS SQUAD LIST

Surname	Christian name	Position	Height (Metric)	Height (Imp)	Weight (Metric)	Weight (Imp)	DOB	Honours
Abraham	Luke	Back row	1.88m	6ft 2in	105kg	16st 5lb	26/09/83	
Ayerza	Marcos	Prop	1.85m	6ft 1in	106kg	16st 9lb	12/01/83	Argentina
Bemand	Scott	Scrum half	1.80m	5ft 11in	85kg	13st 8lb	21/09/78	
Buckland	James	Hooker	1.80m	5ft 11in	107kg	16st 10lb	21/09/81	
Burke	Paul	Fly half	1.73m	5ft 8in	87kg	13st 10lb	01/05/73	Ireland
Castrogiovanni	Martin	Prop	1.88m	6ft 2in	122kg	19st 3lb	21/10/81	Italy
Chuter	George	Hooker	1.79m	5ft 10in	101kg	15st 12lb	09/07/76	England
Cornwell	Matt	Centre/Full back	1.85m	6ft 1in	95kg	15st 0lb	16/01/85	
Corry	Martin	Back row	1.96m	6ft 5in	112kg	17st 10lb	12/10/73	England/Lions
Crane	Jordan	Back row	1.91m	6ft 3in	109kg	17st 2lb	03/06/86	
Croft	Tom	Lock	1.97m	6ft 5in	104kg	16st 4lb	07/11/85	
Cullen	Leo	Lock	1.98m	6ft 6in	110kg	17st 5lb	09/01/78	Ireland
Deacon	Brett	Back row	1.93m	6ft 4in	105kg	16st 8lb	07/03/82	
Deacon	Louis	Lock/Back row	1.98m	6ft 6in	114kg	17st 13lb	07/10/80	England
Ellis	Harry	Scrum half	1.79m	5ft 10in	85kg	13st 5lb	17/05/82	England
Gibson	Daryl	Centre	1.80m	5ft 11in	98kg	15st 4lb	02/03/75	New Zealand
Goode	Andy	Fly half	1.80m	5ft 11in	93kg	14st 13lb	03/04/80	England
Hamilton	James	Lock	2.03m	6ft 8in	123kg	19st 6lb	17/11/82	
Hickie	Gavin	Hooker	1.78m	5ft 10in	100kg	15st 10lb	24/04/80	
Hipkiss	Dan	Centre/Wing	1.79m	5ft 10in	90kg	14st 2lb	04/06/82	
Holford	Michael	Prop	1.81m	5ft 11in	103kg	16st 1lb	11/08/82	
Humphreys	Ian	Fly half	1.80m	5ft 11in	84kg	13st 1lb	24/04/82	
Jennings	Shane	Flanker	1.83m	6ft 0in	103kg	16st 2lb	08/07/81	

210 www.leicestertigers.com

LEICESTER TIGERS SQUAD LIST

Surname	Christian name	Position	Height (Metric)	Height (Imp)	Weight (Metric)	Weight (Imp)	DOB	Honours
Kay	Ben	Lock	1.98m	6ft 6in	112kg	17st 7lb	14/12/75	England/Lions
Lloyd	Leon	Centre/Wing	1.93m	6ft 4in	94kg	14st 11lb	22/09/77	England
Moody	Lewis	Flanker	1.91m	6ft 3in	105kg	16st 8lb	12/06/78	England/Lions
Moreno	Alejandro	Prop	1.85m	6ft 1in	110kg	17st 5lb	26/04/73	Argentina/Italy
Murphy	Frank	Scrum half	1.78m	5ft 10in	88kg	13st 11lb	02/12/81	
Murphy	Geordan	Full back/Wing	1.85m	6ft 1in	85kg	13st 3lb	19/04/78	Ireland/Lions
Murphy	Johne	Full back	1.85m	6ft 1in	92kg	14st 6lb	10/11/84	
Nimmo	Ian	Lock	2.01m	6ft 7in	120kg	18st 12lb	25/07/85	
Rabeni	Seru	Centre/Wing	1.87m	6ft 2in	105kg	16st 5lb	27/12/78	Fiji/Pacific Is
Rowntree	Graham	Prop	1.83m	6ft 0in	109kg	17st 3lb	18/04/71	England/Lions
Smith	Matt	Centre/Full back	1.93m	6ft 4in	96kg	15st 2lb	15/11/85	
Smith	Ollie	Centre	1.85m	6ft 1in	92kg	14st 7lb	14/08/82	England/Lions
Tuilagi	Alesana	Wing	1.85m	6ft 1in	111kg	17st 7lb	24/02/81	Samoa
Tuilagi	Anitelea	Wing/Centre	1.85m	6ft 1in	96kg	15st 2lb	05/06/86	
Tuilagi	Henry	Back row	1.86m	6ft 1in	119kg	18st 8lb	12/08/76	Samoa
Varndell	Tom	Wing	1.92m	6ft 3in	95kg	14st 13lb	16/09/85	
Vesty	Sam	Utility back	1.83m	6ft 0in	90kg	14st 2lb	26/11/81	
White	Julian	Prop	1.85m	6ft 1in	114kg	18st 0lb	14/05/73	England/Lions
Young	David	Prop	1.85m	6ft 1in	112kg	17st 8lb	18/02/85	

CLUB PROFILES

212 www.leicestertigers.com

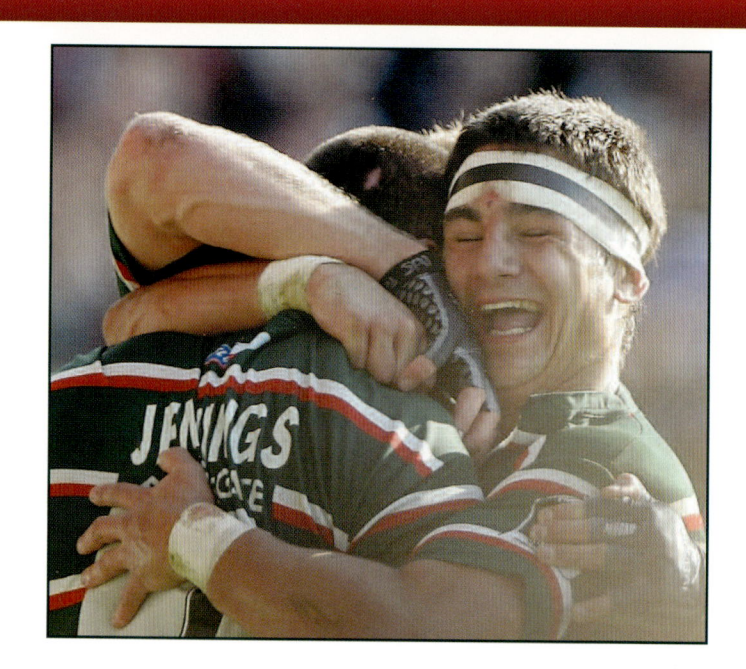

CLUB PROFILES

DIRECTIONS & MAP

By Road: Exit the M1 at Junction 21. Follow the signs for the city centre via Narborough Road (A5460). After 3 miles, at the crossroad junction with Upperton Road, turn right. The stadium is 1/2 mile ahead (past Leicester City football ground on the right).

From A6 (South): Follow the signs for the city centre, coming in via London Road. At the main set of lights opposite the entrance to the railway station (on the right), turn left on to Waterloo Way which becomes Tigers Way. The stadium is 1/2 mile further on.

From A5199 (South): Follow the signs for the city centre, coming in via Welford Road.

From A426 (South): Follow the signs for the city centre, coming in via Aylestone Road.

From A47 (East): Follow the signs for the city centre, coming in via Uppingham Road. At the St Georges Retail Park roundabout, take the second exit into St Georges Way (A594). Carry on past the Leicester Mercury offices on the right, and then filter off right into Waterloo Way just before the Railway Station. This then turns into Tigers Way and the stadium is 1/2 mile further on.

By Rail: Leicester Station is a ten minute walk away, along Waterloo Way and Tigers Way.

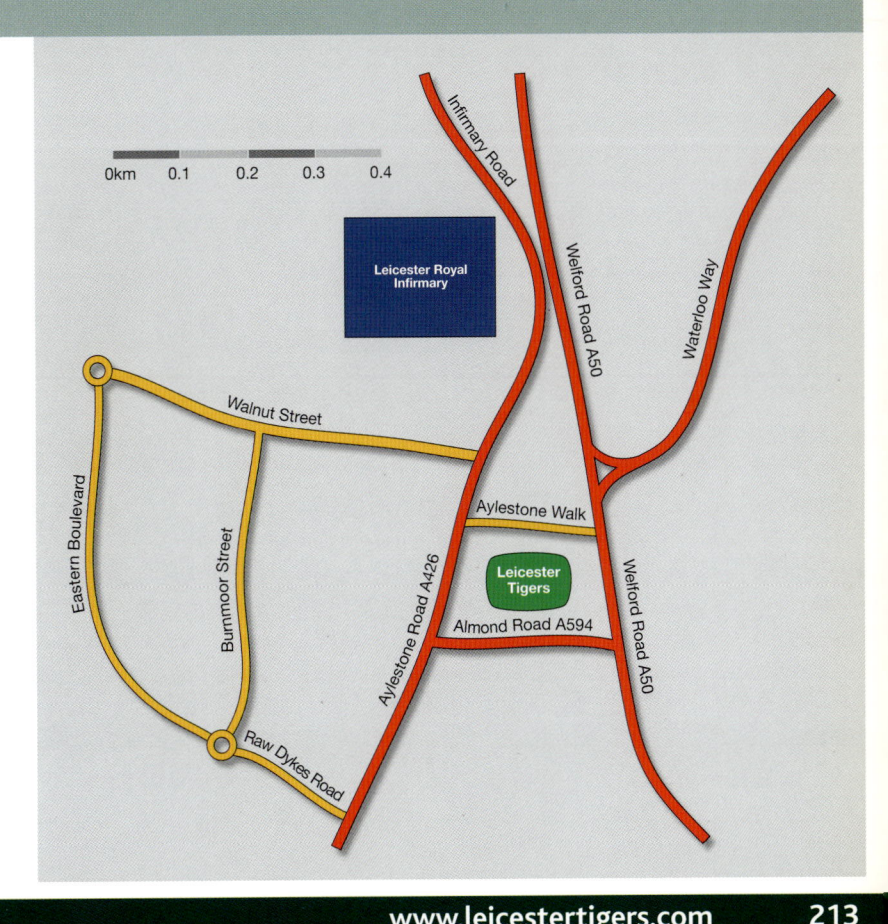

www.leicestertigers.com 213

CLUB PROFILES

London Irish

NAME OF CLUB	London Irish
FOUNDED	1898
STADIUM ADDRESS	Madejski Stadium, Junction 11, M4, Reading RG2 0FL
STADIUM CAPACITY	24,100 (all seated)
CLUB SWITCHBOARD	Tel: 01932 783 034
CLUB OFFICIALS	Chief Executive: Ian Taylor
	Director of Rugby: Brian Smith
	Coaches: Toby Booth
	Tony Stanger
	Captain: Mike Catt
WEBSITE	www.london-irish.com

CLUB PROFILES

PLAYING SQUAD

Last season exceeded all expectations as Irish finished fourth in the table and made it into the Guinness Premiership play-offs before being eliminated by Leicester. Mike Catt was at his influential best and earned an England recall, while lock Nick Kennedy particularly caught the eye in the set-piece. One Exiles era has ended with the departure of stalwarts Ryan Strudwick and Rob Hardwick, but there are more fresh faces coming through. Combined with a willingness to recruit from further afield than just the Irish background, this should be an intriguing season.

ONE TO WATCH

Riki Flutey
Fly-half Flutey arrived in November 2005 after finishing his NPC commitments in New Zealand. The 26-year-old took his opportunity after injury to Barry Everitt and had an immediate impact on Irish's exciting run in the Guinness Premiership. The former Wellington Hurricanes No.10 went on to finish the season with 10 tries and 202 points, but it was his creative contribution within an exciting Exiles back-line that had supporters looking forward to more.

INS & OUTS

IN
Tonga Lea'eatoa *(prop, Pau)*, James Hudson *(lock, Bath)*, Aiden McCullen *(back row, Toulouse)*, Seilala Mapusua *(centre, Otago)*, Richie Rees *(scrum-half, Ospreys)*, Stuart Mackie *(hooker, Newcastle Falcons)*, Steffon Armitage *(flanker, Saracens)*.

OUT
Ryan Strudwick *(lock)*, Kieron Dawson *(back row, Ulster)*, Paul Franze *(centre, Rugby League)*, Ross Laidlaw *(fly-half, Saracens)*, Paul Gustard *(back row, Saracens)*, Rodd Penney *(centre, Saracens)*, Darren Edwards *(scrum-half, Leeds)*, Adrian Flavin *(hooker, Connacht)*, Adam Halsey *(prop, retired)*, Rob Hardwick *(prop, Coventry)*.

CLUB PROFILES

LONDON IRISH SQUAD LIST

Surname	Christian name	Position	Height (Metric)	Height (Imp)	Weight (Metric)	Weight (Imp)	DOB	Honours
Armitage	Delon	Wing/Full back	1.92m	6ft 1in	80kg	12st 8lb	15/12/83	
Armitage	Steffon	Flanker	1.75m	5ft 9in	96kg	15st 12lb	20/09/85	
Bishop	Justin	Wing/Centre	1.84m	6ft 1in	90kg	13st 10lb	08/11/74	Ireland
Casey	Bob	Lock	2.02m	6ft 7in	123kg	19st 3lb	18/07/78	Ireland
Catt	Mike	Centre/Fly half	1.80m	5ft 10in	87kg	13st 8lb	17/09/71	England/Lions
Coetzee	Danie	Hooker	1.85m	6ft 1in	110kg	17st 5lb	02/09/77	South Africa
Collins	Michael	Prop	1.80m	5ft 10in	112kg	17st 9lb	10/05/74	
Danaher	Declan	Back row	1.94m	6ft 4in	104kg	16st 3lb	11/01/80	
Everitt	Barry	Fly half	1.75m	5ft 9in	82kg	12st 13lb	09/03/76	
Feau'nati	Dominic	Wing	1.85m	6ft 1in	110kg	17st 5lb	14/06/78	Samoa
Flutey	Riki	Half back	1.79m	5ft 11in	89kg	13st 9lb	10/02/80	
Hatley	Neal	Prop	1.85m	6ft 1in	119kg	18st 11lb	23/12/69	
Hodgson	Paul	Scrum half	1.73m	5ft 8in	78kg	12st 7lb	25/04/82	
Horak	Michael	Full back	1.90m	6ft 3in	92kg	14st 6lb	03/06/77	England
Hudson	James	Lock	2.03m	6ft 8in	113kg	17st 7lb	28/10/81	
Kennedy	Nick	Lock	2.03m	6ft 8in	113kg	17st 10lb	19/08/81	
Lea'aetoa	Tonga	Prop	1.88m	6ft 2in	130kg	21st 7lb	04/03/77	Tonga
Leguizamon	Juan-Manuel	Back row	1.90m	6ft 2in	102kg	16st 1lb	06/06/83	Argentina
Mackie	Stuart	Hooker	1.80m	5ft 11in	95kg	15st 0lb	12/02/85	
Magne	Olivier	Flanker	1.88m	6ft 2in	95kg	15st 0lb	11/04/73	France
Mapusua	Seilala	Centre	1.80m	5ft 11in	102kg	16st 1lb	27/02/80	
McMullen	Adrian	Flanker	1.94m	6ft 4in	111kg	17st 5lb	05/01/77	Ireland
Mordt	Nils	Centre	1.85m	6ft 1in	94kg	14st 12lb	05/12/83	

www.leicestertigers.com

CLUB PROFILES

LONDON IRISH SQUAD LIST

Surname	Christian name	Position	Height (Metric)	Height (Imp)	Weight (Metric)	Weight (Imp)	DOB	Honours
Murphy	Phil	No 8	1.94m	6ft 5in	114kg	17st 3lb	04/12/76	Canada
Ojo	Topsy	Wing	1.82m	6ft 0in	85kg	13st 4lb	28/07/85	
Paice	David	Hooker	1.85m	6ft 1in	101kg	15st 9lb	24/11/83	
Rautenbach	Faan	Prop	1.90m	6ft 3in	128kg	21st 2lb	22/02/76	South Africa
Rees	Richie	Scrum half	1.76m	5ft 9in	81kg	12st 8lb	21/05/83	
Roche	Kieran	Lock/Back row	2.01m	6ft 7in	115kg	18st 2lb	03/05/79	
Russell	Robbie	Hooker	1.79m	5ft 10in	97kg	15st 4lb	01/05/76	Scotland
Skuse	Richard	Prop	1.80m	5ft 11in	115kg	18st 2lb	11/09/80	
Tagicakibau	Sailosi	Wing	1.94m	6ft 4in	98kg	15st 4lb	14/11/82	Samoa
Thorpe	Richard	Back row	1.85m	6ft 1in	98kg	15st 4lb	01/11/84	
Tiesi	Gonzalo	Centre	1.84m	6ft 0in	88kg	13st 9lb	24/04/85	Argentina
Warren	Tom	Prop	1.85m	6ft 1in	110kg	17st 3lb	4/01/83	
Willis	Ben	Scrum half	1.75m	5ft 9in	88kg	13st 8lb	08/10/76	

www.leicestertigers.com

CLUB PROFILES

218 www.leicestertigers.com

CLUB PROFILES

DIRECTIONS & MAP

By Road: Exit the M4 at junction 11, heading for Reading on the A33. At the first roundabout, take the second left on to the Reading Relief Road, passing the Stadium on your left. At the next roundabout (past McDonald's) take the first left on to Northern Way and follow signs to car parks.

By Rail: Great Western Trains leave Paddington at least five times per hour and take approximately 23 minutes.

South West Trains from London Waterloo to Reading take approximately 90 minutes via Clapham Junction, Putney, Richmond, Twickenham, Egham, Bracknell, Wokingham plus other mainline stations.

Virgin Trains travel via Reading from London Paddington.

On matchdays, a Shuttle Bus Service operates from Reading Station to the Stadium.

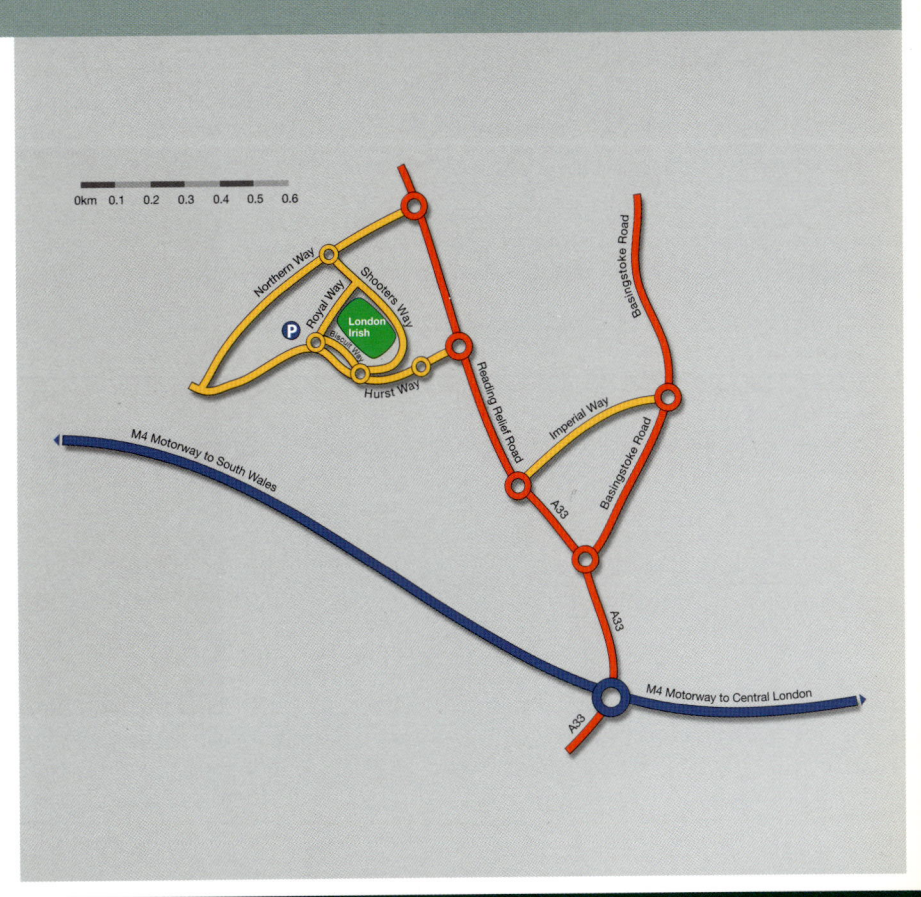

www.leicestertigers.com   219

CLUB PROFILES

NAME OF CLUB	London Wasps
FOUNDED	1867
STADIUM ADDRESS	Causeway Stadium, Hillbottom Road, High Wycombe HP12 4HJ
STADIUM CAPACITY	10,000
CLUB SWITCHBOARD	020 8993 8298
CLUB OFFICIALS	Director of Rugby: Ian McGeechan
	Head Coach: Shaun Edwards
	Coaches: Leon Holden
	Craig Dowd
	Captain: Lawrence Dallaglio
WEBSITE	www.wasps.co.uk

CLUB PROFILES

PLAYING SQUAD

Their run of Premiership victories came to an end in 2005/06, making the club doubly determined to get back on top this term. Stuart Abbott is a big loss in the midfield, but Eoin Reddan's development at scrum-half has compensated for the retirement of World Cup winner Matt Dawson, and the arrival of Tom Palmer from relegated Leeds is a notable one in the second row.

ONE TO WATCH

Eoin Reddan
Scrum-half Reddan joined Wasps at the start of last season and quickly made his mark. By the end of the season he had overtaken England and Lions hero Matt Dawson as first choice and won his first cap for Ireland in the Six Nations clash with France. He was the players' player of the year in 2005/06. Reddan has pace off the mark and a quick pass, and this season he hopes his increasing knowledge of those around him can take his development on again.

INS & OUTS

IN
Tom Palmer (*lock, Leeds Tykes*), Simon Amor (*scrum-half, Gloucester*), Mark McMillan (*scrum-half, Leeds Tykes*), Dave Walder (*fly-half, Newcastle Falcons*), Nick Adams (*prop, Cornish Pirates*), Phil Vickery (*prop, Gloucester*), David Doherty (*wing, Leeds Tykes*).

OUT
Mark Lock (*back row, Leeds Tykes*), Jon Dawson (*prop, South Africa*), Tim Foster (*centre, released*), Rob Laird (*full-back, Northampton Saints*), Stuart Abbott (*centre, Harlequins*), Matt Dawson (*scrum-half, retired*), Thom Evans (*wing, Glasgow*), Ben Gotting (*hooker, Worcester*), Justin Va'a (*prop, Glasgow*).

www.leicestertigers.com 221

CLUB PROFILES

LONDON WASPS SQUAD LIST

Surname	Christian name	Position	Height (Metric)	Height (Imp)	Weight (Metric)	Weight (Imp)	DOB	Honours
Adams	Nick	Prop	1.80m	5ft 10in	118kg	18st 7lb	11/10/77	
Amor	Simon	Scrum half	1.70m	5ft 6in	76kg	11st 13lb	25/04/79	
Barrett	Jonny	Hooker	1.80m	5ft 10in	104kg	16st 4lb	20/12/79	
Baxter	Neil	Wing	1.88m	6ft 2in	98kg	15st 5lb	29/11/82	
Birkett	Richard	Lock	1.93m	6ft 3in	109kg	17st 1lb	01/10/79	
Bracken	Peter	Prop	1.88m	6ft 2in	118kg	18st 7lb	01/12/77	
Brooks	James	Fly half	1.77m	5ft 9in	87kg	13st 9lb	06/04/80	
Corker	Matt	Lock	2.00m	6ft 6in	111kg	17st 6lb	30/11/82	
Dallaglio	Lawrence	Number 8	1.93m	6ft 3in	112kg	17st 8lb	10/08/72	England/Lions
Doherty	David	Full back	1.83m	6ft 0in	83kg	13st 0lb	28/01/87	
Erinle	Ayoola	Centre	1.91m	6ft 3in	110kg	17st 4lb	20/02/80	
Filler	John Paul	Flanker	1.91m	6ft 3in	103kg	16st 2lb	18/01/83	
Fury	Warren	Scrum half	1.83m	6ft 0in	86kg	13st 7lb	10/12/85	
Hart	John	Back row	1.95m	6ft 4in	113kg	17st 10lb	20/03/82	
Haskell	James	Back row	1.93m	6ft 3in	111kg	17st 6lb	02/04/85	
Hoadley	Rob	Centre	1.85m	6ft 0in	89kg	13st 13lb	23/03/80	
Ibanez	Raphael	Hooker	1.80m	5ft 10in	100kg	15st 10lb	17/02/73	France
King	Alex	Fly half	1.83m	6ft 0in	92kg	14st 6lb	17/01/75	England
Leo	Daniel	Lock/Flanker	2.00m	6ft 6in	112kg	17st 8lb	02/10/82	Samoa
Lewsey	Josh	Wing	1.80m	5ft 10in	87kg	13st 9lb	30/11/76	England/Lions
McMillan	Mark	Scrum half	1.81m	5ft 11in	88kg	13st 11lb	17/05/83	
McKenzie	Ali	Prop	1.90m	6ft 2in	120kg	18st 12lb	05/10/81	
O'Connor	Jonny	Flanker	1.80m	5ft 10in	100kg	15st 10lb	09/02/80	Ireland

LONDON WASPS SQUAD LIST

Surname	Christian name	Position	Height (Metric)	Height (Imp)	Weight (Metric)	Weight (Imp)	DOB	Honours
Palmer	Tom	Lock	1.98m	6ft 5in	115kg	18st 1lb	27/03/79	England
Payne	Tim	Prop	1.85m	6ft 0in	116kg	18st 3lb	29/04/79	England
Purdy	Martin	Lock	2.00m	6ft 6in	112kg	17st 8lb	29/10/81	
Reddan	Eoin	Scrum half	1.72m	5ft 7in	80kg	12st 8lbs	20/11/80	Ireland
Rees	Tom	Flanker	1.82m	5ft 11in	100kg	15st 10lb	11/09/84	
Sackey	Paul	Wing	1.86m	6ft 1in	91kg	14st 4lb	08/11/79	
Shaw	Simon	Lock	2.03m	6ft 7in	121kg	19st 0lb	01/09/73	England/Lions
Skivington	George	Lock	2.00m	6ft 6in	111kg	17st 6lb	03/12/82	
Staunton	Jeremy	Fly half/Full back	1.85m	6ft 0in	96kg	15st 1lb	07/05/80	Ireland
Thrower	Edd	Wing	1.84m	6ft 0in	96kg	15st 1lb	01/09/82	
Van Gisbergen	Mark	Full back	1.80m	5ft 10in	89kg	13st 13lb	30/06/77	England
Vickery	Phil	Prop	1.90m	6ft 2in	121kg	19st 0lb	14/03/76	England
Voyce	Tom	Wing	1.85m	6ft 0in	95kg	14st 13lb	05/01/81	England
Walder	Dave	Fly half	1.78m	5ft 10in	86kg	13st 5lb	07/05/78	England
Ward	Joe	Flanker	1.83m	6ft 0in	108kg	16st 13lb	03/06/80	
Waters	Fraser	Centre	1.83m	6ft 0in	94kg	14st 10lb	31/03/76	England
Worsley	Joe	Flanker	1.96m	6ft 5in	111kg	17st 6lb	14/06/77	England

CLUB PROFILES

224 www.leicestertigers.com

CLUB PROFILES

DIRECTIONS & MAP

By Road: Join M40 and head to J4/A404 High Wycombe. At Junction 4 take slip road and turn right, over the motorway, and then take first exit for A4010 (John Hall Way). Follow this road crossing 3 mini roundabouts until the road becomes New Road. Keep on New Road until next mini roundabout, then take left turn on to Lane End Road. Cross next mini roundabout on to Hillbottom Road, this will take you on to Causeway Stadium.

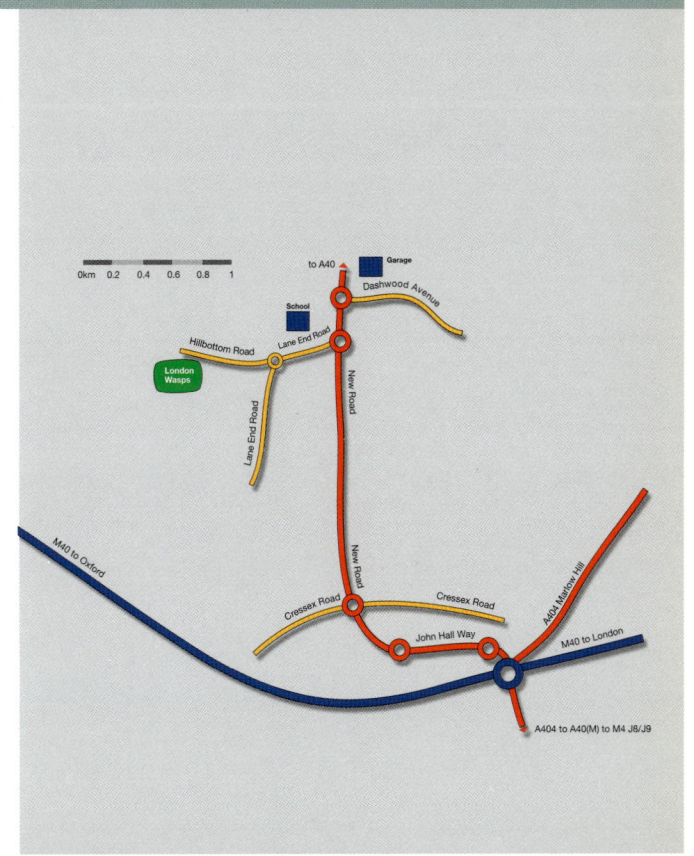

www.leicestertigers.com 225

CLUB PROFILES

NEWCASTLE FALCONS

NAME OF CLUB	Newcastle Falcons
FOUNDED	1877
STADIUM ADDRESS	Kingston Park, Brunton Road, Kenton Bank Foot, Newcastle-upon-Tyne NE13 8AF
STADIUM CAPACITY	10,200
CLUB SWITCHBOARD	0191 214 5588
CLUB OFFICIALS	Chairman: **Dave Thompson** Director of Rugby: **John Fletcher** Forwards Coach: **Peter Walton** Captain: **Matt Burke**
WEBSITE	www.newcastle-falcons.co.uk

CLUB PROFILES

PLAYING SQUAD

Former Academy director John Fletcher steps up into the considerable gap created by Rob Andrew's move to the RFU after 11 years spent establishing top-flight professional rugby in the football hotbed of the North-East. Other experienced members of the set-up have also departed, with Colin Charvis returning to Wales, Owen Finegan moving on to Leinster and Dave Walder a surprise recruit by Wasps. But the production line of young backs talent is still moving, with Toby Flood and Mathew Tait the most obvious eye-catchers. And in Matt Burke, they have the perfect role model on and off the field.

ONE TO WATCH

Ben Woods
Openside flanker Woods made a dramatic comeback from a career-threatening broken leg and picked up where he left off last season following 18 months out of the game. The Yorkshire-born Cambridge Blue made a huge impact with his powerful running and work at the breakdown, earning a place in the Churchill Cup squad with England Saxons.

INS & OUTS

IN
John Rudd (*wing, Northampton Saints*), John Golding (*prop, Rotherham*), Jason Oakes (*lock, Otley*), Brent Wilson (*flanker, North Harbour/Leicester*).

OUT
Dave Walder (*fly-half, London Wasps*), Stuart Grimes (*lock, Scottish Borders*), Colin Charvis (*back row, Newport Gwent Dragons*), Owen Finegan (*back row, Leinster*), Grant Anderson (*prop, Cornish Pirates*), Luke Gross (*lock, Doncaster*), Stuart Mackie (*hooker, London Irish*), Tino Paoletti (*prop, Parma, Italy*), Jason Smithson (*No.8, released*), Mark Wilkinson (*centre, Academy Coach*).

www.leicestertigers.com

CLUB PROFILES

NEWCASTLE FALCONS SQUAD LIST

Surname	Christian name	Position	Height (Metric)	Height (Imp)	Weight (Metric)	Weight (Imp)	DOB	Honours
Batty	Ross	Hooker	1.80m	5ft 11in	96kg	15st 0lb	20/09/86	
Buist	Andy	Lock	1.99m	6ft 6in	108kg	17st 0lb	25/08/84	
Burke	Matthew	Full back	1.82m	6ft 0in	95kg	14st 10lb	26/03/73	Australia
Charlton	Hall	Scrum half	1.80m	5ft 11in	92kg	14st 4lb	25/10/79	
Dawson	Phil	Flanker	1.93m	6ft 4in	96kg	15st 0lb	26/01/86	
Dehaty	Adam	Centre	1.80m	5ft 11in	86kg	13st 5lb	17/04/85	
Dickson	Lee	Scrum half	1.80m	5ft 11in	80kg	12st 6lb	29/03/85	
Dillon	Tom	Centre	1.90m	6ft 3in	90kg	14st 4lb	01/10/83	
Dowson	Phil	Number 8	1.90m	6ft 3in	106kg	16st 10lb	01/10/81	
Elliott	Anthony	Wing/Full back	1.90m	6ft 3in	95kg	14st 9lb	02/02/81	
Flood	Toby	Fly half/Full back	1.87m	6ft 2in	95kg	15st 7lb	08/08/85	
Golding	Jon	Prop	1.83m	6ft 0in	115kg	15st 10lb	06/05/82	
Gesinde	Eni	Flanker	1.93m	6ft 4in	99kg	15st 7lb	25/11/82	
Grindal	James	Scrum half	1.75m	5ft 9in	85kg	13st 4lb	18/08/80	
Harris	Cory	Flanker	1.82m	6ft 0in	100kg	17st 0lb	03/05/75	
Hoyle	James	Wing/Centre	1.85m	6ft 1in	82kg	13st 4lb	04/03/85	
Irvin	Greg	Back row	1.90m	6ft 3in	111kg	17st 6lb	27/03/84	
Long	Andy	Hooker	1.80m	5ft 11in	104kg	16st 3lb	02/09/77	England
May	Tom	Wing	1.77m	5ft 10in	92kg	14st 5lb	05/02/79	
Mayerhofler	Mark	Centre	1.82m	6ft 0in	97kg	15st 2lb	08/10/72	New Zealand
McCarthy	Mike	Flanker	1.93m	6ft 4in	108kg	17st 0lb	27/11/81	
Morris	Robbie	Prop	1.88m	6ft 2in	121kg	18st 11lb	20/02/82	England
Noon	Jamie	Centre	1.77m	5ft 10in	86kg	13st 5lb	09/05/79	England

CLUB PROFILES

NEWCASTLE FALCONS SQUAD LIST

Surname	Christian name	Position	Height (Metric)	Height (Imp)	Weight (Metric)	Weight (Imp)	DOB	Honours
Oakes	Jason	Lock	2.04m	6ft 7in	121kg	19st 0lb	29/09/77	
Parling	Geoff	Lock/Flanker	1.95m	6ft 5in	105kg	16st 5lb	28/10/83	
Perry	Andy	Lock	1.95m	6ft 5in	117kg	18st 7lb	28/12/74	
Phillips	Ollie	Wing	1.80m	5ft 11in	92kg	14st 7lb	08/09/82	
Rudd	John	Centre/Wing	1.88m	6ft 1in	108kg	17st 0lb	26/05/81	
Shaw	Joe	Full back/Centre	1.82m	6ft 0in	97kg	15st 2lb	20/02/80	
Tait	Alex	Centre/Full back	1.82m	6ft 0in	83kg	13st 7lb	18/03/88	
Tait	Mathew	Centre/Wing	1.80m	5ft 11in	85kg	13st 4lb	06/02/86	England
Thompson	Matt	Hooker	1.87m	6ft 2in	115kg	18st 0lb	12/12/82	
Tomes	Sean	Lock	2.01m	6ft 6in	120kg	18st 12lb	19/07/84	
Vickers	Rob	Hooker	1.80m	5ft 11in	102kg	16st 1lb	02/11/81	
Visser	Tim	Flanker	1.95m	6ft 4in	101kg	16st 0lb	29/05/87	
Walker	Stuart	Lock	2.04m	6ft 7in	101kg	16st 0lb	05/12/84	
Ward	Micky	Prop	1.80m	5ft 11in	120kg	18st 9lb	09/01/79	
Wilkinson	Jonny	Fly half	1.77m	5ft 10in	86kg	13st 5lb	25/05/79	England/Lions
Williamson	Ed	Flanker	1.87m	6ft 2in	95kg	14st 9lb	31/03/84	
Wilson	Brent	Flanker	1.95m	6ft 4in	108kg	17st 0lb	09/09/81	
Wilson	David	Prop	1.84m	6ft 1in	117kg	18st 7lb	09/04/85	
Woods	Ben	Flanker	1.87m	6ft 2in	105kg	16st 5lb	09/06/82	

www.leicestertigers.com

CLUB PROFILES

CLUB PROFILES

DIRECTIONS & MAP

By Road: From the A1 Western Bypass, take the turn off for Newcastle Airport at Junction 6, and follow signs for Kingston Park on the B6918. Go straight over two roundabouts, under a bridge and then turn right on to Brunton Road after around half a mile. The stadium is then visible on your left in approximately 300 metres.

By Rail: The main railway station is Central Station in Newcastle city centre. From there, take the Metro marked for 'Airport' and get off at Kingston Park station, which is ten stops and approximately 15-20 minutes away.

By Metro: Kingston Park is connected to most parts of Newcastle, Gateshead and Sunderland by the Metro train network. Kingston Park Metro station is a five minute walk from Kingston Park or Bank Foot Metro stations on the Airport branch of the line. The station is nine stops from the Monument Station in Newcastle city centre, with a journey time of approximately 15-20 minutes. Services arrive and depart Kingston Park approximately every ten minutes, with the last train at around midnight. For a detailed Metro map and full timetables for all Metro services, go to www.tyneandwearmetro.co.uk

By Bus: Local bus services run from Kingston Park to Newcastle city centre and numerous other parts of the city on a regular basis. National Express coach services connect Newcastle with many parts of Britain from the station in the Gallowgate area of the city centre, next to St James's Park football stadium. From Gallowgate bus station to get to Kingston Park, take the Metro one stop from St James's Park station to Monument, and then change to trains marked for 'Airport' and Kingston Park station is nine stops away, with a journey time of approximately 15-20 minutes.

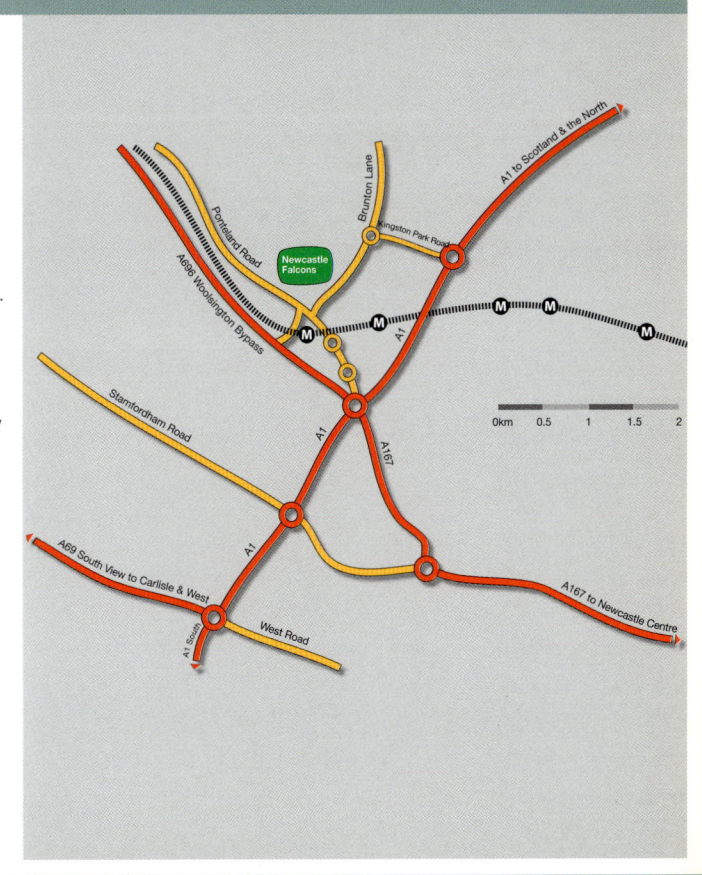

www.leicestertigers.com

CLUB PROFILES

NAME OF CLUB	Northampton Saints
FOUNDED	1880
STADIUM ADDRESS	Franklin's Gardens, Weedon Road, Northampton NN5 5BG
STADIUM CAPACITY	13,500
CLUB SWITCHBOARD	01604 751543
CLUB OFFICIALS	Chairman: **Keith Barwell**
	Chief Executive: **Allan Robson**
	Director of Rugby: **Budge Pountney**
	Head Coach: **Paul Grayson**
	Coaches: **Peter Sloane**
	Frank Ponissi
	Paul Larkin
	Tim Exeter
	Captain: **Bruce Reihana**
WEBSITE	www.northamptonsaints.co.uk

CLUB PROFILES

PLAYING SQUAD

After finishing sixth and 11th in the last two seasons, Saints are determined to get back in the play-off frame. Carlos Spencer is still the big attraction, with his sublime skills at fly-half, but skipper Bruce Reihana is among the Premiership's most consistent players, either at full-back or in the centre. After the much-heralded arrival of All Blacks star Spencer last summer, it is little wonder things were a little quieter on the recruitment front in 2006 and Saints have gone for potential rather than experience.

ONE TO WATCH

James Percival

After a career-threatening fracture of the neck in a pre-season game in the summer of 2005, young lock Percival spent all of last term in rehabilitation but Saints say he is now fitter and stronger than ever. He was signed from Worcester Warriors following some impressive form in England's Under-21 Six Nations squad.

INS & OUTS

IN

Ian Vass *(scrum-half, Harlequins)*, Matias Cortese *(hooker, Argentina)*, Rob Laird *(full-back, London Wasps)*, David Akinluyi *(wing, Cambridge University)*, Christian Short *(lock, Connacht)*, Soane Tonga'uiha *(prop, Bedford)*.

OUT

John Rudd *(wing, Newcastle Falcons)*, Ross Beattie *(flanker, Borders)*, Selborne Boome *(lock, Western Province)*, Luke Harbut *(prop, Brive)*, Ben Jones *(flanker, Doncaster)*, Brett McNamee *(back row, London Welsh)*, Colin Noon *(prop, Biarritz)*, James Pritchard *(full-back, Bedford)*, Grant Seely *(retired)*, Mark Soden *(back row, Capitolina, Rome)*, Brett Sturgess *(prop, released)*, Andy Vilk *(centre, Sale Sharks)*.

www.leicestertigers.com

CLUB PROFILES

NORTHAMPTON SAINTS SQUAD LIST

Surname	Christian name	Position	Height (Metric)	Height (Imp)	Weight (Metric)	Weight (Imp)	DOB	Honours
Akinluyi	David	Wing	1.85m	6ft 1in	99kg	15st 8lb	10/02/84	
Appleford	Geoff	Centre	1.91m	6ft 3in	95kg	14st 13lb	26/09/77	England
Barnard	Pat	Prop	1.83m	6ft 0in	115kg	18st 1lb	03/07/81	
Browne	Damien	Lock	1.98m	6ft 6in	123kg	19st 5lb	17/05/80	
Browne	Daniel	Number 8	1.95m	6ft 5in	106kg	16st 10lb	16/04/79	
Budgen	Chris	Prop	1.73m	5ft 8in	113kg	17st 11lb	21/01/73	
Clarke	Jon	Full back/Wing	1.90m	6ft 3in	95kg	15st 0lb	22/10/83	
Cohen	Ben	Wing	1.88m	6ft 2in	100kg	15st 10lb	14/09/78	England/Lions
Davies	Rhodri	Centre	1.75m	5ft 9in	87kg	13st 10lb	11/01/83	
Diggin	Paul	Wing	1.73m	5ft 8in	84kg	13st 3lb	23/01/85	
Easter	Mark	Back row	1.90m	6ft 3in	102kg	16st 2lb	19/10/82	
Emms	Simon	Prop	1.80m	5ft 11in	111kg	17st 7lb	27/01/75	
Fox	Darren	Flanker	1.82m	6ft 0in	102kg	16st 1lb	20/01/81	
Gerard	David	Lock	1.99m	6ft 6in	121kg	19st 1lb	26/11/77	France
Harding	Sam	Flanker	1.84m	6ft 1in	104kg	16st 5lb	01/12/80	New Zealand
Hartley	Dylan	Hooker	1.85m	6ft 1in	113kg	17st 11lb	24/03/86	
Hopley	Mark	No.8	1.91m	6ft 3in	108kg	17st 0lb	01/05/84	
Howard	Johnny	Scrum half	1.75m	5ft 9in	82kg	12st 13lb	02/10/80	
Kydd	Robbie	Utility back	1.80m	5ft 11in	90kg	14st 3lb	19/01/82	
Lamont	Sean	Wing	1.88m	6ft 2in	100kg	15st 10lb	15/01/81	Scotland
Laird	Rob	Utility back	1.83m	6ft 0in	90kg	14st 3lb	28/09/82	
Lewitt	Ben	Flanker	1.90m	6ft 3in	97kg	15st 4lb	23/10/79	
Lord	Matt	Lock	1.93m	6ft 4in	109kg	17st 12lb	07/01/78	

NORTHAMPTON SAINTS SQUAD LIST

Surname	Christian name	Position	Height (Metric)	Height (Imp)	Weight (Metric)	Weight (Imp)	DOB	Honours
Mallon	Seamus	Centre	1.91m	6ft 3in	94kg	14st 11lb	21/11/80	
Myring	Luke	Fly half	1.80m	5ft 11in	93kg	14st 9lb	20/12/83	
Percival	James	Lock	1.95m	6ft 5in	110kg	17st 5lb	09/11/83	
Quinlan	David	Centre	1.94m	6ft 4in	103kg	16st 3lb	04/01/78	Ireland
Reihana	Bruce	Full back	1.82m	6ft 0in	86kg	13st 8lb	06/04/76	New Zealand
Richmond	Dan	Hooker	1.80m	5ft 11in	105kg	16st 8lb	12/02/79	
Robinson	Mark	Scrum half	1.78m	5ft 10in	88kg	13st 12lb	21/08/75	New Zealand
Short	Christian	Lock	2.00m	6ft 7in	104kg	16st 5lb	15/11/79	
Smith	Tom	Prop	1.78m	5ft 10in	103kg	16st 3lb	31/10/71	Scotland/Lions
Spencer	Carlos	Fly half	1.84m	6ft 1in	95kg	15st 0lb	14/10/75	New Zealand
Starling	Neil	Centre	1.97m	6ft 5in	95kg	15st 0lb	08/06/82	
Thompson	Steve	Hooker	1.88m	6ft 2in	115kg	18st 2lb	15/07/78	England/Lions
Tonga'uhia	Soane	Prop	1.95m	6ft 5in	130kg	20st 7lb	21/02/82	Tonga
Tupai	Paul	Lock/Back row	1.93m	6ft 4in	115kg	18st 2lb	16/09/74	Samoa
Vass	Ian	Scrum half	1.80m	5ft 11in	98kg	15st 5lb	17/08/81	

CLUB PROFILES

www.leicestertigers.com

CLUB PROFILES

DIRECTIONS & MAP

By Road: From South - Leave M1 at junction 15A and follow signs for Northampton then Sixfields. Go past retail park that includes the Sixfields Stadium on the right before turning right at a major roundabout towards the town centre. Proceed across two more roundabouts before bearing right off Weedon Road to follow signs for the Supporters' Car Park.

From North - Exit M1 at junction 16 and follow signs to Northampton and the town centre. Go over four roundabouts before bearing right off Weedon Road for the Supporters' Car Park.

By Rail: Taxi rank available at Northampton station or catch the number 27 bus from the other side of the main road opposite the station. However, a 10-minute walk is just as easy: turn right out of the main car park and follow the road past BP garage, Thomas A Becket pub, bus depot, post office and working men's club. Franklin's Gardens can be clearly seen from the left hand side of the road.

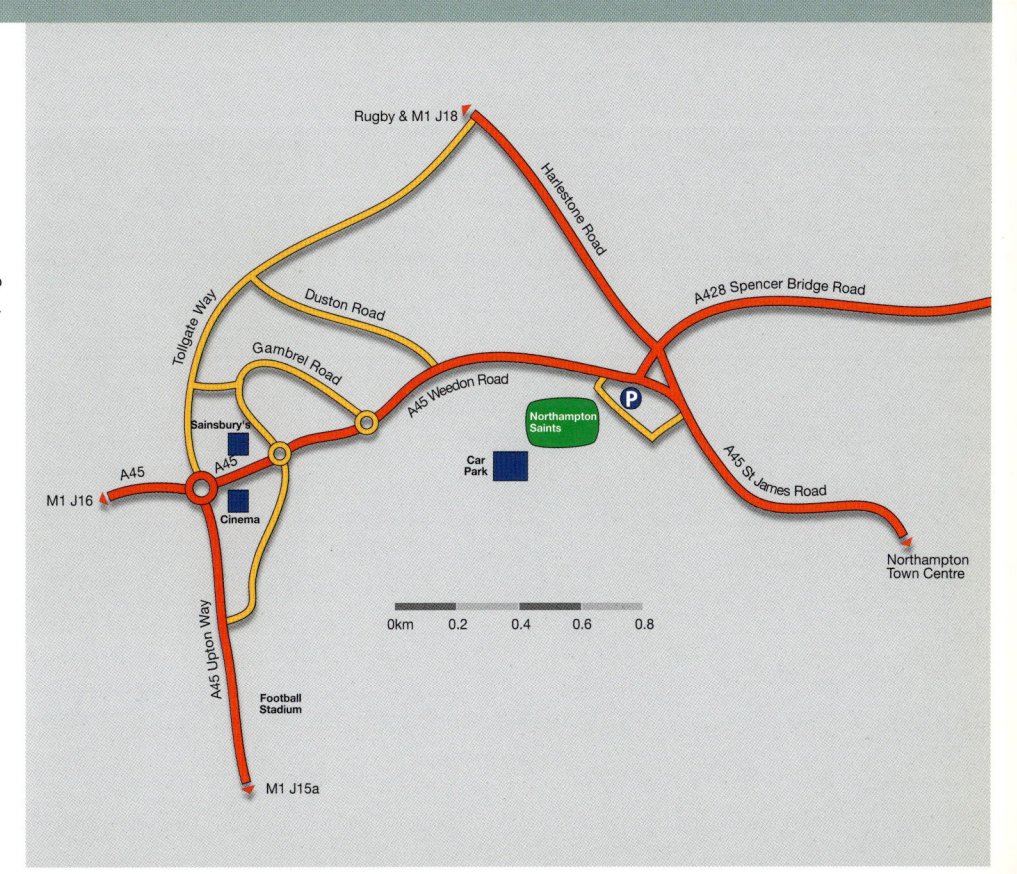

www.leicestertigers.com 237

CLUB PROFILES

SALE SHARKS

NAME OF CLUB	Sale Sharks
STADIUM ADDRESS	Edgeley Park, Hardcastle Road, Stockport, Cheshire SK3 9DD
STADIUM CAPACITY	10,641
CLUB SWITCHBOARD	0161 286 8888
CLUB OFFICIALS	Chairman: **Brian Kennedy** Chief Executive: **Niels de Vos** Director of Rugby: **Philippe Saint Andre** Coaches: **Kingsley Jones and Mark Nelson** Captain: **Jason Robinson**
WEBSITE	www.salesharks.com

CLUB PROFILES

PLAYING SQUAD

As the defending Guinness Premiership champions, you would not expect many changes this season and Sharks have been relatively conservative in the market. The signing of centre Chris Bell will make some others green with envy, though Philippe Saint Andre has a lot of established international figures to call upon as well as potential for the future. A lot depends on Charlie Hodgson's form at fly-half, but he has rarely been found wanting so far. Sebastien Chabal is still the talisman in the pack, but it is by no means a one-man show with the likes of Sherdian, Bruno, Lund, Chris Jones and Jason White all masters of their arts. International calls can hit hard, especially if Jason Robinson makes his way back into the England fold.

ONE TO WATCH

Ben Foden

A prominent member of the England Sevens and Under-21 squads in recent seasons, Foden is primarily a scrum-half, though his pace also allows him to come into consideration on the wing. He has waited for his opportunities and scored a quality try at Northampton at the end of last season, as well as getting off the bench in the Premiership Final victory over Leicester at Twickenham.

INS & OUTS

IN
Chris Bell (*centre, Leeds Tykes*), Andrew Vilk (*wing, Northampton Saints*), Juan Martin Fernandez Lobbe (*back row, Liceo Naval*), John Bryant (*centre, Newport Gwent Dragons*), Ben Evans (*prop, Cardiff Blues*), Lee Thomas (*fly-half, Cardiff Blues*).

OUT
Pete Anglesea (*flanker, retired*), Valentin Courrent (*scrum-half, Toulouse*), Ben Coutts (*prop, Queensland*), Epi Taione (*centre, released*), Robert Todd (*centre, retired*), Nick Wakley (*released*).

www.leicestertigers.com

CLUB PROFILES

SALE SHARKS SQUAD LIST

Surname	Christian name	Position	Height (Metric)	Height (Imp)	Weight (Metric)	Weight (Imp)	DOB	Honours
Blair	David	Fly half	1.75m	5ft 9in	73kg	11st 7lb	14/07/85	
Briggs	Neil	Hooker	1.78m	5ft 10in	95kg	15st 0lb	01/06/85	
Bruno	Sebastien	Hooker	1.75m	5ft 9in	105kg	16st 9lb	26/08/74	France
Bryant	Jon	Centre	1.81m	5ft 11in	98kg	15st 6lb	14/10/76	Wales
Carter	John	Flanker	1.90m	6ft 3in	108kg	17st 0lb	16/02/81	
Chabal	Sebastien	Number 8	1.90m	6ft 3in	108kg	17st 0lb	08/12/77	France
Cox	Sean	Lock	1.96m	6ft 5in	109kg	17st 2lb	16/01/85	
Cueto	Mark	Wing	1.83m	6ft 0in	93kg	14st 9lb	26/12/79	England/Lions
Day	Christian	Lock	1.98m	6ft 6in	106kg	16st 10lb	24/06/83	
Evans	Ben	Prop	1.90m	6ft 3in	119kg	18st 10lb	31/07/75	Wales
Faure	Lionel	Prop	1.86m	6ft 1in	114kg	18st 0lb	26/11/77	
Fernandez Lobbe	Ignacio	Lock	1.95m	6ft 5in	109kg	17st 4lb	20/11/74	Argentina
Fernandez Lobbe	Juan Martin	Back row	1.93m	6ft 4in	102kg	16st 0lb	19/11/81	Argentina
Foden	Ben	Scrum half	1.83m	6ft 0in	85kg	13st 7lb	22/07/85	
Halsall	Martin	Prop	1.81m	5ft 11in	111kg	17st 10lb	25/12/84	
Hanley	Steve	Wing	1.93m	6ft 4in	101kg	15st 13lb	11/06/79	England
Hodgson	Charlie	Fly half	1.78m	5ft 10in	82kg	12st 13lb	12/11/80	England/Lions
Hills	Mike	Flanker	1.86m	6ft 1in	93kg	14st 7lb	11/06/85	
Jones	Chris	Lock/Back row	2.00m	6ft 7in	102kg	16st 1lb	24/06/80	England
Jones	Marc	Hooker	1.86m	6ft 1in	99kg	15st 9lb	03/04/87	
Kuadey	Selorm	Wing	1.80m	5ft 11in	84kg	13st 4lb	05/05/87	
Larrechea	Daniel	Fly half	1.83m	6ft 0in	90kg	14st 3lb	09/07/77	
Lloyd	Ben	Lock	1.96m	6ft 5in	109kg	17st 3lb	07/10/84	

CLUB PROFILES

SALE SHARKS SQUAD LIST

Surname	Christian name	Position	Height (Metric)	Height (Imp)	Weight (Metric)	Weight (Imp)	DOB	Honours
Lund	Magnus	Flanker	1.91m	6ft 3in	105kg	16st 9lb	25/06/83	England
Martens	Sililo	Scrum half	1.80m	5ft 11in	93kg	14st 7lb	27/04/77	Tonga
Mayor	Chris	Centre/Wing	1.88m	6ft 2in	95kg	15st 0lb	19/05/82	
Riley	Matt	Centre	1.88m	6ft 2in	101kg	15st 1lb	19/05/82	
Ripol	Oriol	Wing	1.75m	5ft 9in	78kg	12st 6lb	06/09/75	Spain
Roberts	Eifion	Prop	1.86m	6ft 1in	135kg	21st 3lb	13/02/81	
Robinson	Jason	Full back	1.73m	5ft 8in	84kg	13st 4lb	30/07/74	England/Lions
Schofield	Dean	Lock	1.98m	6ft 6in	114kg	18st 0lb	19/01/79	
Seveali'i	Elvis	Centre/Wing	1.78m	5ft 10in	89kg	14st 0lb	20/06/78	Samoa
Sheridan	Andrew	Prop	1.96m	6ft 5in	119kg	18st 10lb	01/11/79	England/Lions
Stewart	Barry	Prop	1.88m	6ft 2in	114kg	18st 0lb	03/06/76	Scotland
Tait	David	No.8	1.93m	6ft 4in	110kg	17st 3lb	05/07/87	
Taylor	Mark	Centre	1.85m	6ft 1in	95kg	15st 0lb	27/02/73	Wales/Lions
Thomas	Lee	Full-back	1.83m	6ft 0in	96kg	15st 3lb	02/06/84	
Titterrell	Andy	Hooker	1.73m	5ft 8in	93kg	14st 9lb	10/01/81	England/Lions
Turner	Stuart	Prop	1.83m	6ft 0in	112kg	17st 9lb	22/04/72	England
Vilk	Andy	Centre/Wing	1.80m	5ft 11in	98kg	15st 6lb	11/06/81	
White	Jason	Flanker	1.96m	6ft 5in	117kg	18st 6lb	17/04/78	Scotland/Lions
Wigglesworth	Richard	Scrum half	1.76m	5ft 9in	83kg	13st 3lb	09/06/83	

www.leicestertigers.com

CLUB PROFILES

242 www.leicestertigers.com

CLUB PROFILES

DIRECTIONS & MAP

By Road:

From the South (M6) - Leave the M6 at J19 and follow A556 (SP Manchester) to Bowdon Roundabout, then follow Manchester M56. Pass Airport (on right), keep in left hand lanes and follow signs (J3) Stockport M60, Sheffield M67. Soon after joining the M60, leave at J2. Follow slip road, take 2nd left at roundabout (SP A560 Stockport) and take right turn at traffic lights by Farmers Arms. Turn into Edgeley Road, through mini roundabout (Morrison's on left) and carry on along to second set of lights (after the bowling club on your right), where turn right into Dale Street. Ground is on Hardcastle Road; 4th on left. If you miss the exit at J2, come off at J1 (by Pyramid), take third exit at roundabout and follow Yorkshire instructions below.

From Yorkshire (M62, M60) - Leave M60 at J1 and take first exit left at roundabout. Over bridge and left along Brinksway/Chestergate (A560). Right at lights and up King Street West hill (bus garages on your left.) Climb to top of hill (Stockport Station on your left) and take right turn at roundabout into Mercian Way. You can see ground and floodlights ahead. Access to Hardcastle Road by Caroline Street or Dale Street: only access roads on left.

From Peak District (A6) - Approach Stockport through Hazel Grove. Pass St. George's Church and A5102 Bramhall Lane (on left) and turn left at lights at Longshut Lane West (B5465,) then right at lights in Shaw Heath. Ground and floodlights can be seen on your left. Through one more set of lights, then approach ground via Booth Street (on left) or go to roundabout, where turn left into Mercian Way. Access to ground via Caroline Street or Dale Street onto Hardcastle Road. If you miss the turn at Longshut Lane West, carry on along A6 and turn left into Greek Street (before Town Hall) which takes you to the roundabout and Mercian Way.

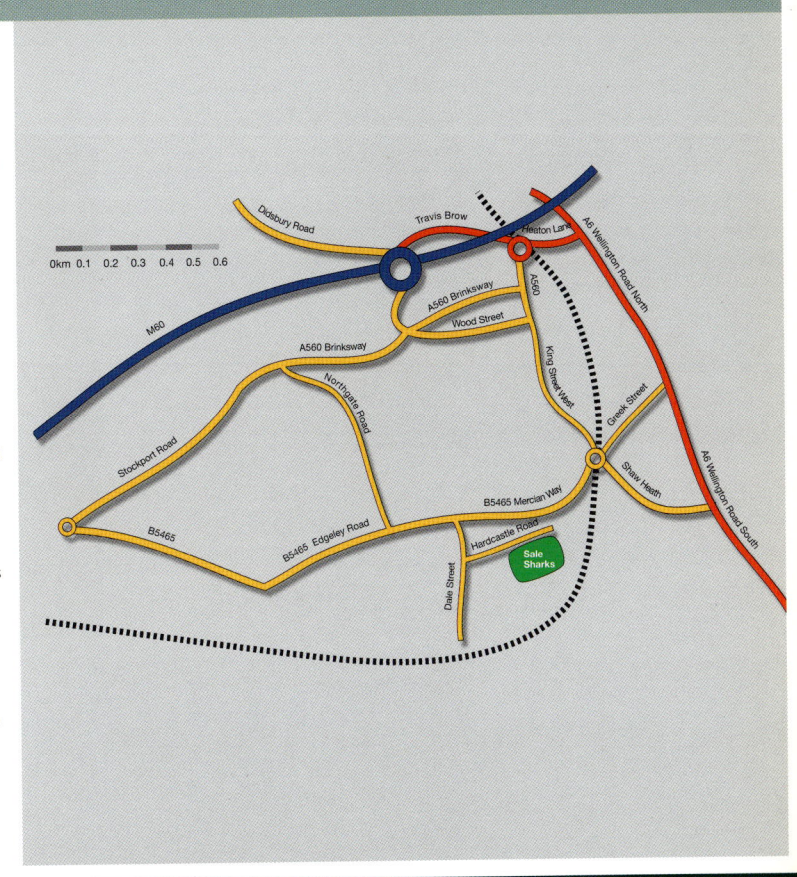

www.leicestertigers.com   243

CLUB PROFILES

SARACENS

NAME OF CLUB	Saracens
FOUNDED	1876
STADIUM ADDRESS	Vicarage Road Stadium, Watford WD18 0EP
STADIUM CAPACITY	19,108
CLUB SWITCHBOARD	01923 475222
CLUB OFFICIALS	Chief Executive: Mark Sinderberry
	Director of Rugby: Alan Gaffney
	Coaches: Richard Graham
	Adrian Kennedy
	Captain: Hugh Vyvyan
WEBSITE	www.saracens.com

CLUB PROFILES

PLAYING SQUAD

Only one top-five finish in the last five years, Sarries are now under the expert gaze of Alan Gaffney. Most eyes, however, will be on rugby league legend Andrew Farrell as he plays his first serious rugby since his code switch and a year of injury problems. If he is going to make it to the World Cup, he is going to need to get off to a good start – and that is just what Saracens need too. Few major changes in personnel should help with stability and continuity at Vicarage Road.

ONE TO WATCH

David Seymour

It was not just his distinctive long blond hair that got Seymour noticed last season as he cemented his place in the Saracens team, won a Commonwealth Games silver medal with the Sevens squad and then earned rave reviews with the Saxons at the Churchill Cup. Seymour's performances as an out-and-out No.7 who lives for his work at the breakdown saw him pushed forward as a potential late runner into the World Cup squad this term.

INS & OUTS

IN
Fabio Ongaro *(hooker, Treviso)*, Census Johnson *(prop, Biarritz)*, Ross Laidlaw *(fly-half, London Irish)*, Rodd Penney *(centre, London Irish)*, Paul Gustard *(back row, London Irish)*, Pelu Taele Pavihi *(lock, Otago)*, Tomas De Vedia *(Centre, San Isidro)*, Kameli Ratuvou *(centre, Fiji)*.

OUT
Emmanuel Amapakabo *(flanker, released)*, Steffon Armitage *(flanker, London Irish)*, Paul Bailey *(wing, released)*, Mark Bartholomeusz *(full-back, Ulster)*, Kyran Bracken *(scrum-half, retired)*, Hamish Mitchell *(prop, released)*, Nnamdi Obi *(wing, released)*, Billy O'Driscoll *(centre, released)*, Ben J Russell *(flanker, released)*.

CLUB PROFILES

SARACENS SQUAD LIST

Surname	Christian name	Position	Height (Metric)	Height (Imp)	Weight (Metric)	Weight (Imp)	DOB	Honours
Broster	Ben	Prop	1.81m	5ft 11in	105kg	16st 7lb	07/05/82	Wales
Byrne	Shane	Hooker	1.78m	5ft 10in	98kg	15st 6lb	18/07/71	Ireland/Lions
Cairns	Matt	Hooker	1.80m	5ft 11in	102kg	16st 0lb	31/03/79	
Castaignede	Thomas	Fly half	1.76m	5ft 9in	84kg	13st 3lb	21/01/75	France
Chesney	Kris	Lock	1.99m	6ft 6in	116kg	18st 4lb	02/03/74	
De Vedia	Tomas	Wing	1.88m	6ft 2in	98kg	15st 6lb	31/05/82	
Dickens	Alan	Scrum half	1.78m	5ft 10in	80kg	12st 9lb	02/04/76	
Farrell	Andy	Centre/Back row	1.90m	6ft 3in	102kg	16st 0lb	30/05/75	
Fullarton	Iain	Lock	2.01m	6ft 7in	107kg	16st 12lb	25/04/76	Scotland
Gustard	Paul	Back row	1.93m	6ft 4in	108kg	17st 0lb	02/02/76	
Harris	Dan	Centre	1.78m	5ft 11in	96kg	15st 12lb	17/05/77	
Haughton	Richard	Wing	1.88m	6ft 2in	86kg	13st 7lb	08/11/80	
Hill	Richard	Back row	1.88m	6ft 2in	102kg	16st 0lb	23/05/73	England/Lions
Jackson	Glen	Fly half	1.80m	5ft 11in	85kg	13st 6lb	23/10/75	
Johnson	Census	Prop	1.89m	6ft 2in	130kg	20st 0lb	01/01/82	Samoa
Johnston	Ben	Centre	1.91m	6ft 3in	105kg	16st 7lb	08/11/78	England
Kyriacou	Andy	Hooker	1.80m	5ft 11in	96kg	15st 2lb	04/01/83	
Laidlaw	Ross	Fly-half	1.78m	5ft 10in	80kg	12st 9lb	08/10/83	
Lloyd	Nick	Prop	1.83m	6ft 0in	106kg	16st 9lb	12/10/76	
Ongaro	Fabio	Hooker	1.83m	6ft 0in	104kg	16st 3lb	23/09/77	Italy
Penney	Rodd	Centre	1.83m	6ft 0in	93kg	14st 6lb	22/07/78	
Powell	Adam	Centre	1.80m	5ft 11in	94kg	14st 12lb	01/01/87	
Pavihi	Pelu-Taele	Lock	1.98m	6ft 6in	114kg	17st 13lb	28/09/81	Samoa

www.leicestertigers.com

CLUB PROFILES

SARACENS SQUAD LIST

Surname	Christian name	Position	Height (Metric)	Height (Imp)	Weight (Metric)	Weight (Imp)	DOB	Honours
Raiwalui	Simon	Lock	1.99m	6ft 6in	120kg	18st 13lb	08/09/74	Fiji
Ratuvou	Kameli	Centre	1.90m	6ft 3in	89kg	14st 0lb	06/11/83	Fiji
Raluni	Moses	Scrum half	1.77m	5ft 10in	86kg	13st 7lb	27/06/75	Fiji
Russell	Ben T	Back row	1.91m	6ft 3in	100kg	15st 10lb	10/01/83	
Ryder	Tom	Lock	1.96m	6ft 5in	105kg	16st 7lb	21/02/85	
Scarbrough	Dan	Full back	1.86m	6ft 1in	84kg	13st 3lb	16/02/78	
Seymour	David	Back row	1.80m	5ft 11in	89kg	14st 2lb	27/09/84	
Skirving	Ben	Back row	1.93m	6ft 4in	107kg	16st 12lb	09/10/83	
Sorrell	Kevin	Centre	1.80m	5ft 11in	87kg	13st 8lb	06/03/77	
Vaikona	Tevita	Wing	1.88m	6ft 2in	103kg	16st 2lb	18/08/74	Tonga
Visagie	Cobus	Prop	1.85m	6ft 1in	117kg	18st 0lb	31/10/73	South Africa
Vyvyan	Hugh	Back row	1.98m	6ft 6in	102kg	16st 0lb	08/09/76	England
Yates	Kevin	Prop	1.80m	5ft 11in	114kg	17st 14lb	06/11/72	England

www.leicestertigers.com

CLUB PROFILES

CLUB PROFILES

DIRECTIONS & MAP

By Road: From the North - Exit M1 at Junction 5 and take third exit off roundabout, A4008 (Stephenson Way), signposted Watford Town Centre. Bear left on dual carriageway, by-passing the roundabout, towards Town Centre. At next roundabout follow signs to Town Centre. Immediately ahead is the Harlequin Centre. Stay in the middle lane of the three-lane carriageway on the ring road. After the second set of traffic lights (Watford High Street Station is on your left), move into the left-hand lane and head left at traffic lights to Stadium.

From the West - Exit M25 at Junction 19 and take third exit off roundabout, A411 (Hempstead Road), signposted Watford. Continue for approximately 2 miles and at roundabout go straight across, then follow signs to Rickmansworth (A412).

From the South - Exit M1 at Junction 5 and take first exit off roundabout, then as north.

From the East - Exit M25 at Junction 21A and then join the M1 Southbound (J6). Exit at Junction 5, then as North.

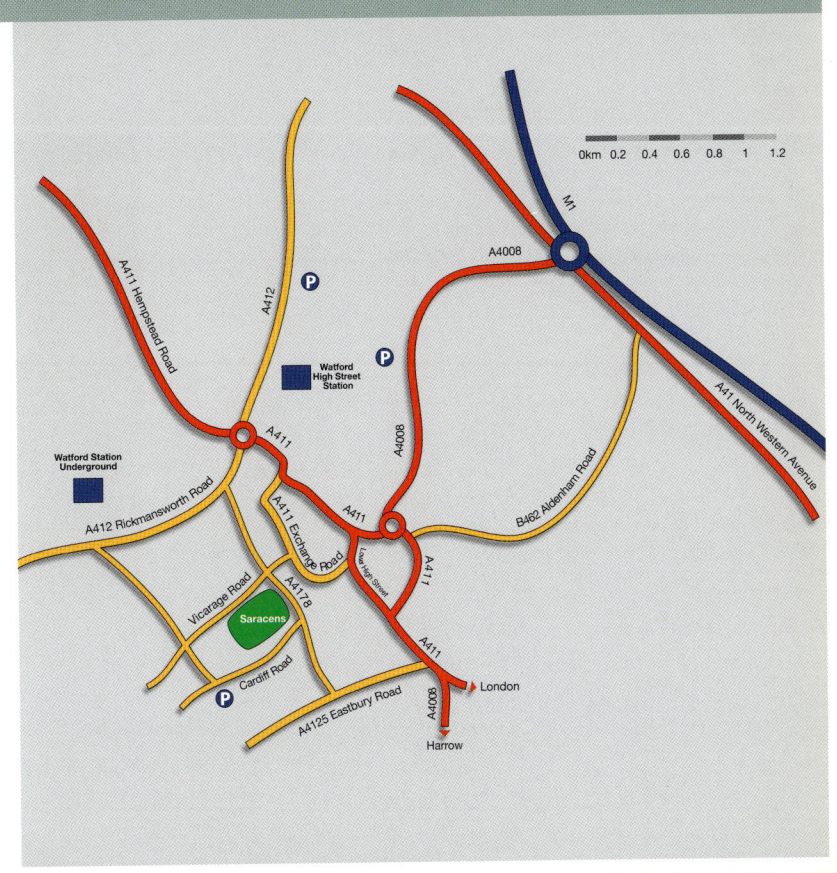

CLUB PROFILES

NAME OF CLUB	Worcester Warriors
STADIUM ADDRESS	Sixways, Pershore Lane, Hindlip, Worcester WR3 8ZE
STADIUM CAPACITY	10,221
CLUB SWITCHBOARD	01905 454183
CLUB OFFICIALS	Chief Executive: **Cecil Duckworth** Director of Rugby: **John Brain** Head Coach: **Anthony Eddy** Captain: **Pat Sanderson**
WEBSITE	www.wrfc.co.uk

CLUB PROFILES

PLAYING SQUAD

Eighth last season represented an improvement of one place on their debut efforts in 2004/05, though they scored considerably better last term and earned five more points than a year earlier. There was a Welsh influence on their summer signings, as well as attracting attention for the move to take Gloucester wing Marcel Garvey to Sixways. Fly-half Shane Drahm is a key man for the Warriors, especially now that England scrum-half Andy Gomarsall is no longer in the picture.

ONE TO WATCH

Marcel Garvey
The winger's links with Warriors director of rugby John Brain go back a long way as it was Brain who gave Garvey his break as a schoolboy winger at Gloucester. Two years ago he was viewed as an international certainty but failed to build on that early promise. Now he has linked up with Brain again and, still just 23 years old, he will feel he can rekindle that early form. His development in new pastures will be fascinating to watch – just as long as you're not defending his wing!

INS & OUTS

IN
Lee Best *(full-back, Bath)*, Marcel Garvey *(wing, Gloucester)*, Gavin Quinnell *(lock, Llanelli Scarlets)*, Ben Gotting *(hooker, London Wasps)*, Darren Morris *(prop, Leicester Tigers)*, Ryan Powell *(scrum-half, Cardiff Blues)*, Miguel Avramovic *(centre, Alumni)*.

OUT
Andre Van Niekerk *(hooker, South Africa)*, Gavin Hickie *(hooker, Leicester Tigers)*, Nicholas Le Roux *(full-back, Brive)*, John Hylton *(winger, Cornish Pirates)*, Mike McDonald *(prop, Leeds Tykes)*, Andy Gomarsall *(scrum-half)*, Ed O'Donoghue *(lock, Queensland)*, Mike Maguire *(winger, Ulster)*, Saioso Vaili *(flanker Viadana)*, Jonny Tuamoheloa *(flanker, Tarbes)*.

www.leicestertigers.com

CLUB PROFILES

WORCESTER WARRIORS SQUAD LIST

Surname	Christian name	Position	Height (Metric)	Height (Imp)	Weight (Metric)	Weight (Imp)	DOB	Honours
Avramovic	Miguel	Centre	1.83m	6ft 0in	95kg	15st 0lb	18/07/81	Argentina
Best	Lee	Full back	1.90m	6ft 3in	102kg	16st 0lb	16/10/78	
Black	Callum	Prop	1.82m	5ft 11in	112kg	17st 6lb	25/02/86	
Blaze	Richard	Lock	2.02m	6ft 7in	115kg	18st 0lb	19/04/85	
Bowley	Will	Lock	2.01m	6ft 5in	115kg	18st 0lb	05/03/84	
Brown	James	Fly half	1.80m	5ft 10in	84kg	13st 0lb	25/05/78	
Collier	Tim	Lock	1.99m	6ft 6in	135kg	21st 3lb	22/10/77	
Collins	James	Back row	1.93m	6ft 4in	98kg	15st 6lb	08/02/86	
Delport	Thinus	Full back	1.88m	6ft 2in	92kg	14st 6lb	02/02/75	South Africa
Drahm	Shane	Fly half	1.76m	5ft 9in	81kg	12st 10lb	29/08/77	
Fortey	Chris	Hooker	1.81m	5ft 11in	112kg	17st 8lb	25/08/75	
Fortey	Lee	Prop	1.80m	5ft 10in	108kg	16st 3lb	25/08/75	
Garvey	Marcel	Wing	1.72m	5ft 8in	92kg	14st 6lb	21/04/83	
Gillies	Craig	Lock	2.03m	6ft 7in	112kg	17st 8lb	06/05/76	
Gotting	Ben	Hooker	1.83m	6ft 0in	104kg	16st 5lb	15/02/81	
Harding	Tom	Back row	1.82m	5ft 11in	96kg	15st 2lb	03/05/82	
Havili	Alsea	Wing	1.78m	5ft 10in	97kg	15st 4lb	1/03/77	
Hickey	Drew	Back row	1.93m	6ft 3in	101kg	15st 12lb	16/05/78	
Horsman	Chris	Prop	1.90m	6ft 2in	111kg	17st 6lb	02/02/78	Wales
Horstmann	Kai	Back row	1.91m	6ft 3in	106kg	16st 9lb	21/09/81	
Lennard	Jamie	Full back	1.85m	6ft 1in	109kg	17st 2lb	23/02/87	
Lombard	Thomas	Centre	1.89m	6ft 2in	85kg	13st 5lb	05/06/75	France
Lutui	Aleki	Hooker	1.85m	6ft 1in	113kg	17st 8lb	01/07/78	Tonga

CLUB PROFILES

WORCESTER WARRIORS SQUAD LIST

Surname	Christian name	Position	Height (Metric)	Height (Imp)	Weight (Metric)	Weight (Imp)	DOB	Honours
Morris	Darren	Prop	1.85m	6ft 1in	122kg	19st 4lb	24/09/74	Wales/Lions
Mullan	Matt	Prop	1.82m	5ft 11in	89kg	14st 0lb	15/03/86	
Murphy	Phil	Lock	2.02m	6ft 7in	111kg	17st 6lb	01/04/80	
Oduoza	Uche	Wing	1.91m	6ft 3in	91kg	14st 4lb	15/10/86	
Powell	Matt	Scrum half	1.78m	5ft 10in	87kg	13st 9lb	08/05/78	
Powell	Ryan	Scrum half	1.72m	5ft 8in	85kg	13st 4lb	01/07/80	Wales
Quinnell	Gavin	Lock	2.02m	6ft 7in	140kg	22st 0lb	25/22/83	
Rasmussen	Dale	Centre	1.88m	6ft 2in	95kg	14st 13lb	05/07/77	Samoa
Runciman	Nick	Scrum half	1.78m	5ft 10in	80kg	12st 7lb	01/09/85	
Sanderson	Pat	Back row	1.90m	6ft 2in	93kg	14st 8lb	06/09/77	England
Taumoepeau	Tevita	Prop	1.83m	6ft 0in	120kg	19st 0lb	16/05/74	Tonga
Trueman	Gary	Centre	1.85m	6ft 0in	90kg	14st 2lb	21/08/80	
Tucker	Mark	Centre/Wing	1.83m	6ft 0in	100kg	15st 10lb	16/04/80	
Whatling	Simon	Centre	1.76m	5ft 9in	93kg	14st 6lb	16/09/84	
Windo	Tony	Prop	1.83m	6ft 0in	108kg	16st 13lb	30/04/69	

www.leicestertigers.com

CLUB PROFILES

CLUB PROFILES

DIRECTIONS & MAP

By Road: Take Junction 6 off the M5 motorway. Take the A4538 to Droitwich.

By Rail: Depart at Worcester Shrub Hill Station. There is a taxi rank outside the station. A taxi to Sixways will cost approximately £6.

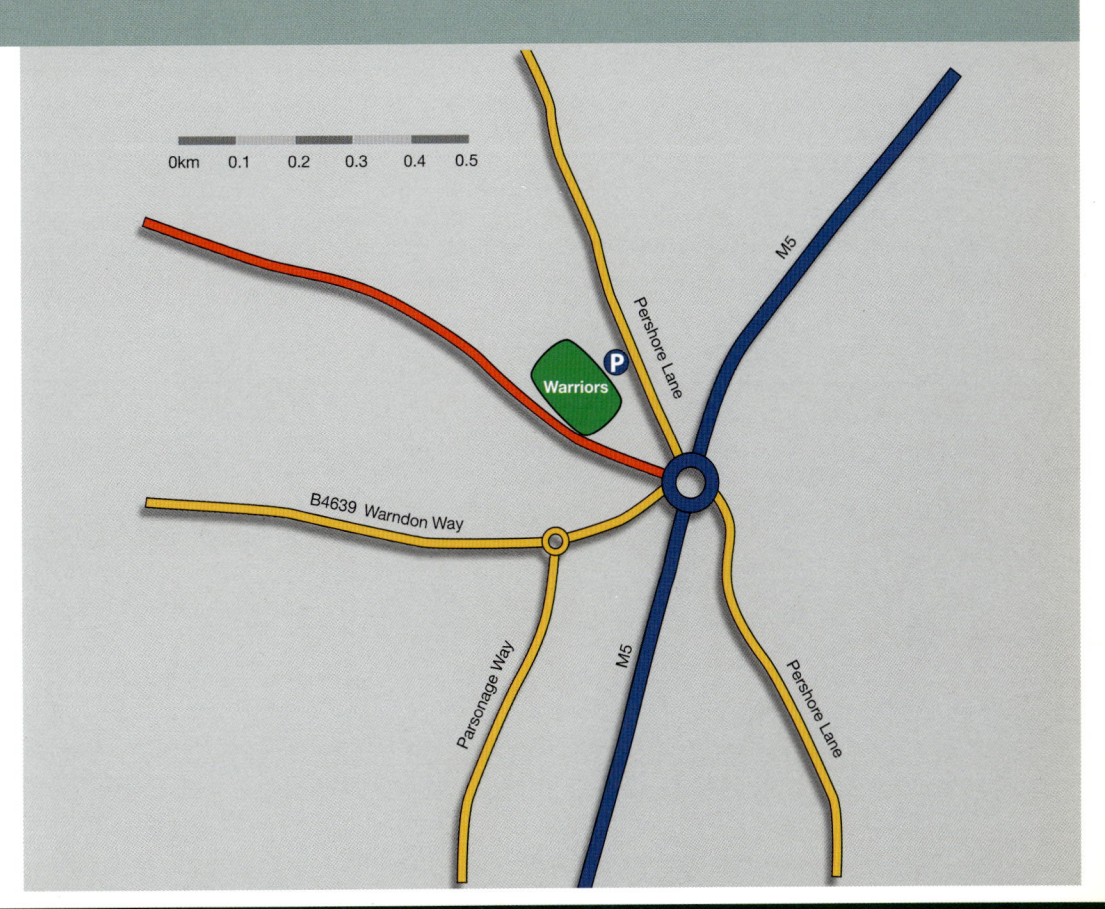

www.leicestertigers.com 255